# English Agriculture

For Jill, Susan, Catherine and Stephen, with much love.

# English Agriculture

## *An Historical Perspective*

### David Grigg

Basil Blackwell

Copyright © David Grigg 1989

First published 1989

Basil Blackwell Ltd
108 Cowley Road, Oxford, OX4 1JF, UK

Basil Blackwell Inc.
432 Park Avenue South, Suite 1503
New York, NY 10016, USA

*British Library Cataloguing in Publication Data*

Grigg, David, 1934–
English agriculture: an historical perspective.
1. England. Agriculture, to 1980
I. Title
630′.942

ISBN 0–631–16033–7

*Library of Congress Cataloging in Publication Data*

Grigg, David B.
English agriculture: an historical perspective / David Grigg.
p.    cm.
Includes index.
ISBN 0-631-16033-7 :
1. Agricultural geography—England. 2. Agricultural geography—Wales. 3. Agriculture—England—History. 4. Agriculture—Wales—History. 5. Agriculture—Economic aspects—England—History. 6. Agriculture—Economic aspects—Wales—History. 7. Agriculture and state—England. 8. Agriculture and state—Wales. I. Title.
S455.G78   1989                                                    88-31741
630′.942—dc19                                                      CIP

Typeset in 10 on 11½pt Baskerville
by Photo-Graphics Ltd., Honiton, Devon
Printed in Great Britain by T J Press (Padstow) Ltd.

Endpapers: '*Ploughing on the uplands*'-*Ambleside* (BBC Hulton Picture Library)

# Contents

# Acknowledgements

I am grateful for some considerable help in producing the manuscript of this book. Margaret Gray typed the manuscript most efficiently and promptly, while Graham Allsopp and Paul Coles drew the maps and graphs with their customary skill. John Owen and David Maddison produced some excellent photographs for me. To all of them, many thanks.

David Grigg

# 1
# Introduction

Over the last ten years much has been written on farming in England and Wales, much of it highly critical. The Common Agricultural Policy of the European Economic Community and its consequences have attracted most attention. The imposition of high import levies on cheap food from outside the Community, the cost of supporting high farm prices within the Community and the absurdities of the food surpluses have all been attacked. But this is not all; the financial protection of British farmers has allowed them to adopt technologies which, it has been argued, are destroying the environment. Thus the excessive use of nitrogen fertilizers has polluted some rivers, pesticides have damaged flora and fauna, and the use of large machines has led farmers to destroy hedgerows. The treatment of animals has received much criticism, notably that of poultry and pigs confined indoors under cramped conditions.

There is a large and often impassioned literature on these topics. The aim of this book is more prosaic, but it is hoped no less useful: it is to describe farming in England and Wales in the 1980s. The centre of interest is what farmers produce, how they produce it and where. The approach adopted here differs from that of many other books on modern farming in that it is concerned with the great regional variations in the way farming is carried on in this country. All too often it seems to be assumed by the press, television and radio that all farmers live and farm in East Anglia and grow nothing but cereals.

Thus the first aim of this book is to give a systematic account of the agricultural *geography* of England and Wales at a time when a long period of prosperity is coming to an end and great changes are imminent. The output of the industry and the broad pattern of land use are dealt with, and then the crops that are grown and the livestock that are kept are discussed. The farms on which the production takes place are examined – their size, ownership and layout – and then the technology of the times is related to the long decline of the English agricultural population. The last part of the book deals with different types of farming, farming systems that have characteristic combinations of land use, livestock, tenure and technology.

Although one aim of this book is to describe present conditions, of equal importance is to explain how the pattern and types of farming became established. To some writers there is no doubt that current problems result from the entry of Britain into the Common Market; the expansion of crops into moors and fens, the pollution of rivers, the destruction of hedgerows, high-priced food and food surpluses are all seen as a response to the Common Agricultural Policy. However, many of these features were well established long before 1973. A more suitable period for consideration might then be the post-war era. Certainly the Agricultural Act of 1947 established the system of guarantees and subsidies that provided farmers with prosperity long before Britain entered Europe. But again it is soon found that the antecedents of much that is characteristic of the present day has its beginnings much further back than 1947. Thus the number of people working on the land has fallen dramatically since 1950 – but it had been falling for a century before. If the application of inorganic power to the land is a sign of modernity, the first steam engine on a farm was erected in Wales in 1798. If mechanization is the acme of modern farming, the threshing machine dates from the early 1790s and the first reapers were used – not with much success – in the 1820s.

The second aim of this book is to give an historical account of how the present patterns of farming came into being. This presents a problem. It could be argued that some of the features of modern farming can be traced back to before the Roman occupation; doubtless some of the enclosures and field boundaries have a Saxon origin, and medieval historians would argue that understanding present land tenure needs some knowledge of the fourteenth and fifteenth centuries. But for the most part this book does not go back beyond the early seventeenth century. By then English farmers were largely commercial farmers, and between the 1620s and the 1850s there were two slow but critical changes that constitute the Agricultural Revolution. First was the virtual completion of enclosure, of both open fields and common land. Second, the introduction of two new crops, turnips and clover, integrated crop and livestock husbandry to produce the mixed farming, or High Farming, of the early and mid-Victorian period. From the 1870s this elegant and productive system of farming which had made England the leading agricultural country was undermined by imports of wheat, wool, meat and dairy products from overseas. The salvation of English farmers was in the production of milk, or vegetables, or good quality beef or lamb. By the 1930s some farmers had taken this course. Others were grappling with the problems of mechanization and experimenting with the new chemical technologies. The Second World War brought a return of prosperity and the years after the war brought a revival of traditional farming methods. But by the late 1950s the old ways were swept aside by the advance of mechanization and the almost universal adoption of chemical methods. Thus the last 30 years have seen the transformation of an agriculture that took 200 years – from the 1620s to the 1870s – to develop; in contrast it took half a century – from the 1870s to 1930s – to be undermined by low prices and a couple of decades to be transformed by modern technology. To understand the 1980s it is necessary to understand the technological changes of the last quarter century, but to understand them fully it is necessary to have some knowledge of the last three centuries. This book aims to provide at least some of that knowledge.

# 2

# The Growth and Structure of Agricultural Output

SURPLUSES AND GROWTH

Much of the criticism of British farming over the last decade and a half has been prompted by the existence of cereal and other surpluses. Since the United Kingdom's entry into the Common Market farmers have been protected from overseas competition by import levies. In addition *target* prices for a wide range of commodities are set each year; if the price falls below this to an *intervention* price – a tenth or so below the *target* price – then the government must buy from farmers at that price. Some of this produce can be exported, although usually only with the aid of a subsidy, for EEC prices have generally been above world prices since 1977; otherwise it must be stored, at high cost. At the end of 1986 nearly 4 million tons of cereals were in store, together with one-quarter million tons of butter and 53,000 tons of beef.[1]

The reasons for these surpluses are rather more complex than is usually allowed, but of prime importance has been the dramatic rise of agricultural output since 1950 – indeed since the 1930s. The increase in the physical quantities of individual commodities since before the Second World War is shown in table 2.1. The output of a few products has actually declined; potato production reached a peak in the immediate post-war food scarcity, while the dwindling of the horse population has led to the eclipse of oats. But the output of most commodities has increased substantially: barley and poultry meat are exceptional, but that of many other products has doubled, or nearly doubled.

Estimates of the total *value* of the output of United Kingdom agriculture year by year provide perhaps a simpler way of measuring the increase. By using the estimates of the Ministry of Agriculture, which date from the late 1930s, and the work of economists and historians on earlier

1 *Intervention Board for Agricultural Produce: report for the calendar year 1986*, HMSO, Cm. 167 (1987).

periods it is possible to demonstrate the remarkable rise of output over the last half century and to compare it with earlier periods. Most of the estimates used (see table 2.2 and figure 2.1) are of net agricultural output and in constant prices.

The great increase in output over the last half century is best illustrated by placing this period into a longer historical context. Most historians would put the beginnings of modern agriculture in the mid-seventeenth century. Until 1800 rates of increase in total output were well below 1 per cent per annum (see table 2.2), but then they steadily rose to the 1860s; during the Great Depression in agriculture in the last two decades of the nineteenth century output actually fell. There was little or no increase in the first two decades of the twentieth century, but from the 1920s the average annual rate of increase rose until after 1940 it was well above any previous level. Figure 2.1 is an attempt to show an index of net agricultural output from varied and sometimes conflicting sources; it perhaps should be treated with caution. (See Appendix, pp. 14–15.) However, there is little doubt of the great surge of output since the 1920s. Agricultural output in the early 1980s was two and a half times that of the 1930s, four times that of the 1870s and nearly nine times what it was in the first decade of the nineteenth century.

The existence of considerable surpluses of cereals, butter and beef in the early 1980s indicates that British agricultural output has outrun demand. There is no difficulty in explaining how this came about. Although English farmers had been protected by the state before entry into the Common Market, the system of guaranteed prices and deficiency payments used before 1973 allowed supply to be controlled reasonably effectively. Under the Common Agricultural Policy, however, prices are established not with reference to demand, but as a result of political bargaining in which member countries try to ensure target prices that will give their least efficient farmers a livelihood.

There are other factors of course. Behind a system of production subsidies and guaranteed prices, which has lasted for over 50 years, British farmers have adopted technical advances that have made possible the remarkable increase in output. Indeed in many ways it is surprising that the surpluses are not larger, given the magnitude of the increase; they are not larger because first, far less of British consumption is imported than in the past, and second, because increases in population and income have absorbed some of the great increases in output since the 1930s.

### TRADE AND SELF-SUFFICIENCY

Until the late eighteenth century Britain was largely self-sufficient in food supplies, although of course the population was then much smaller and average calorie consumption per capita at most only three-quarters

Table 2.1 Changes in the physical output of United Kingdom agriculture, 1930s to 1980s (thousand tons)

| Product | Average | | | | | 1980 | 1985 | % increase 1936–9 to 1985 |
|---|---|---|---|---|---|---|---|---|
| | 1936–9 | 1946–7 | 1950–1 | 1959–60 | 1969–70 | | | |
| Wheat | 1,677 | 1,998 | 2,647 | 2,827 | 3,364 | 8,472 | 12,046 | 618 |
| Barley | 777 | 1,994 | 1,738 | 4,080 | 8,663 | 10,326 | 9,740 | 1,153 |
| Oats | 1,971 | 2,949 | 2,735 | 2,212 | 1,307 | 601 | 614 | −70 |
| Potatoes | 4,950 | 10,328 | 9,659 | 7,026 | 5,798 | 7,110 | 6,892 | 39 |
| Sugar-beet | 2,784 | 4,594 | 5,299 | 5,598 | – | 7,380 | 7,717 | 177 |
| Milk (million litres) | 7,105 | 7,569 | 9,156 | 10,488 | 12,138 | 15,340 | 15,408 | 117 |
| Eggs (million dozen) | 541 | 451 | – | 1,069 | 1,231 | 1,100 | 1,059 | 96 |
| Beef and Veal | 587 | 545 | 610 | 759 | 929 | 1,096 | 1,124 | 91 |
| Mutton and Lamb | 198 | 143 | 149 | 240 | 218 | 286 | 313 | 103 |
| Pig meat | 442 | 147 | 320 | 704 | 867 | 917 | 945 | 113 |
| Poultry meat | – | 71 | – | 262 | 560 | 754 | 874 | 1,130 |
| Wool | 34 | 27 | 27 | 38 | – | 39 | 41 | 21 |

Source: Ministry of Agriculture, Annual Reviews of Agriculture.

Table 2.2    Average rate of increase of agricultural output, 1700–1985 (per cent per annum)

| | |
|---|---|
| 1700 to 1760[a] | 0.6 |
| 1760 to 1780[a] | 0.13 |
| 1780 to 1801[a] | 0.75 |
| 1801/11 to 1831/41[b] | 1.2 |
| 1811/21 to 1841/51[b] | 1.5 |
| 1821/31 to 1851/61[b] | 1.8 |
| 1831/41 to 1861/71[b] | 1.3 |
| 1841/51 to 1871/81[b] | 0.7 |
| 1851/61 to 1881/91[b] | 0.5 |
| 1861/71 to 1891/1901[b] | 0.7 |
| 1885/9 to 1900/4[a] | − 0.8 |
| 1900/4 to 1922/4[a] | 0.0 |
| 1922/4 to 1936/9[a] | 1.6 |
| 1936/9 to 1960[c] | 2.9 |
| 1960 to 1985[c] | 2.7 |

[a] England and Wales.
[b] Compound percentage rates per annum for decade averages measured over 30-year periods for Great Britain.
[c] United Kingdom of Great Britain and Northern Ireland.
*Sources*: N. F. R. Crafts, *British Economic Growth during the Industrial Revolution* (1985), p. 42; P. Deane and W. A. Cole, *British Economic Growth 1688–1959* (Cambridge, 1962), p. 170; O. J. Beilby, 'Changes in agricultural production in England and Wales', *Journal of the Royal Agricultural Society of England*, 100 (1930), pp. 62–73; Central Statistical Office, *Economic Trends, Annual Supplement 1986* (1986), p. 84; British Parliamentary Papers, *Accounts and Papers*, 26, 7 (1956–7), p. 384.

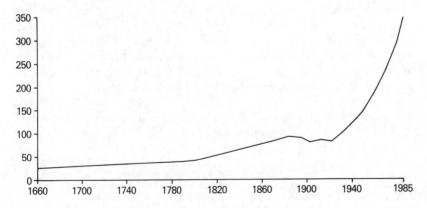

Figure 2.1 An index of agricultural output, 1660–1985 (1936–9 = 100).
*Source*: see Appendix to chapter 1, pp. 14–15.

of the present. Indeed for much of the late seventeenth and early eighteenth centuries England was a major cereal exporter, but as population began to grow after 1740 so exports were diverted to home use, and they had largely disappeared by the 1760s.[2] By the end of the century one-sixth of British food consumption was imported, much of it from Ireland, but some also from Eastern Europe and from North America. The rapid rate of population growth in the early nineteenth century – much higher than that before or since – meant that by 1841 one-fifth of food supplies came from abroad.[3] This was at a time when cereal and other products were still protected by import duties, while the difficulty of moving perishable produce before the age of refrigeration also protected British farmers. The repeal of the Corn Laws in 1846 removed the former protection. Britain's continued population growth combined with rising real incomes after the 1860s came at a time when the introduction of refrigeration and the decline in oceanic and railway freight rates combined with the opening up of cheap land in the interior of North America, Australia and temperate South America provided the British consumer with a variety of cheap foods – but at the expense of the British farmer. By the end of the nineteenth century Britain was not only importing a great variety of tropical products such as tea, coffee, cocoa and citrus fruits, but had become dependent upon overseas suppliers for many of the staple foods that were also produced in Britain. In 1905–7 the United Kingdom imported three-quarters of its wheat, 75 to 80 per cent of its butter and cheese and half its meat (see table 2.3). this system of provisioning the country, whereby cheap food was paid for by the export of manufactured goods, received a rude shock in the U-boat campaign of the First World War; but by the eve of the Second World War Britain's imports were an even greater proportion of consumption than in 1905–7.

In the Second World War Britain had to reduce food consumption; after the war the world food shortages of the late 1940s led the government to encourage a policy of self-sufficiency, so that, although the system of agricultural support allowed the entry of foreign food, Britain did not return to pre-war levels of imports. The increases in home output in the 1950s and 1960s also eroded the need for imports. But it was entry into the Common Market, with a system of levies on imported goods, that effectively ended Britain's import of cheap food. Consequently much of the increase in home food output since 1973 has replaced imports, generally of course at a higher cost (see table 2.3). Not all Britain's consumption can be produced at home. Tropical

---

2 D. Ormrod, *English Grain Exports and the Structure of Agrarian Capitalism 1700–1760*, Occasional Papers in Economic and Social History no. 12 (Hull, 1985).

3 N. F. R. Crafts, *British Economic Growth during the Industrial Revolution* (London, 1985), pp. 127, 138; B. Thomas, "Food supply in the UK during the Industrial Revolution", *Agricultural History*, 56 (1982), pp. 328–42.

Table 2.3   Long-term changes in United Kingdom self-sufficiency (percentage home-produced)

| Product | 1905–7 | 1937 | 1946–7 | 1953–4 | 1963–4 | 1972–3 | 1983 |
|---|---|---|---|---|---|---|---|
| Wheat | 25 | 23 | 30 | 41 | 40 | 52 | 101 |
| Barley | 60 | 46 | 96 | 67 | 94 | 97 | 143 |
| Oats | 74 | 94 | 95 | 97 | 97 | 99 | 95 |
| Potatoes | 92 | – | 99 | 100 | 100 | 93 | 89 |
| Butter | 13 | 9 | 8 | 9 | 9 | 22 | 65 |
| Cheese | 24 | 24 | 8 | 28 | 44 | 54 | 65 |
| Eggs | 32 | 61 | 51 | 86 | 96 | 97 | 97 |
| Beef and Veal | 53 | 49 | 58 | 66 | 73 | 85 | 101 |
| Lamb and Mutton | 52 | 36 | 24 | 35 | 43 | 43 | 77 |

*Sources*: S. J. Fallows and J. V. Wheelock, 'Self sufficiency and United Kingdom food policy', *Agricultural Administration*, 11 (1982), pp. 107–25; Ministry of Agriculture, *Annual Reviews of Agriculture*.

beverages and fruits have to be imported, so that in 1983 Britain was still importing 37.9 per cent of its total food supplies, compared with 50.8 per cent before entry into the Common Market (see table 2.4). Of temperate products, which can be grown in Britain, the country now produces nearly four-fifths compared with only 61.8 per cent in 1970 and only 50 per cent in the 1930s (see table 2.4).

CHANGING CONSUMPTION NEEDS

Britain has needed an increase in food output since the 1930s because the population rose by 20 per cent between the censuses of 1931 and 1981. This alone would have required an increase in output or further imports. Income increases have also led to rising demand. In the 1930s a significant proportion of the population was living on very low real

Table 2.4   Measures of self-sufficiency, United Kingdom (home output as a percentage of consumption)

| | 1930s | 1955–6 to 1957–8 | 1966–7 to 1968–9 | 1970 | 1975 | 1980 | 1983 |
|---|---|---|---|---|---|---|---|
| All foods | c.33 | 46.7 | 46.2 | 49.2 | 51.4 | 59.3 | 62.1 |
| Indigenous-type foods | c.50 | 61.1 | 58.1 | 61.8 | 63.4 | 73.9 | 78.1 |

*Sources*: Central Statistical Office, *Annual Abstract of Statistics, 1985* (1986); R. Mordue and J. Parrett, 'United Kingdom self sufficiency in food, 1970–78', *Economic Trends*, 312 (1979), pp. 151–5.

incomes, and widespread malnutrition was one symptom of this poverty.[4] The war reduced unemployment and raised incomes, and from the late 1940s real incomes have risen continuously. Initially, increased incomes among the poor led to increased food consumption, but by the 1960s little of the higher wages and salaries went on extra food. In contrast, in nineteenth century England the bulk of the population was poor and spent a high proportion of its income on food – and on the foods that would give most calories per penny. Households in Lancashire towns in the 1840s obtained 70 per cent of their calorie intake from potatoes and bread.[5] Later in the century as real incomes rose there was an increased demand for more expensive foods – meat, milk, fruit and fresh vegetables – which was met partly by imports, partly by home production. British farmers for all their problems had an expanding market, with both population and incomes increasing.

But by the 1960s most of the British population, with rising incomes and little unemployment, was spending its increased income, not on extra or more expensive food, but on televisions, refrigerators, houses and holidays, while the rate of population growth, which since the 1920s had been well below nineteenth-century rates, was falling even lower. Thus the increase in the potential market for food was falling behind the growth of food output. This has to be qualified to some extent. First, since the 1950s the British consumer has spent more on the processing and marketing of food – on canned, dried, frozen and pre-cooked foods and washed potatoes – while much more food expenditure has gone on meals bought outside the home. Second, there have been some changes in per capita consumption (see table 2.5). Most noticeable has been the decline in the consumption of bread; potato consumption, however, has held up well. But while preferences for meat have changed from beef and mutton to poultry and pork, total meat consumption per capita has changed little since the 1930s, and the increase in cheese has been matched by a fall in butter consumption.[6] Thus the market for English farmers has increased very slowly over the post-war period.

4 Sir John Boyd Orr, *Food, Health and Income* (London, 1937); F. Le Gros Clark and R. M. Titmus, *Our Food Problem and its Relation to our National Defences* (Harmondsworth, 1939) p. 125.

5 J. C. McKenzie, "The composition and nutritional value of diets in Manchester and Dukinfield, 1841", *Lancashire and Cheshire Antiquarian Society Transactions*, 72 (1962), pp. 126–39.

6 L. J. Angel and G. E. Hurdle, "The nation's food – forty years of change", *Economic Trends*, 294 (1978), pp. 97–105; J. P. Greaves and D. F. Hollingsworth, "Trends in food consumption in the United Kingdom", *World Review of Nutrition and Dietetics*, 6 (1966), pp. 34–89; Ministry of Agriculture, *Household Food Consumption and Expenditure: annual report of the National Food Survey Committee, 1985* (London, 1987).

Table 2.5   Changes in supply of principal foods moving into consumption, 1934–1980 (lbs per head per annum)

| Product | 1934–8 | 1950–2 | 1960–2 | 1970–2 | 1978–80 |
|---|---|---|---|---|---|
| Dairy products[a] | 38.3 | 53.5 | 55.1 | 56.2 | 53.4 |
| Meat | 110.0 | 85.6 | 117.5 | 115.5 | 107.9 |
| Poultry, Game | 32.7[b] | 28.4[b] | 10.0 | 23.3 | 20.6 |
| Fish | – | – | 20.8 | 18.7 | 15.4 |
| Eggs | 28.3 | 28.5 | 33.4 | 35.0 | 31.4 |
| Oils and Fats[c] | 46.9 | 47.4 | 49.4 | 49.9 | 49.3 |
| Sugar and Syrup | 104.6 | 90.9 | 115.5 | 114.1 | 103.2 |
| Pulses, Nuts | 9.5 | 10.3 | 11.2 | 12.3 | 12.3 |
| Potatoes | 181.9 | 241.3 | 221.3 | 221.5 | 229.5 |
| Fruit | 137.4 | 127.0 | 143.2 | 125.9 | 128.2 |
| Vegetables | 107.0 | 105.4 | 103.0 | 137.2[d] | 148.1 |
| Cereal products | 210.1 | 221.1 | 178.3 | 160.0 | 157.3 |
| Tea | 9.3 | 8.3 | 9.5 | 8.3 | 6.7 |
| Coffee | 0.7 | 1.6 | 2.3 | 4.5 | 4.8 |

[a] Excluding butter.
[b] Includes fish.
[c] Butter, margarine, lard, other edible oils.
[d] Change in method of classification.
Sources: Ministry of Agriculture, Domestic Food Consumption and Expenditure: 1956 (1958); Thereafter annually Household Food Consumption and Expenditure.

THE STRUCTURE OF BRITISH AGRICULTURAL OUTPUT

The recent growth of *total* agricultural output has been outlined; it is now necessary to look at what different items British farmers produce and how this has changed over time.

Although cereals have received a great deal of attention from many writers, they do not dominate the output of British agriculture. Indeed no one item does, and the national farm produces a wide variety of products; of individual items only milk, fat cattle and wheat account for more than one-tenth of the value of total output (see table 2.6). However, it is livestock and livestock products and not crops that are of most significance. Livestock sold fat together with livestock products such as eggs, milk and wool account for over 60 per cent of total output; and it should be recalled that half the cereal output is sold to make feeds for livestock. Thus although there is no gainsaying the rising importance of cereals since entry into the Common Market – wheat and barley now accounting for nearly one-fifth of the value of output compared with nearer one-tenth in 1969–70 – livestock remains the primary product of British agriculture.

The dominance of livestock and livestock products is relatively new. In the eighteenth century, crops – mainly cereals – probably accounted

Table 2.6   The structure of United Kingdom agricultural output, 1969–1970 and 1985 (current prices)

| Product | 1969–70 £ (million) | % | 1985 £ (million) | % |
|---|---|---|---|---|
| Cereals | 245 | 11.3 | 2,283 | 19.3 |
| Wheat | 91 | 4.2 | 1,408 | 11.9 |
| Barley | 144 | 6.7 | 843 | 7.1 |
| Other | 10 | 0.4 | 32 | 0.3 |
| Other crops | 184.1 | 8.5 | 814 | 6.9 |
| Potatoes | 125 | 5.8 | 324 | 2.7 |
| Sugar-beet | 41 | 1.9 | 231 | 2.0 |
| Hops | | | 15 | 0.1 |
| Oilseed rape | 18.1 | 0.8 | 244 | 2.1 |
| Fodder | | | | |
| Horticulture | 271 | 12.5 | 1,256 | 10.6 |
| Vegetables | 153 | 7.0 | 771 | 6.5 |
| Fruit | 58 | 2.7 | 231 | 2.0 |
| Flowers, etc. | 60 | 2.8 | 254 | 2.1 |
| | | | | |
| All crops | 700.1 | 32.3 | 4,353 | 36.8 |
| | | | | |
| Livestock | 796 | 36.9 | 4,321 | 36.5 |
| Fat cattle and calves | 336 | 15.6 | 1,932 | 16.3 |
| Fat sheep and lambs | 85 | 3.9 | 609 | 5.1 |
| Fat pigs | 248 | 11.5 | 974 | 8.2 |
| Poultry | 127 | 5.9 | 702 | 6.0 |
| Other | – | – | 104 | 0.9 |
| | | | | |
| Livestock products | 661 | 30.6 | 3,009 | 25.4 |
| Milk and milk products | 455 | 21.1 | 2,398 | 20.3 |
| Eggs | 192 | 8.9 | 528 | 4.5 |
| Clipwool | 14 | 0.6 | 41 | 0.3 |
| Other | – | – | 42 | 0.3 |
| | | | | |
| Total: | 2,157.1 | | 11,683 | |

*Source*: Ministry of Agriculture, *Annual Reviews of Agriculture*.

for two-thirds or more of the value of output (see table 2.7). This declined as the output of livestock increased in the nineteenth century. But it was not until the 1850s that the value of livestock equalled the value of crops. Thereafter, rising incomes and an increased demand for milk, meat, butter, cheese, vegetables and fruit slowly changed the structure of British agricultural output. Part of the demand for livestock products was met by imports from abroad – New Zealand butter, Dutch cheese and Argentine beef entered the British diet in the late nineteenth century – but the eclipse of cereals by imports pushed farmers slowly and reluctantly towards livestock products and arable farmers in particular

Table 2.7 The changing structure of British agricultural output, 1785–1985 (percentage per annum)

| Product | 1785[a] | 1831[a] | 1856[a] | 1867–73[a] | 1908[b] | 1925[b] | 1951[c] | 1970[c] | 1985[c] |
|---|---|---|---|---|---|---|---|---|---|
| Milk and dairy products | – | – | – | 15 | 19.1 | 25.6 | 31.5 | 21.1 | 20.3 |
| Fatstock | – | – | – | 37 | 43.7 | 35.0 | 22.7 | 31.0 | 29.6 |
| Eggs and Poultry | – | – | – | 3 | 3.2 | 6.7 | 13.9 | 14.8 | 10.5 |
| All livestock | 37.8 | 45.5 | 51.3 | 55 | 66.0 | 67.3 | 68.1 | 66.9 | 62.1 |
| Crops | – | – | – | 36 | 29.5 | 20.5 | 20.4 | 19.9 | 27.3 |
| Horticulture | – | – | – | 5 | 2.9 | 10.9 | 9.6 | 12.5 | 10.6 |
| All crops | 62.2 | 54.5 | 48.7 | 41 | 32.4 | 31.4 | 30.0 | 32.4 | 37.9 |
| Other | | | | 4 | 1.6 | 1.3 | 1.9 | 0.7 | – |

[a] Great Britain.
[b] England and Wales.
[c] United Kingdom.
Sources: P. O'Brien and C. Keyder, *Economic Growth in Britain and France 1780–1914* (London, 1978), p. 44; E. Ojala, *Agriculture and Economic Progress* (Oxford, 1952), p. 208; E. H. Whetham, *The Agrarian History of England and Wales*, vol. VIII: *1914–1939* (Cambridge, 1978), p. 5; Ministry of Agriculture and Fisheries, *The Agricultural Output of England and Wales 1925* (London, 1927), Cmd. 2815; Ministry of Agriculture, Fisheries and Food, *Annual Reviews of Agriculture*.

towards potatoes and other vegetables. By the beginning of the twentieth century two-thirds of the value of British output was from livestock and only a third from crops. This ratio remained unchanged – although horticulture accounted for a rising proportion of crop output – until the 1970s. Since entry to the Common Market, the favourable prices for cereals and oilseed rape and the introduction of dairy quotas and their effect on milk output have increased the crop share of total output.

SUMMARY

This chapter has demonstrated the remarkable growth of output since the 1930s as a result of government support and technical advance, both of which are explored in more detail in later chapters. At the same time demand for food – or for the raw materials farmers produce – has slowed: population growth has been well below nineteenth-century rates and a progressively more affluent population has spent its income increases not on food but on consumer durables. Under the Common Agricultural Policy the imposition of import levies has led to the substitution of imports by home-grown food – although Britain still remains a major food importer. But the EEC's pricing system has led to the growth of surpluses, in spite of the half-hearted attempts to curtail output by the introduction of quotas for dairy produce and thresholds to the payment of target prices. Clearly, government policy has been critical in accounting for the growth of output, and this must now be considered.

## Appendix

The Ministry of Agriculture has published an index of net agricultural output for the United Kingdom in the *Annual Review of Agriculture* since 1952–3; before that indices were published annually in the *Journal* of the Ministry of Agriculture. The index is in constant prices, and before 1960 is net of seeds, feeding stuffs and livestock; after 1960 machinery, fertilizers and other costs are also deducted. However, the indices have been rebased periodically and cannot be linked.[7]

*Economic Trends, Annual Supplement* publishes an index of output of agriculture, forestry and fisheries, net of inputs and in constant prices. The index in figure 2.1 has been constructed by taking the Ministry of Agriculture index, base year 1936–9 as 100, to 1954, and extending it by a percentage increase based on the 1987 *Economic Trends* index for 1954–84. Note this conflicts with the

7 Ministry of Agriculture, "The new index of agricultural net output in the United Kingdom", *Economic Trends*, 77 (1960), pp. viii–x; "The index of agricultural net output in the United Kingdom: rebasing on 1964/65–1966/67", *Economic Trends*, 194 (1969), pp. xxxvii–xxxviii; J. E. Outlaw and G. Croft, "Recent developments in economic accounting for agriculture", *Economic Trends*, 339 (1981), pp. 94–9.

Ministry's index, which shows a decline from 1975 to 1983, and Nix and Edwards, which shows a greater increase from 1954 to 1984.[8]

The period for the 1880s to the 1930s is based upon Bielby: his index is spliced on to the Ministry's index. The difference between 1885–9 and the 1870s is covered by using Drescher's index of change.[9]

From 1801 to 1871 there is assumed to have been a doubling of net ouput, although Deane and Cole's figures, the only series available for the first three-quarters of the century, give for 1801–71 a 73 per cent increase in the agricultural income of Great Britain at current prices, and a 150 per cent increase at constant prices. The latter seems too high: the increase used, of 100 per cent from 1801 to 1871, is a guess.[10]

Jackson suggests an index of output for England and Wales of 100 for 1660, 140 for 1740 and 160 for 1790. 1801 is taken as 170 and spliced onto the later figure. All the indices before 1936–9 are by calculation backwards.[11]

8 *Annual Review of Agriculture 1987*, HMSO, Cm. 67 (1987); J. Nix and Angela Edwards, "Trends in agricultural productivity: the UK, USA and Greece compared", *Outlook in Agriculture*, 16 (1987), pp. 82–98.

9 O. J. Beilby, "Changes in agricultural production in England and Wales", *Journal of the Royal Agricultural Society of England*, 100 (1939), pp. 62–73; L. Drescher, "The development of agricultural production in Great Britain and Ireland from the early nineteenth century", *Manchester School*, 23 (1955), pp. 193–75. See also E. M. Ojala, *Agriculture and Economic Progress* (London, 1952); T. W. Fletcher, "Drescher's index: a comment", *Manchester School*, 23 (1955), pp. 176–83; P. O'Brien, *Economic Growth in Britain and France 1780–1914*, (London, 1978).

10 P. Deane and W. A. Cole, *Britain's Economic Growth 1685–1959: trends and structure* (Cambridge, 1962), pp. 166, 282, 291.

11 R. V. Jackson, "Growth and deceleration in English agriculture 1660–1790", *Economic History Review*, 38 (1985), pp. 333–51. See also Deane and Cole, *op. cit.* (1962), p. 78, which gives a 43% increase in real agricultural output in the 18th century; and W. A. Cole, "Factors in demand 1700–80", in R. Floud and D. McCloskey (eds), *The Economic History of Britain since 1700*, vol. 1: *1700–1860* (Cambridge, 1981), p. 64; this gives an 80% increase in output at 1700 prices. E. L. Jones in Floud and McCloskey, p. 68, gives an increase of 61% in the 18th century, 25 to 36% in the 17th century and 25 to 37% in the sixteenth century.

# 3

# Prices, Policies and Prosperity

The post-war growth of output has been accompanied by prosperity for farmers in England and Wales, both when compared with the past or with many other groups in post-war English society.[1] But this has been due as much to the financial support farmers have received from the British government, and later from the policies of the EEC, as to their own enterprise. Stanley Evans, the Parliamentary Secretary for the Ministry of Food in the Labour government, summarized in 1950 the feelings of many when he said that 'no other nation feather-beds its agriculture like Britain'.[2] Yet it is by no means easy to trace the changing prosperity of farmers. Even in the 1950s some 90 per cent of British farmers did not keep reliable farm accounts,[3] and the evidence on post-war farm incomes is based on government estimates of national farm prices and costs rather than on farmers' actual incomes. Before 1939–45 the changing fortunes of agriculture can be traced only by inference from long-term movements in prices, rents and production costs and the comments of contemporaries, none of which is a reliable guide to net income.

## POST-WAR PROSPERITY

At first sight there is little doubt about the post-war growth in farming prosperity. In the 1920s and 1930s prices were falling, rents were low, bankruptcies were common and much land was out of cultivation. Agricultural prices rose dramatically from 1939 to the early 1950s, then stabilized until the great inflation of the 1970s and 1980s (see figure 3.1). But in *real* terms agricultural prices did little more than hold their own in the 1940s and 1950s, and since 1973 have trended downwards

1 J. K. Bowers and P. Cheshire, *Agriculture, the Countryside and Land Use: an economic critique* (London, 1983), pp. 83–5.
2 *The Times* (17 April 1950).
3 T. Beresford, *We Plough the Fields* (Harmondsworth, 1975), p. 47.

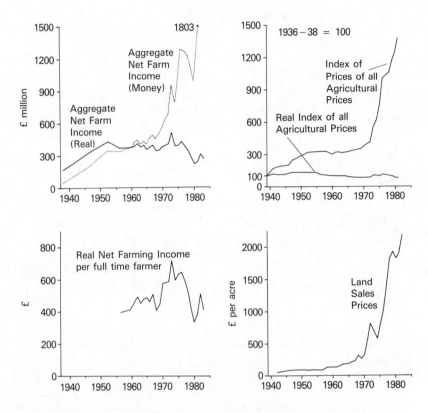

Figure 3.1 Trends in farm income, agricultural prices and land prices.
*Source*: R. W. Howarth, *Farming for Farmers: a critique of agricultural support policy* (London, 1985), pp. 79–80.

(see figure 3.1). The Ministry of Agriculture has provided estimates of the net aggregate income of the United Kingdom farming industry since the 1930s. This income has risen steeply since 1940; but in *real* terms most of the progress was made between 1939 and 1953, when real net income increased two and a half times. Thereafter, until the 1970s real income was relatively little changed; in the 1970s the method of measuring real net income was altered, but there is little doubt that it has declined since the peak of 1973 (figure 3.1). Since 1940 the number of full-time farmers has declined, and so the average farmer's income has risen, but as there are no reliable statistics on the number of farmers, estimates of the average farm income are debatable. Evidence from several sources suggests a steady increase in real income per farmer from the pre-war period until the 1970s and a decline since then (see figure 3.1 and table 3.1). Farm incomes underestimate British farmers' income, for fully one-third have incomes from a source other than farming, while

Table 3.1   Farmers' incomes, 1938–1982

| Date | United Kingdom[a] | England and Wales[b] | United Kingdom[c] |
|------|------|------|------|
| 1938 | 1,177 | – | – |
| 1939 | 2,414 | – | – |
| 1940–4 | 3,573 | 5,975 | – |
| 1945–7 | 3,164 | 3,443 | – |
| 1948–52 | 3,826 | 4,975 | – |
| 1953–7 | 3,403 | 5,002 | – |
| 1958–62 | 3,569 | 5,564 | – |
| 1963–7 | 3,961 | 6,825 | – |
| 1968–72 | 4,904 | 8,066 | 9,263 |
| 1973–7 | 7,384 | 10,368 | 9,796 |
| 1978–82 | – | – | 6,342 |

[a] Agricultural net income divided by estimate of the number of farmers, in £ per annum at 1976 prices.
[b] Incomes from Farm Management Survey. A sample of 2,250 farms; in 1976 prices.
[c] Real net farm income per full-time farmer at 1980 prices.
*Sources*: J. K. Bowers and Paul Cheshire, *Agriculture, the Countryside and Land Use: an economique critique* (London, 1983), p. 82; Richard W. Howarth, *Farming for Farmers? A critique of agricultural support policy*, Institute of Economic Affairs (London, 1985), p. 65.

in terms of *wealth*, occupier-owners and landlords have gained from the rise in land values, particularly since 1970 (see figure 3.1); these, like farm incomes, however, have begun to fall in the uncertain times of the 1980s.[4] Nor, of course, have all farmers shared equally in the post-war growth of incomes. There are very marked differences in income both by type of farming (see table 3.2a) and by size of business (table 3.2b). Not surprisingly, net incomes are largest on farms with a large annual turnover, while farmers producing crops do better than the producers of livestock (table 3.2a); as crop producers are mainly in the east and livestock producers in the west, there are also regional variations in farm incomes (table 3.2c).

TRENDS IN FARMING PROSPERITY, 1770–1870s

There have of course been periods of very varying farming prosperity in the past, and the fortunes of the post-war period should be set in a rather longer perspective. The late eighteenth century was a period of rising prices, both for cereals and livestock products and of rents (see figures 3.2 and 3.3). During the Napoleonic Wars cereal prices reached remarkable heights in the general inflation and shortages of food supplies.

4 B. Hill, "Farm incomes: myths and perspectives", *Lloyds Bank Review*, 149 (1983), pp. 35–48; "Concepts and measurement of the incomes, wealth and economic well-being of farmers", *Journal of Agricultural Economics*, 34 (1983), pp. 311–24.

Table 3.2   Variations in farm income, England, 1983–1984 (average per farm)

| *(a)*<br>*by type of farming* | | *(b)*<br>*by size of holding in BSU*[a] | |
|---|---|---|---|
| | £ | | £ |
| General cropping | 22,485 | 100 and over | 67,419 |
| Specialist cereals | 17,529 | 40–99.9 | 23,389 |
| Horticulture | 16,774 | 24–39.9 | 10,922 |
| Hill and upland sheep | 10,769 | 16–23.9 | 6,053 |
| Mainly dairying | 10,475 | 8–15.9 | 4,350 |
| Pigs and poultry | 8,708 | 4– 7.9 | 738 |
| Hill cattle and sheep | 7,979 | Average | 12,261 |
| Specialist dairying | 6,664 | | |

| *(a)*<br>*by type of farming* | | *(c)*<br>*by region* | |
|---|---|---|---|
| Lowland cropping, cattle and sheep | 5,618 | | |
| Lowland cattle and sheep | 2,963 | | |
| Average (excluding horticulture) | 12,261 | | £ |
| | | East | 16,472 |
| | | North | 11,954 |
| | | West | 8,095 |

[a] British Size Unit is a measure of the size of a farm business. One BSU equals 2,000 European Units of Account of Standard Gross Margin at 1978–80 average value. Large Pig and Poultry and Horticulture Units have been excluded from the sample.
*Source*: Ministry of Agriculture, *Farm Incomes in England 1984*, Farm Income Series no. 37, (London, 1985).

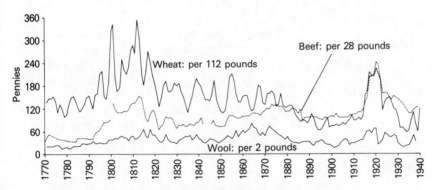

Figure 3.2   Wheat, beef and wool prices, 1770–1940.
*Sources*: J. D. Chambers and G. E. Mingay, *The Agricultural Revolution, 1750–1880* (London, 1966), p. 167; Lord Ernle, *English Farming, Past and Present* (London, 1961), pp. 488–9.

The price of wheat in 1812 was £1.9.6 per hundredweight, a level not reached again until 1953. Although rents doubled between 1790 and 1815 and labour costs also increased, farm profits rose substantially in this period.[5]

5 J. D. Chambers and G. E. Mingay, *The Agricultural Revolution 1750–1880* (London, 1966), p. 167; G. Hueckel, "English farming profits during the Napoleonic Wars 1793–1815", *Explorations in Economic History*, 13 (1976), pp. 331–49.

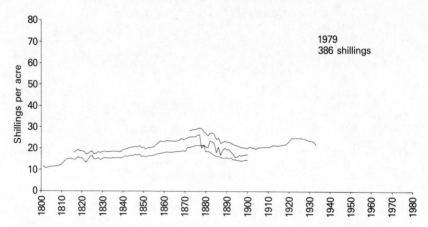

Figure 3.3 Rent per acre on selected estates in England and Wales from 1800.
Sources: R. J. Thompson, 'An inquiry into the rent of agricultural land in England and Wales during the nineteenth century', *Journal of the Royal Statistical Society*, 70 (1907), pp. 587–624; A. Rhee, *The Rent of Agricultural Land in England and Wales* (London, 1949).

After 1812 both cereal and livestock prices fell, and the 1820s and 1830s have been seen as a period of agricultural depression. Certainly arrears of rent accumulated in some parts of the country, and the farming press and witnesses to Select Committees of the House of Commons were full of compaints.[6] It seems likely that the principal sufferers, as in the 1730s and later in the 1880s and 1890s, were cereal producers, particularly on the heavy clays of the Midlands. Falling prices did not halt the expansion of the area in wheat;[7] during this period, however, a relative movement in favour of livestock products became apparent (see table 3.3). Rents did not decline in most of the country (see figure 3.3) and by the 1830s farmers in the east and south were making substantial outlays on new inputs such as oil-cake, fertilizers and buildings, particularly for cattle. The repeal of the Corn Laws in 1846 did not lead to the disaster that many farmers expected; wheat prices fluctuated but did not fall substantially (see figure 3.2). Wool and meat prices, in contrast, rose considerably; wool prices in the 1860s and 1870s were twice their level in 1850 and beef rose over 50 per cent from 1850 to the 1870s.[8] The High Farming in the 1850s and 1860s is seen by most historians – with some justification – as a period of considerable agricultural prosperity for farmers and landlords: rents rose

6 G. E. Fussell and M. Compton, "Agricultural adjustments after the Napoleonic Wars", *Economic History*, 4 (1939), pp. 18–24; D. Grigg, "A note on agricultural rent and expenditure in nineteenth century England", *Agricultural History*, 39 (1965), pp. 147–54.

7 A. R. Wilkes, "Adjustments in arable farming after the Napoleonic Wars", *Agricultural History Review*, 28 (1980), pp. 90–103.

8 Chambers and Mingay, *op. cit.* (1966), p. 110.

Table 3.3    Trends in agricultural prices, 1790–1870 (average annual percentage rates of change)

|  | 1790–1815 | 1812–22 | 1822–45 | 1846–70 |
|---|---|---|---|---|
| Grain prices | + 2.5 | − 6.6 | − 0.1 | + 0.2 |
| Animal product prices | + 2.7 | − 4.5 | + 0.2 | + 0.7 |

*Source*: G. Hueckel, 'Agriculture during industrialisation', in R. Floud and D. McCloskey (eds), *The Economic History of Britain since 1700*, vol. 1: *1700–1860 (Cambridge, 1981), p. 183.*

from between 35 and 50 per cent from 1820 to 1870 (see figure 3.3). Even agricultural labourers had some gain in real wages after 1850. Perhaps of most significance was the continued shift of prices in favour of livestock production (see table 3.3).[9]

### THE GREAT DEPRESSION

The repeal of the Corn Laws reduced import duties on nearly all agricultural products, and Britain's dependence upon food imports increased. But it was not until the 1870s that there was any great impact upon home prices. The continued fall in oceanic and railway freight rates, the introduction of refrigeration to ships, and the rapid opening up of new land overseas in the later nineteenth century led to a dramatic fall in prices. Unlike most of the rest of Europe – elsewhere only the Netherlands and Denmark maintained free trade – Britain did not impose any tariffs upon this flood of cheap imports and the British farmer suffered accordingly, although the British consumer gained. The rent of agricultural land fell by 29 per cent between the late 1870s and 1901 (see figure 3.3) and average farm income slumped.[10] The only other gainers were farm-workers, whose numbers were falling and whose real wages were rising. However the prices of different products did not fall by equal amounts and so not all farmers were equally affected. The greatest fall was in wheat and wool (see figure 3.2 and table 3.4), while livestock farmers, particularly those producing milk, whose price fell hardly at all, suffered less. Consequently, there was a marked regional difference in the impact of the depression – the arable farmers of the

9 E. L. Jones, "The changing basis of English agricultural prosperity 1853–73", in W. E. Minchinton (ed.), *Essays in Agrarian History*, 2 (London, 1968), pp. 219–37.
    10 R. J. Thompson, "An inquiry into the rent of agricultural land in England and Wales during the nineteenth century", *Journal of the Royal Statistical Society*, 70 (1907), pp. 587–624; J. R. Bellerby, "Distribution of farm income in the United Kingdom, 1867–1938", in W. E. Minchinton (ed.), *Essays in Agrarian History*, 2 (London, 1968), pp. 261–78.

Table 3.4 Decline in agricultural prices,
from 1876–1878 to 1893–1894

| Product | % |
| --- | --- |
| Wheat | 52 |
| Barley | 37 |
| Oats | 34 |
| Potatoes | 20 |
| Wool | 40–50 |
| Cheese and Butter | 25–33 |
| Fat cattle | 24–30 |
| Fat sheep | 23 |

*Sources*: G. R. Porter, *The Progress of the Nation*
(new edition, revised by F. W. Hirst, London,
1912), pp. 203–4; P. J. Perry, *British Farming in
the Great Depression 1870–1914: an historical
geography* (Newton Abbot, 1974), pp. 42–51.

east and south, for whom cereals and wool were important, suffering most, the livestock producers of the Midlands and the west suffering least, while arable farmers, who turned to vegetables or fruit, rode out the bad years.

The decline in prices halted in the mid-1890s and the Edwardian period was one of stability. During the First World War the prices of all agricultural commodities soared; in 1917 the government guaranteed cereal prices and farm profits rose. But when the guarantee was withdrawn in 1921 cereal prices slumped, as did other prices, as world shortages gave way to oversupply.[11] In 1934 wheat reached its lowest price since the Corn Returns began in 1771 (see figure 3.2). The 1920s and early 1930s were bad years for farmers, but as in the earlier depression livestock farmers suffered less than cereal producers, and potato, vegetable and sugar-beet prices were enough to encourage some arable farmers. In the mid-1930s confidence was returning to farming, and incomes were well above their low point in the 1890s.[12]

POLICIES AND PROSPERITY

The prosperity of farming in the post-war period, and indeed much of the technical change in the industry, is largely due to the support policies of the British government. Although the calculation is difficult to make,

11 E. H. Whetham, "The Agriculture Act, 1920, and its repeal – the 'Great Betrayal'", *Agricultural History Review*, 22 (1974), pp. 36–49; P. Dewey, "British farming profits and government policy during the First World War", *Economic History Review*, 37 (1984), pp. 373–90; A. Cooper, "Another look at the Great Betrayal", *Agricultural History*, 60 (1986), pp. 81–104.
12 Bellerby, *op. cit.* (1968), pp. 261–78.

it has nonetheless been estimated that the cost of agricultural support was equal to the UK aggregate farm net income in the mid-1950s, between half and four-fifths of farm income until the early 1970s; in the late 1970s government support was again equal to net farm income.[13] The nature of government support, although often discussed, needs some comment here, as does its origin.

In 1846 Sir Robert Peel steered an Act repealing the Corn Laws through the House of Commons, split the Conservative party and ended his own political career. The Act also ended some 200 years of protection for British farmers and landlords and initiated a comparatively short period of free trade. Before 1846 duties had been imposed upon the import of cereals into the United Kingdom, one aim being to maintain a reasonable price for wheat. This was often incompatible with a reasonable price for bread, and the Corn Laws had been the centre of prolonged debate, which became particularly heated after the 1815 Act that established a sliding scale of duties. Political hostility to the duties was backed by a large growing urban population, and the urban consumer won the battle. Import duties were reduced on cereals and nearly all other agricultural products; at the same time Peel's Act introduced the first producer subsidy – financial incentives to landlords and tenants to underdrain their land.[14]

By the 1870s free trade was too embedded in the political philosophy of both parties for much change to be likely when prices began to fall. The first return to protection did not come until war caused shortages, and in 1917 the government guaranteed a price for cereals and later promised to maintain fixed prices after the end of the war. The post-war fall in world prices made this extremely costly and the promise was broken in 1921.[15] But the deep depression in both industry and agriculture in the 1920s and 1930s made protection for farmers at last politically possible.

Protection for farming came in by the back door. In 1924 farmers were exempted from local rates and in 1925 British sugar production was granted a subsidy. But in 1932 more overt protection was offered. In the Wheat Act of that year farmers were given a deficiency payment, the difference between a notional price set by the government and the price at which the farmer sold. This was financed by a levy on flour. In addition a system of import quotas was negotiated with the leading

13 B. Hill and K. A. Ingersent, *An Economic Analysis of Agriculture* (London, 1982), pp. 106–7; R. Body, *Agriculture: the triumph and the shame* (London, 1982), p. 5; R. W. Howarth, *Farming for Farmers? A critique of agricultural support policy*, Institute of Economic Affairs (London 1985), pp. 79–80.

14 D. C. Moore, "The Corn Laws and High Farming", *Economic History Review*, 18 (1965), pp. 544–61; N. Longmate, *The Breadstealers: the fight against the Corn Laws 1838–1846* (London, 1984).

15 Whetham, *op. cit.* (1974); E. A. Attwood, "The origins of state support for British agriculture", *Manchester School*, 31 (1963), pp. 129–48.

wheat exporters. Earlier tariffs had been imposed in 1931 on some horticultural imports, a subsidy on fat cattle was introduced in 1934, and in 1937 the Ministry of Agriculture began to pay a subsidy on the use of lime. In the early 1930s Agricultural Marketing Acts were passed to reorganize the marketing of milk, potatoes and hops. But although here were nearly all the methods of price support and organization to be used in the 1947 Agricultural Act, the cost to the British Exchequer in the 1930s was negligible – no more than 5 per cent of the value of gross output in 1937–8.[16]

The outbreak of war transformed the attitude towards farming of both the government and the nation, which was suddenly required to produce as much food as possible, almost regardless of cost. Food was rationed and the government became the sole purchaser of agricultural products. The price of cereals and milk was raised, and producer subsidies were given to hill sheep. Farming prospered, even though machinery and feeding stuffs were rationed and allocated by the government and inefficient farmers could be evicted by local Agricultural Executive Committees.[17]

During the war there was much discussion of post-war policies, and there was agreement between the political parties and by landlords, tenants and farm-workers that there should be no return to the 1930s. The U-boat campaign left a deep mark on the legislators of the time – as it had not done in 1918 – and few were prepared to leave Britain so greatly dependent on food imports again. Some wished to see some support for farming to reduce the income gap between the rural and urban economies and to reduce rural poverty, while to others, government support was seen as a reward for the hard work of farmers during the war.[18]

Whatever the motives, there was little opposition to the 1947 Agricultural Act of the Labour government which promised, in remarkably vague terms, support for the industry. The means of support were to hand, for they had been tried in the 1930s. Between 1947 and 1973 the government assisted farming in a number of ways. From 1953 agricultural imports were allowed into the country without duty and British farmers sold their products at the market price. However, each year the government announced a guaranteed price for a wide range of commodities; the farmer received, in addition to his sale price, the difference between the guaranteed price and his sale price, the deficiency

16 E. H. Whetham, *The Agrarian History of England and Wales*, vol. VIII: *1914–1939* (Cambridge, 1978), pp. 89–102, 118–22, 163–5, 241–58; *British Farming 1939–49* (London, 1952), pp. 15–16; J. A. Mollett, "The Wheat Act of 1932: a forerunner of modern farm price support programmes", *Agricultural History Review*, 8 (1960), pp. 20–35; T. Rooth, "Trade agreements and the evolution of British agricultural policy in the 1930s", *Agricultural History Review*, 33 (1985), pp. 173–90.

17 Whetham, *op. cit.* (1952); K. Murray, *Agriculture: history of the Second World War*, 6 (London, 1955).

18 P. Self and H. J. Storing, *The State and the Farmer* (London, 1962), pp. 20–4.

price. In 1956 the Conservative government agreed not to reduce prices more than $2\frac{1}{2}$ per cent a year, to allow long-range planning. Although not all farm produce was covered by this system – horticulture, pigs and poultry-meat were excluded – this was a very considerable burden on the exchequer, particularly as world food prices fell in the 1950s with the recovery of world farming after the disruption of the war. In addition, a wide range of producer subsidies were introduced in order to encourage greater efficiency, and farmers were paid part of their outlay on liming, the purchase of chemical fertilizers (until 1974), improved underdrainage, water supplies, measures to eliminate animal disease, some buildings (such as silos), and the number of hill sheep and cattle kept.[19]

This system had some advantages. Consumers paid world prices for food; increased production reduced the need for expensive dollar imports; prosperous farmers invested and improved productivity substantially. But this was all at a growing cost to the exchequer and to the tax-payer. From the late 1950s the proportion of total government expenditure on producer subsidies was increased and that on guaranteeing prices diminished; in 1960 only 37 per cent of government subsidy to agriculture was on producer subsidies, by 1972, 70 per cent. In the late 1950s and the 1960s governments of either party were increasingly loath to subsidize farmers. Criticism of the policies grew. As the memory of the war faded there seemed less reason to single out farmers for special treatment; increasingly it was pointed out that most of the subsidy went not to the small and poor farmers, but to the large and rich farmers. By 1970 the 20 per cent largest farm businesses received 70 per cent of the support. Nor was it simply subsidies that were provoking the public. From the 1960s criticisms of the use of agrochemicals began to mount and the destruction of hedgerows was under attack.[20] But once Britain had joined the Common Market these criticisms rose to a crescendo.

BRITAIN AND THE EEC

Britain joined the EEC on 1 January 1973; for a short period world agricultural prices were above those of the EEC, but this was a temporary phase. The Common Agricultural Policy has since ensured that agricultural prices are above world prices.

Each year a *target* price for a range of agricultural commodities is established. This is generally such as to allow the least efficient producers

19 J. K. Bowers, "British agricultural policy since the Second World War", *Agricultural History Review*, 33 (1985), pp. 66–76; Self and Storing, *op. cit.* (1962); Anon, "Britain's farming policy from guarantees to intervention", *Midland Bank Review* (November 1976), pp. 9–23.

20 A. Winegarten, "British agriculture and the 1947 Agricultural Act", *Journal of the Royal Agricultural Society of England*, 139 (1978), pp. 74–82; H. Wagstaff, "EEC food surpluses: controlling production by two-tier prices", *National Westminster Bank Quarterly Review* (November 1982), pp. 30–41.

to break even, and is invariably above the price of the traditional food exporters. Imports of agricultural products from outside the EEC have levies imposed upon them, so that cheap foods are excluded. Within the EEC, prices vary according to supply and demand, but if the price falls below the target price to a previously announced intervention price, then the agents of the government must buy any products offered by farmers. These surpluses have to be stored – the celebrated wine lakes and butter mountains – and have to be disposed of if storage costs are to be kept down. Some are exported – but only with the aid of a subsidy, and to the indignation of traditional exporters such as the USA and Australia – or are sent as food aid to developing countries. By the late 1970s some attempt to control output was being made. In 1977 a co-responsibility levy was imposed on the dairy producers of countries that exceeded specified quotas of milk output, and in 1984 dairy quotas that were significantly below output in earlier years were announced for each farmer in the EEC; the quotas have since been further reduced. A half-hearted attempt to control cereal surpluses was made in 1982, when it was announced that the guaranteed – or target – price would not be paid on amounts offered above a given quantity.[21] But as yet no decisive change in the Common Agricultural Policy has been agreed. Since Britain's entry into the EEC prices have favoured arable farmers, particularly those producing cereals and oilseed rape, to the disadvantage of those who buy grains for feeding livestock, while the sheep-meat regime introduced in 1980 has brought some cheer to Britain's upland farmers, long the poorest of all. The upland areas also benefit from the subsidies allowed in the Least Favoured Area policy introduced in 1975. Many of the production grants established before entry into the EEC are still available to British farmers.

The failure of EEC ministers to reform the Common Agricultural Policy has prompted the British government to suggest measures that might reduce output; in Britain alone the relaxation of planning controls on the sale of agricultural land, the encouragement of forestry and the possibility of paying farmers not to grow crops have all been discussed.[22] There seems to be a stoic acceptance among British farmers that fundamental and, for them, adverse changes are now inevitable. The 1980s mark the end of a long period of favourable treatment for British farmers. During these years the agriculture of England and Wales has been greatly changed and it is these changes that must now be discussed.

21 G. Avery, "Guaranteed thresholds and the Common Agricultural Policy", *Journal of Agricultural Economics*, 36 (1985), pp. 355–64; Anon, "The Common Agricultural Policy", *Midland Bank Review* (Winter 1984), pp. 10–16; J. S. Marsh, "The CAP and the British interest – a general review", *Journal of Agricultural Economics*, 26 (1976), pp. 183–95; B. Hill, *The Common Agricultural Policy: past, present and future* (London, 1984).

22 W. F. Raymond, "Options for reducing inputs to agriculture: a non-economist's view", *Journal of Agricultural Economics*, 36 (1985), pp. 345–54; Stephen Trudgill, "Alternative land use", *Geography Review*, 1 (1987), pp. 10–12.

# 4
# Making and Using the Land

Currently about three-quarters of the total area of England and Wales is used for agriculture, 8 per cent is occupied by woodland and the rest is used for housing, industry and transport (see table 4.1). Just over 4 million acres of rough grazing – largely semi-natural vegetation that would revert to scrub and eventually woodland if not grazed and occasionally burnt – are used by farmers for grazing sheep and cattle. The *improved land*, under crops and grass, which is enclosed and cultivated, occupies over 23 million acres. But this improved land has taken centuries to produce. In the last two decades there has been much criticism of farmers for draining wetlands, ploughing moors and cutting down woodland. In an age of food surpluses it may be unnecessary to destroy the little semi-natural vegetation left in the country. But in the longer context farmland has been created not simply by removing the deciduous woodland that once covered all but the highest parts of Wales, but by fundamentally changing the environment. Agricultural soils are essentially man-made.

Much of the original woodland was destroyed in pre-Roman times; the Anglo-Saxon settlers who arrived over one and a half millennia ago continued the process; by the time of Domesday nearly all modern villages were in existence and late-medieval farmers slowly occupied the few remaining empty areas. By the seventeenth century most of the woodland in lowlands and uplands had gone.[1] But the production of modern farmland was far from complete. In the last two decades farmers have been draining fens, ploughing the uplands and draining heavy clays. But these are long-established activities, not simply a response to EEC cereal prices. They are a continuation of a millennia or more of land improvement.

---

1 J. N. L. Baker, 'England in the seventeenth century', in H. C. Darby (ed.), *An Historical Geography of England before 1800* (Cambridge, 1951), pp. 387–443.

Table 4.1 Land use in England and Wales

### (a)
### (thousand acres)

| Date | Crops and grass | Rough grazing | Total agricultural area | Woodland | Urban land | Other land | Total land area |
|---|---|---|---|---|---|---|---|
| 1901 | 27,505 | 3,556 | 31,061 | 1,847 | 1,664 | 4,981 | 39,553 |
| 1921 | 26,135 | 4,730 | 30,865 | 1,803 | 2,109 | 2,344 | 37,121 |
| 1939 | 24,633 | 5,537 | 30,171 | 2,502 | 2,978 | 1,679 | 37,330 |
| 1951 | 24,455 | 5,441 | 29,896 | 2,398 | 3,307 | 1,516 | 37,117 |
| 1961 | 24,383 | 4,959 | 29,342 | 2,553 | 3,680 | 1,538 | 37,116 |
| 1971 | 23,788 | 4,653 | 28,441 | 2,754 | 4,065 | 1,852 | 37,112 |
| 1980 | 23,694 | 4,280 | 27,974 | – | – | – | – |

### (b)
### (percentage)

| 1901 | 74.1 | 9.6 | 83.7 | 5.0 | 4.5 | 6.8 | 100.0 |
|---|---|---|---|---|---|---|---|
| 1921 | 70.4 | 12.7 | 83.1 | 4.9 | 5.7 | 6.3 | 100.0 |
| 1939 | 66.4 | 14.9 | 81.3 | 6.2 | 8.0 | 4.5 | 100.0 |
| 1951 | 65.9 | 14.7 | 80.6 | 6.5 | 8.9 | 4.1 | 100.0 |
| 1961 | 65.7 | 13.4 | 79.1 | 6.9 | 9.9 | 4.1 | 100.0 |
| 1971 | 64.1 | 12.5 | 76.6 | 7.4 | 11.0 | 5.0 | 100.0 |
| 1980 | 62.7 | 11.4 | 74.1 | 8.0 | 11.6 | 6.3 | 100.0 |

*Sources*: R. Best, *Land Use and Living Space* (London, 1981), pp. 46–47; M. L. Parry, 'The changing use of land', in *The Changing Geography of the United Kingdom*, ed. R. J. Johnston and J.Doornkamp (London, 1982), p. 23.

### DRAINING MARSH AND FEN

A great deal of the present agricultural land of England and Wales was once too wet to be used for intensive farming; indeed much of Wales and northern England is still too wet and cold to be used other than for rough grazing. In the lowlands there are three types of location which have been poorly drained in the past, and some so remain. First are coastal marshes where flooding occurs at times of high tide, disastrously so when high spring tides combine with a following high wind – as has happened in recent times at Canvey and in the Lincolnshire marshes.[2] Although long used for grazing livestock, their intensive use awaited

2 A. H. W. Robinson, 'The storm surge of 31st January–1st February, 1953', *Geography*, 38 (1953), pp. 134–41; F. A. Barnes and C. A. M. King, 'The Lincolnshire coastline and the 1953 storm flood', *Geography*, 38 (1953), pp. 141–66; A. H. W. Robinson, 'The sea floods around the Thames Estuary', *Geography*, 38 (1953), pp. 170–6; D. R. MacGregor, 'A note on Canvey Island', *Geography*, 38 (1953), pp. 176–7.

Table 4.2   Areas containing extensive drainage systems

| Area | 000 acres | % |
|------|-----------|---|
| Fen District | 772 | 55.6 |
| Somerset Levels | 127 | 9.3 |
| Lancashire Mosses | 89 | 6.4 |
| Thorne and Hatfield Moors | 86 | 6.3 |
| Lincolnshire Marshes | 61 | 4.4 |
| Romney Marsh | 57 | 4.1 |
| North Kent Marshes | 50 | 3.6 |
| Norfolk River Valleys | 46 | 3.3 |
| Monmouth Moors | 20 | 1.4 |
| Essex Coast | 18 | 1.3 |
| Ancholme Valley | 16 | 1.2 |
| Pevensey Levels | 12 | 0.8 |
| Beverley and Holderness | 10 | 0.7 |
| Suffolk Coast | 10 | 0.7 |
| Vale of Pickering | 7 | 0.5 |
| Other | 5 | 0.4 |
| Total: | 1386 | 100.0 |

*Source*: E. Marshall, P. M. Wade and P. Clare, 'Land drainage channels in England and Wales', *Geographical Journal*, 144 (1978), pp. 254–63.

embankment against the sea. Second are low and flat areas often near the coast, surrounded inland by higher lands. Rivers have little power with such low gradients, and heavy rainfall in the surrounding uplands invariably leads to flooding. The Fens and Somerset Levels are the most important of these lands (see table 4.2). They were used only for summer grazing until artificial drains were cut; these had to be scoured constantly and embanked, while the outfalls of the rivers needed to be deepened and provided with sluice-gates that could be shut to exclude the sea at high tide and opened to release the rivers and their floodwaters at low tide. But drainage did not work efficiently until pumps were available to lift water from the tributary ditches and drains into the main drains and rivers. The third type of location is the heavy clays. Here it is not surface water that is the problem but underdrainage; rainfall cannot move easily downwards through the minute pores between the very small particles that make up heavy clay soils, and they need underdrainage to carry subsoil moisture to ditches at the edge of fields.

Attempts have been made to drain and embank coastal marsh and inland fen since Roman times, but effective drainage began only in the mid-seventeenth century, when Dutch engineers cut drains in the Fens and in the Isle of Axholme; attempts to drain the Hull Valley date from the same period. The Ancholme valley in north Lincolnshire and the Somerset Levels were not attempted until the later eighteenth century,

*The ridge and furrow of medieval fields was the only form of drainage. Depth of furrow is clear from the figure in foreground. (Author)*

and most of the Lancashire and Cheshire mosses were undrained until the nineteenth century.[3]

However, while the chronology of drainage is well known – most drainage schemes required an Act of Parliament – the effectiveness of drainage and the consequences for land use are less clear. Initially, improvements, such as the cutting of drains in the southern Fens after 1653, led to the conversion of land to arable; but flooding soon returned, and the permanent conversion of summer grazing and fen to arable awaited efficient pumping. Windmills were only partially successful. However, the first steam pump was erected in the Fens in 1817, and these spread rapidly in the 1830s. Together with the deepening of the outfalls of the Witham, Nene and Ouse, this secured the drainage of much of the Fenland. By the late nineteenth century the Fens were, as they are now, overwhelmingly in arable. Indeed so successful has been the drainage of the interior Fens that the peat soils have shrunk to reveal

3 H. C. Darby, *The Changing Fenland* (Cambridge, 1983); June Sheppard, 'The Hull Valley: the evolution of a pattern of artificial drainage', *Geographical Studies*, 5 (1958), pp. 33–44; M. Williams, *The Draining of the Somerset Levels* (Cambridge, 1970); A. Straw, 'The Ancholme Levels North of Brigg: a history of drainage and its effect on land utilization', *East Midland Geographer*, 3 (1955), pp. 37–42; A. D. M. Phillips, 'Mossland reclamation in nineteenth century Cheshire', *Transactions of the Historic Society of Lancashire and Cheshire, 1979*, 129 (1980), pp. 93–108; R. Millward, *Lancashire: an illustrated essay in the history of the landscape* (London, 1955), pp. 21, 51, 55, 116; J. Thirsk, 'The Isle of Axholme before Vermuyden', *Agricultural History Review*, 1 (1953), pp. 16–28.

the underlying clays, and little of this fertile soil is left. The nineteenth century also saw the successful drainage of the Lancashire mosses. By the 1870s, 70 per cent of their area was in arable.[4]

Not all the drained marsh and fens became arable, for not all drainage schemes successfully reduced water-tables. In the 1930s Romney Marsh, the Monmouth Levels and the Norfolk Broads remained mainly in grassland, as did the marshes between the Lincolnshire Wolds and the sea; but the Second World War and the prosperous times for arable farming since 1945 have prompted further drainage. In 1939 only one-tenth of Romney Marsh was in tillage, by 1950 one-half; while in 1933 three-quarters of the Ancholme Valley was in grass, in 1953 only half.[5]

Between the two national land-use surveys of the 1930s and the 1960s there was little change in the proportion of drained land in arable in the Fens, but in other districts the arable area increased by one-fifth (see table 4.3). Since the 1960s drainage of fen and marsh has continued, although no comprehensive statistics are available. However, conservation interests have been successful – in parts of Norfolk for example – in blocking some proposals to drain further.[6]

The importance of the drained lands in England and Wales should not be under-estimated. One and one-third million acres are dependent

Table 4.3  Land use in drained areas at the time of the first and second land use surveys (1930–1937 and 1960–1968) (thousand acres)

| Area | | Woodland | Arable | Grass | Industry and urban | Roughland |
|---|---|---|---|---|---|---|
| All areas | 1930–7 | 16 | 764 | 430 | 81 | 393 |
| | 1960–8 | 20 | 799 | 383 | 99 | 869 |
| Fens | 1930–7 | 0 | 617 | 77 | 38 | 38 |
| | 1960–8 | 0 | 617 | 77 | 38 | 38 |
| Other districts | 1930–7 | 16 | 146 | 352 | 42 | 58 |
| | 1960–8 | 20 | 181 | 306 | 61 | 48 |

*Source*: E. J. P. Marshall, P. M. Wade and P. Clare, 'Land drainage and channels in England and Wales', *Geographical Journal*, 144 (1978), pp. 254–63.

4 Darby, *op. cit.* (1983), pp. 92, 96; Phillips, *op. cit.* (1980), pp. 93–108; G. Fowler, 'Shrinkage of the peat-covered fenlands', *Geographical Journal*, 81 (1933), pp. 149–50.

5 J. Sheail and J. Owen Montford, 'Changes in the perception of agricultural land improvement: the post-war trends in Romney Marsh', *Journal of the Royal Agricultural Society of England*, 145 (1984), pp. 45–85; C. N. H. Scotter, P. M. Wade, E. P. S. Marsh and R. W. Edwards, 'The Monmouth Levels' drainage system: its ecology and relation to agriculture', *Journal of Environmental Management*, 5 (1977), pp. 75–86; M. George, 'Land use and nature conservation in Broadland', *Geography*, 61 (1976), pp. 137–42; Straw, *op. cit.* (1955), pp. 37–42; H. Harris, 'Reclaiming the Norfolk Marshes', *The Field* (6 September 1978), pp. 332–3.

6 George, *op. cit.* (1976), pp. 137–42.

upon artificial drainage, and nearly a million acres are in arable; although this is only 7 per cent of the total arable, most of it is Grade 1 agricultural land and much of the rest is Grade II. By far the largest area dependent upon drains is the Fens (see table 4.2), which, together with the Thorne and Hatfield Moors and the Lancashire Mosses, carry much intensive crop production. The Somerset Levels, the second largest drained area, remain mainly in grass.

It is worth emphasizing that, until the introduction of steam pumping, little of the drained area was in arable land; much of the country's most valuable land has been added to the national total only since the 1820s.

DRAINING THE CLAYS

Clay soils that need underdrainage make up one-quarter of the land area of England and Wales, and proportionally more of the agricultural area (see figure 4.1).[7] Until the eighteenth century they were the prime agricultural soils of the country, perhaps due to their inherent fertility and suitability for wheat. However, from the late seventeenth century it was their disadvantages, particularly when compared with light soils, that were the subject of much contemporary comment. The very narrow pores of clay soils prevents rainfall from draining freely downwards, and this in turn impedes root development and reduces crop yields. In spring wet soils warm up slowly, reducing the length of the growing season and hence also crop yields, while very wet autumns and springs often preclude cultivation at all. When under grass, wet clays are easily poached by cattle. But the texture of clays is such that, whether wet or dry, they need more energy to plough than loams or light soils and thus are more costly to cultivate. This problem was not really resolved until the introduction of more powerful tractors after 1945. However, clay soils occupy much of eastern and midland England and have long been farmed. Although expensive to drain and cultivate they give good wheat yields, while their retention of soil moisture in summer is an advantage for grass growing in the drier Midlands, the south and the east.[8]

Until the late seventeenth century the clays received only surface drainage. Ploughing land into alternately ridge and furrow increased run-off and limited percolation. However, in the late seventeenth century farmers in Essex began to underdrain; trenches were dug downslope, partially filled with stones or thorn-bushes and then covered in with soil. It was not until the nineteenth century that this method was

7 Ministry of Agriculture, Fisheries and Food, *Modern Farming and the Soil* (London, 1970) p. 122.

8 Ministry of Agriculture, *op. cit.* (1970), p. 31; M. H. R. Soper, 'Heavy land farming', *Agriculture*, 67 (1960), pp. 174–8; R. W. Sturgess, 'The agricultural revolution on the English clays', *Agricultural History Review*, 14 (1966), pp. 104–21.

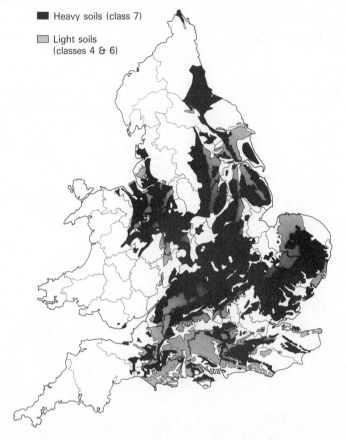

Figure 4.1   Heavy and light soils in England and Wales.
*Source*: compiled from maps in Ministry of Agriculture, Fisheries and Food, *Modern Farming and the Soil* (London, 1970), p. 122 *et seq*.

improved upon. The use of tiles for drains was common in the 1820s, although there was controversy about their optimum depth, and received a great boost in the 1840s with the invention of a tile-making machine; in 1846 Peel introduced financial assistance for land drainage as a sop to landlords at the repeal of the Corn Laws.[9] The period from 1840 to 1880 was one of great drainage activity, although precisely how much was underdrained is in doubt; contemporaries thought about 3 million acres, modern writers believe as much as 12 million. Drainage was not limited to the clays of the Midlands or the east, although substantial

9 H. C. Darby, 'The draining of the English clay lands', *Geographische Zeitschrift*, 52 (1964), pp. 190–201; F. H. W. Green, 'Ridge and furrow, mole and tile', *Geographical Journal*, 141 (1975), pp. 88–93.

proportions of these were drained; so too was much of the north-west, the Lake District, Devon and the Weald.[10]

The declining prices and rents of the 1880s caused a halt in underdrainage schemes; nor were existing systems properly maintained, and in many areas drainage deteriorated. There was no revival until 1939, when a government subsidy for underdrainage was introduced: by 1968–9, 1.7 million acres had been drained, mainly in eastern England, but it was estimated that there were still 7 million acres in need of drainage. Underdrainage has allowed the intensification of land use; on some grassland higher livestock densities are now possible, and elsewhere grass has been converted to arable. In upland areas drainage has allowed the sowing of good grass where before only rough grazing was possible.[11]

LIGHT LANDS

In the seventeenth century light soils were not highly valued by farmers; limestone uplands and lowland sandy soils were not held to be very fertile and were often either in heath or used only as sheep walks (see figure 4.1). However, the adoption of turnips and rotational grasses, and the integration of sheep into the arable system by folding them on turnips, helped to increase soil fertility and led to the development in these regions of an intensive arable system producing cereals, wool, beef and mutton. Much of the best High Farming in the early Victorian period was found on the limestone uplands – Lincoln Heath and the Yorkshire Wolds, for example. These soils, although thin and not naturally fertile, did have two advantages; first, they were easily and naturally drained; second, they were easily and cheaply cultivated. Thus in the eighteenth and nineteenth centuries they slowly replaced the clays as the major cereal producers. Low fertility, however, meant that many of the light soil areas long resisted the plough; much of the southern chalk was not ploughed until the Second World War, and the successful farming of light soils such as those on the Bunter Sands in Sherwood Forest has also come only in the last 30 years.[12]

10 M. Robinson, 'The extent of farm underdrainage in England and Wales, prior to 1939', *Agricultural History Review*, 34 (1986), pp. 79–85; R. D. Trafford, 'Recent progress in field drainage, part 1', *Journal of the Royal Agricultural Society of England*, 138 (1977), pp. 27–43; F. W. H. Green, 'Field underdrainage before and after 1940', *Agricultural History Review*, 28 (1980), pp. 120–3; E. H. Whetham, 'Sectoral advance in English agriculture 1850–1880', *Agricultural History Review*, 16 (1968), pp. 46–8.

11 E. T. Belding, 'Drainage survey in England and Wales', *Agriculture*, 78 (1971), pp. 250–4.

12 J. D. Chambers, 'The problem of Sherwood Forest', *Agriculture*, 62 (1955), pp. 177–80; P. H. Armstrong, 'Changes in the land use of the Suffolk sandings: a study of the disintegration of an ecosystem', *Geography*, 58 (1973), pp. 1–8; G. R. Field, 'Heathland

RECLAIMING THE UPLANDS

Although lowland England has presented problems to farmers, it is the hills that have most effectively resisted cultivation. Well over one-third of the total land area of England and Wales consists of upland and hill soils at altitudes generally 800 feet (see figure 4.2) or more above sea level, where temperatures are low, the growing season short, rainfall high and soils acid. Since 1939 farmers have made substantial advances in this area, converting rough grazing into permanent grass and, less commonly, into arable land. Between 1952 and 1972 some 250,000 acres of rough grazing were ploughed up and sown with improved grasses in Wales, and in England about 370,000 acres may have been reclaimed in the hills – there are no accurate figures. In some regions – Exmoor, for example – there have been strong protests at the cultivation of one of the few surviving wildscapes.[13]

But the attack in the hills is far from new. Farms were recorded in the Middle Ages at heights not attained later. On Dartmoor, settlements above 1,000 feet in the eleventh century were deserted in the fourteenth century, in the north settlements at 1,235 feet in Weardale were abandoned in the fourteenth century. Places settled in the North Yorkshire Moors between 1150 and 1300 at 1,000 feet and over were later abandoned. The sixteenth century, with its long upward movement of wool and wheat prices, encouraged further attempts to settle the uplands, as did the inflationary prices of the Napoleonic Wars, when land was ploughed for crops as high as 1,700 feet in parts of Wales.[14]

reclamation in East Suffolk', *Agriculture*, 73 (1966), pp. 160–3; D. Grigg, 'Changing regional values during the Agricultural Revolution in South Lincolnshire', *Transactions and Papers of the Institute of British Geographers*, 30 (1962), pp. 91–104; E. J. T. Collins and E. L. Jones, 'Sectoral advance in English agriculture, 1850–1880', *Agricultural History Review*, 15 (1967), pp. 65–81; R. J. P. Kain and H. C. Prince, *The Tithe Surveys of England and Wales* (Cambridge, 1985), pp. 199–200; J. T. Coppock, *An Agricultural Geography of Great Britain* (London, 1971), p. 138.

13 J. A. Taylor, 'Upland Climates', in T. J. Chandler and S. Gregory (eds), *The Climate of the British Isles* (London, 1976), pp. 264–87; M. L. Parry, Ann Bruce and Claire Harkness, 'The plight of British moorlands', *New Scientist* (28 May 1981), pp. 550–1; Emrys Jones, 'The future of the uplands', Ministry of Agriculture, *Conference Report on Upland Farming, Forestry and Wildlife Conservation* (London, 1973), p. 4; L. Curtis, 'Reflections on management agreements for conservation of Exmoor moorlands', *Journal of Agricultural Economics*, 34 (1983), pp. 397–406.

14 J. S. Cocks, 'Exploitation', in C. Gill (ed.), *Dartmoor: a new study* (Newton Abbot, 1970), pp. 245–76; M. L. Parry, *Climatic Change, Agriculture and Settlement* (Folkestone, 1978), p. 22; R. I. Hodgson, 'Medieval colonization in Northern Ryedale, Yorkshire', *Geographical Journal*, 135 (1969), pp. 44–54; S. R. Eyre, 'The upward limit of enclosure in the East Moor of North Derbyshire', *Transactions of the Instititue of British Geographers*, 23 (1957), pp. 61–74; J. Porter, 'Waste land reclamation in the sixteenth and seventeenth centuries: the case of southeast Bowland 1550–1630, *Transactions of the Historic Society of Lancashire and Cheshire for the year 1977*, 127 (1978), pp. 1–23; R. G. Stapledon, 'Climate and the improvement of hill land', *Geography*, 18 (1933), pp. 17–25.

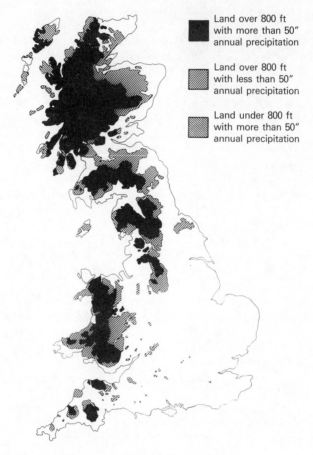

Land over 800 ft
with more than 50"
annual precipitation

Land over 800 ft
with less than 50"
annual precipitation

Land under 800 ft
with more than 50"
annual precipitation

Figure 4.2 The uplands of Britain.

In some upland areas – Westmorland, for example – the upper limits of settlement were not reached until 1850–75. In a few areas – such as Pembrokeshire – crop cultivation had reached its highest point in the 1850s and was retreating long before the collapse of grain prices in the 1870s. From then on cultivation in the uplands was abandoned; permanent grass was neglected and reverted to rough grazing, cropland tumbled down to grass, and bracken began a long expansion in the hills of Britain. This trend was not reversed until the outbreak of the Second World War, when cultivation reached into the hills again. After the war subsidies on hill sheep and cows were maintained, while production subsidies on lime, fertilizers, underdrainage and reseeding, together with plough-up grants, have encouraged a return to the hills. Indeed much of the reclamation of land which has occurred since 1940 is of improved land abandoned in the 1880s and later.[15]

IMPROVED LAND AND URBAN EXPANSION

Until the 1870s the country's improved land had long been increasing; only occasionally had there been a decline, and that temporary, as in the fourteenth and fifteenth centuries. There are of course no national agricultural statistics before 1866, but it seems likely that a peak was reached somewhere between the 1850s and the 1870s. The early agricultural census understates the area in crops and grass, and so the improved land was almost certainly over 28 million acres in 1870–4 (see table 4.4).[16] Since then the area in crops and grass has declined continuously (see figure 4.3) and is now 3 or 4 million acres less than in the Victorian apogee of High Farming. There are various reasons for this decline. In some lowland areas afforestation has taken place; in a few areas agricultural land was abandoned in the 1920s and 1930s. Some land claimed by the Ministry of Defence during the war has not been returned, while the dropping of small holdings from the census in the 1960s and 1970s reduced the *recorded* area in crops and grass. But the principal reason has been the expansion of the urban area. Records of the transfer of agricultural land to other purposes have been kept since 1922, and over that period (see table 4.5) nearly 2½ million acres of agricultural land have been lost to urban expansion and 600,000 acres to woodland. However, most of the afforestation has been upon rough grazing and does not help account for the decline in the area in crops and grass. Before 1922 no records were kept of the transfer of agricultural land: however, the urban area expanded by 440,000 acres between 1901 and 1921 (see table 4.1).

No similar data are available for the nineteenth century, but it has been estimated that the urban area increased by 2 million acres between 1801 and 1891. Clearly, even if not all this urban expansion was onto improved land, much was; the loss of farmland thus began well before the suburban expansion of the inter-war period.[17]

15 L. D. Stamp, *The Land of Britain, Westmorland*, pt. 50: (London, 1943); E. J. T. Collins, *The Economy of Upland Britain, 1750–1950: an illustrated review*, CAS Paper no. 4 (Reading, 1978), pp. 14, 16; R. J. P. Kain and H. C. Prince, *The Tithe Surveys of England and Wales* (Cambridge 1985), pp. 173, 183, 196, 198; M. L. Parry, A. Bruce and C. E. Harkness, *Changes in the Extent of Moorland and Roughland in the Northumberland National Park*, Surveys of Moorland and Roughland Change no. 4 (1982), p. 45.

16 R. H. Best and J. T. Coppock, *The Changing Use of Land in Britain* (London, 1962), p. 73.

17 T. A. Welton, 'On the distribution of population in England and Wales and its progress in the period of ninety years from 1801–1891', *Journal of the Royal Statistical Society*, 63 (1900), pp. 527–95.

Table 4.4 Land use in England and Wales, 1801–1984 (thousand acres)

| Date | Arable | Fallow | Temporary grass | Tillage | Permanent grass | All grass | Arable and permanent grass |
|---|---|---|---|---|---|---|---|
| 1801 | – | – | – | 7,977 | – | – | – |
| 1801 | 11,350 | – | – | – | 16,796 | – | 28,146 |
| 1808 | 11,591 | 2,297 | 1,149 | 10,442 | 17,495 | 18,644 | 29,086 |
| 1812 | 12,000 | 2,400 | 1,200 | 10,800 | – | – | – |
| 1827 | 11,143 | – | – | – | 17,605 | – | 28,748 |
| 1836 | 12,700 | 1,200 | 2,600 | 10,100 | 16,363 | 18,963 | 29,063 |
| 1846 | 13,100 | 1,500 | 1,300 | 11,800 | – | – | – |
| 1851 | 13,667 | 1,300 | 2,277 | 11,390 | 13,332 | 15,609 | 26,999 |
| 1854 | 14,847 | 896 | 2,820 | 12,027 | 12,987 | – | 27,834 |
| 1870–4 | 14,815 | 558 | 3,090 | 11,725 | 11,579 | 14,669 | 26,394 |
| 1890–4 | 12,800 | 447 | 3,056 | 9,744 | 15,029 | 18,085 | 27,829 |
| 1910–14 | 11,201 | 340 | 2,586 | 8,615 | 15,989 | 18,575 | 27,190 |
| 1935–9 | 9,071 | 370 | 2,351 | 6,720 | 15,720 | 18,071 | 24,791 |
| 1940–4 | 12,668 | 248 | 2,260 | 10,408 | 11,804 | 14,776 | 24,472 |
| 1960–4 | 13,780 | 206 | 4,528 | 9,252 | 10,626 | 15,154 | 24,406 |
| 1980–4 | 13,676 | 150 | 2,811 | 10,865 | 9,961 | 12,772 | 23,637 |

Arable is crops plus fallow plus temporary grass. Tillage is crops and fallow, excluding temporary grass.

Sources: M. Turner, 'Arable in England and Wales, estimates from the 1801 crop returns', Journal of Historical Geography, 7 (1981), pp. 291–302; H. C. Prince, 'England circa 1800', A New Historical Geography of England after 1600, ed. H. C. Darby (Cambridge, 1976), p. 103; J. R. McCulloch, A Statistical Account of the British Empire, 1 (London, 1937), p. 529; G. R. Porter, The Progress of the Nation (London, 1847), pp. 155–7; R. J. P. Kain, An Atlas and Index of the Tithe Files of Mid-nineteenth Century England and Wales (Cambridge, 1986), p. 4; L. Drescher, 'The development of agricultural production in Great Britain and Ireland from the early nineteenth century', Manchester School, 25 (1955), pp. 155–75; James Caird, English Agriculture in 1850–51 (London, 1852), p. 522; Ministry of Agriculture, Agricultural Statistics, England and Wales.

ARABLE AND GRASS

The improved land in England and Wales increased continuously until the 1860s and 1870s, and has since slowly declined until, in the 1980s, it is only four-fifths of the area it was in the 1870s. Equally dramatic has been the change in the area in crops compared with that in grass. Although the area in crops – in tillage – is currently two-thirds greater than it was in 1939, it is less than it was in 1944 at the height of the war-time plough-up, and substantially less than it was in the 1870s (see table 4.4 and figure 4.3).

From the 1770s to the 1870s there was a continual increase in the improved land of England and Wales, an increase in the arable area, and in the arable area as a percentage of the area in crops and grass (see table 4.6). But the most striking feature of this period was the decline of the fallow, from over 2 million acres in the early nineteenth century, and one-fifth of the arable, to only half a million acres in the 1870s (see table 4.4). In the same period the arable area rose from only 40 per cent of the total area of crops and grass to 56 per cent. In the 1870s, then, the improved land, the arable area and the tillage area reached their highest point (see table 4.4).

The falling cereal prices from the 1870s to the 1930s transformed this pattern. The area in grass increased and that in arable slumped (see figure 4.3) until in 1939 it was only 59 per cent of that in 1875, and indeed only two-thirds of the arable area in 1801. The only interruption to this 60-year decline came in the First World War. The government guaranteed cereal prices in 1917, and the area in tillage rose by 1.8

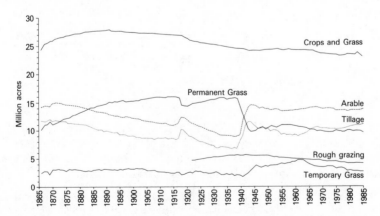

Figure 4.3 Trends in agricultural land-use in England and Wales, 1866–1985.
*Source:* Ministry of Agriculture, *Agricultural Statistics, England and Wales* (London, 1866–1985).

Table 4.5   Average annual transfer of agricultural
land to urban use and to woodland in England and
Wales, 1922–1980

| Date | Thousand acres per annum urban | wood |
|---|---|---|
| 1922–6 | 22.5 | 1.5 |
| 1926–31 | 52.1 | 6.7 |
| 1931–6 | 62.0 | 4.0 |
| 1936–9 | 62.0 | 16.8 |
| 1939–45 | 13.1 | 19.0 |
| 1945–50 | 43.2 | 18.0 |
| 1950–5 | 38.3 | 22.5 |
| 1955–60 | 34.6 | 19.8 |
| 1960–5 | 37.8 | 16.3 |
| 1965–70 | 41.5 | 13.6 |
| 1970–5 | 36.8 | 7.4 |
| 1975–80 | 23.0 | 2.2 |

*Sources*: R. Best, 'Are we really losing the land?' *Town
and Country Planning*, 53 (1984), pp. 10–11; *Land Use
and Living Space* (London, 1981), p. 86.

Table 4.6   Land-use changes, 1801–1984 (as a percentage of total area of crops and
grass)

| Date | Arable | Tillage | Temporary grass | Permanent grass | All grass |
|---|---|---|---|---|---|
| 1808 | 39.3 | 35.4 | 3.9 | 60.7 | 64.6 |
| 1827 | 38.8 | – | – | 61.2 | – |
| 1836 | 43.6 | 34.7 | 8.9 | 56.4 | 65.3 |
| 1851 | 50.6 | – | – | 49.4 | – |
| 1870–4 | 56.1 | 44.4 | 11.7 | 43.9 | 55.6 |
| 1890–4 | 46.0 | 35.0 | 11.0 | 54.0 | 65.0 |
| 1910–14 | 41.2 | 31.7 | 9.5 | 58.8 | 68.3 |
| 1935–9 | 36.6 | 27.1 | 9.5 | 63.4 | 72.9 |
| 1940–4 | 51.8 | 42.4 | 9.4 | 48.2 | 60.3 |
| 1960–4 | 56.6 | 37.9 | 18.6 | 43.5 | 62.0 |
| 1980–4 | 57.9 | 46.0 | 11.9 | 42.1 | 54.0 |

*Sources*: As for Table 4.4.

million acres from 1916 to 1918.[18] But this increase was dwarfed by
the events of the Second World War. Between 1939 and 1944, 5.6
million acres were added to the arable area, an increase of 63 per cent,
and an increase unique in English agricultural history. The changes

18  J. Sheail, 'Land improvement and reclamation: the experience of the First World
War in England and Wales', *Agricultural History Review*, 24 (1976), pp. 110–25; D. Grigg,
'From Gregory King to Alure: the changing amount and distribution of arable land in
England and Wales 1700–1985', *Tijdschrift voor economische en sociale geografie* 79 (1988),
pp. 199–209.

since 1945 are modest if set against this background. In the post-war period a distinction needs to be made between the trend in *tillage* as against *arable*; tillage includes crops and fallow – unimportant by the 1940s – but excludes rotational grasses; arable includes fallow, crops *and* rotational grasses. At the end of the war there was a decline in tillage from the peak of 1944, and a return to ley farming. Hence while the area in tillage declined, principally because of a reduction in the cereal acreage, because rotational grasses increased (figure 4.3) the arable area showed little change. From the late 1950s the use of fertilizers, pesticides and herbicides made rotations and ley farming less necessary; hence the area in rotational grasses declined. On the other hand the area in crops – or tillage – increased, and, it should be noted, this increase began long before entry to the EEC. The net effect has been that there was relatively little change in the arable area between the 1960s and the 1980s, but a substantial increase in tillage – although in 1985 the tillage area was still below that of 1944 or the 1870s (see table 4.7).

Although there has been relatively little change in the *arable* area since 1950, and it remains well below that of the Victorian zenith, it does not follow that reclamation of new land has not taken place. Since the 1930s approximately 2.4 million acres have been reclaimed by farmers in the United Kingdom, roughly equal to the area of farmland lost to urban expansion in England and Wales in the same period.[19] Farmers have, as it were, been running to stand in the same place. Whether they needed to add to their cropland, given the great increases in crop yields, is another matter.

Table 4.7 Periods of change in the tillage area (thousand acres)

| Date | Area in arable | Area in tillage | Percentage change in arable | Percentage change in tillage |
|------|------|------|------|------|
| 1801[a] | 11,500 | 10,300 | – | – |
| 1875[b] | 14,606 | 11,637 | + 27.0 | + 13.0 |
| 1913[b] | 11,058 | 8,505 | – 24.3 | – 14.0 |
| 1919[b] | 12,399 | 10,012 | + 12.1 | + 17.7 |
| 1939[b] | 8,935 | 6,830 | – 27.9 | – 31.8 |
| 1944[b] | 14,566 | 11,595 | + 63.0 | + 69.8 |
| 1961[b] | 13,645 | 8,940 | – 6.3 | – 22.9 |
| 1985[b] | 13,867 | 11,161 | + 1.6 | + 24.8 |

*Source*: [a] See table 4.4.
[b] Ministry of Agriculture, *Agricultural Statistics, England and Wales*.

19 M. L. Parry, 'The changing use of land', in R. J. Johnston and J. C. Doornkamp (eds), *The Changing Geography of the United Kingdom* (London, 1982), p. 32.

## THE DISTRIBUTION OF ARABLE AND GRASS

In 1985 the proportion of improved land in tillage was greatest in the eastern counties (see figure 4.6), least in Wales, the north-west and the south-west; this difference between east and west seems always to have existed (see figures 4.4 to 4.6). The reasons for this are not entirely clear. However, in much of Wales, the Pennines and the south-west, *upland* areas are cool and wet, with acid soils and many steep slopes. Much of this area is in rough grazing, and where the land has been improved it is generally in grass, not crops. The western *lowlands* in contrast have some considerable advantages for growing crops, notably the much longer growing season that has led to early potato and other vegetable production in Cornwall, Lancashire and Pembrokeshire. There have always been sizable areas of arable land in these counties, as there

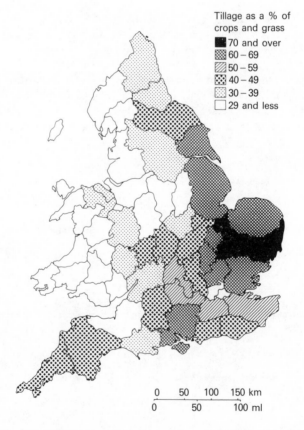

Tillage as a % of
crops and grass
■ 70 and over
▨ 60 – 69
▨ 50 – 59
▨ 40 – 49
▨ 30 – 39
☐ 29 and less

0    50    100    150 km
0         50         100 ml

Figure 4.4   Area in tillage as a percentage of the area in crops and grass, 1875.
*Source*: Board of Agriculture, *Agricultural Statistics, England and Wales 1875* (London, 1876).

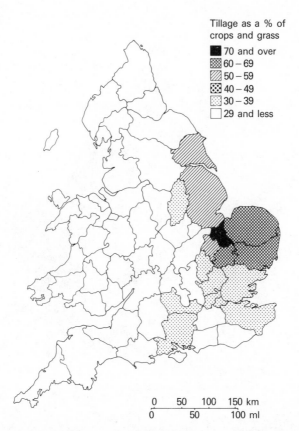

Figure 4.5   Area in tillage as a percentage of the area in crops and grass, 1938.
*Source*: Ministry of Agriculture, *Agricultural Statistics, England and Wales 1938* (London, 1939).

have been in Devon, the coastal regions of Cumberland and the Welsh border counties. The principal disadvantage for crop production is the high rainfall that sometimes makes autumn cultivation difficult and can also damage harvests. But cereal production has always been possible in these areas; indeed it is estimated that 38 per cent of the area now in grass in England offers no physical obstacle to cultivation. Cereal production in the west may have been more important before the improved transport of the eighteenth and nineteenth centuries allowed regional specialization.[20]

20 J. O. Green and R. D. Baker, 'Classification, distribution and productivity of UK grasslands', in J. L. Jollans (ed.), *Grassland in the British Economy* (Reading, 1981), pp. 237–60; L. P. Smith and H. E. Croxall, 'Autumn weather and cereal growing in England', *ADAS Quarterly Review*, 8 (1973), pp. 177–83.

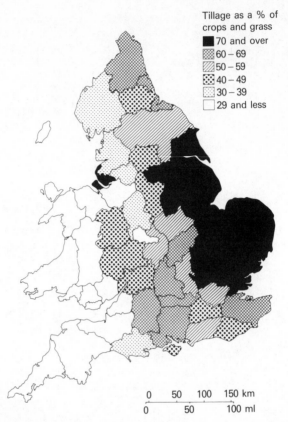

Tillage as a % of
crops and grass

■ 70 and over
▨ 60 – 69
▨ 50 – 59
▨ 40 – 49
▨ 30 – 39
☐ 29 and less

0    50    100    150 km
0        50       100 ml

Figure 4.6   Area in tillage as a percentage of the area in crops and grass, 1985.
*Sources*: Ministry of Agriculture, *Agricultural Statistics, United Kingdom 1985* (London, 1986); Welsh Office, *Welsh Agricultural Statistics no. 8, 1986* (Cardiff, 1986).

In the east and south-east of England cereals have advantages when compared with the west; the hours of sunshine are longer, summer temperatures higher, and autumn and spring drier, as are the harvest periods. In addition there is far more flat land, while farms are larger, an advantage in an age of mechanized farming. A problem is the possibility of drought in the summer, which has led modern farmers to use irrigation on high value crops and has always limited grass growth in the east. Good permanent grass is found only on heavy clay soils that retain soil moisture or in areas with a high water-table. Westwards the rate of grass growth increases, and hay yields have generally been higher in the west than in the east.[21]

21 A. Lazenby and C. J. Doyle, 'Grassland in the British economy – some problems, possibilities and speculations', in Jollans, *op. cit.* (1981); D. K. Britton, *Cereals in the United Kingdom: production, marketing and utilisation* (Oxford, 1969), pp. 695–702.

The midland counties, between the extremes of the east and west, have less pronounced advantages for grass or crop production; over much of this area both are climatically feasible. It is this region – between Hereford and Leicester, and the Pennines and Hampshire, that has the most diversified farming at present (see figures 13.2 and 13.3, pp. 171–2) and has shown the most marked responses to price and technological changes in the past. This is particularly true in terms of the changes in tillage and grass.

In 1875 arable England ran from the East Riding to London (see figure 4.4); there were outliers in Hampshire, Oxfordshire and Berkshire, and this corresponded to James Caird's corn counties, with the grazing districts to the west, including most of the East Midlands (see figure 13.5, p. 175).[22] The fall in cereal prices led to a dramatic decline in the area in tillage between 1875 and 1938; in the latter year only East Anglia, Lincolnshire and the East Riding had more than half their improved land in tillage (see figure 4.5). The area in tillage fell in every county, but the decline was smallest in the east, where the possibilities of switching to grass and livestock production were more limited than they were in the Midlands and Wales, where the decline in tillage was very marked (see table 4.8a). From 1938 until 1944 there was a dramatic increase in tillage, in 1945–61 a decline, and then a resurgence (see figure 4.3). By 1985 (see figure 4.6) the area in tillage was 63 per cent above that in 1938. But this increase as in the earlier period of decline, was not uniform across the country (see table 4.8a). In the south-west, Wales and the north-west, the decline in tillage which had begun after 1875, and was briefly interrupted 1939–45, continued; in eastern arable England there were increases, but these were modest compared with the great increase in tillage in midland England, most notably in Leicestershire and Northamptonshire, where many of the celebrated summer grazing pastures were ploughed up.[23] The principal regional change since 1875 has been the decline of tillage in the west, which then had 22 per cent of the country's tillage, but now has only 12 per cent (see table 4.8b).

SUMMARY

The present pattern of land use in England and Wales is the result of many centuries of reclamation of land from forest, marsh, fen and moor. The expansion of arable in the last 15 years under the stimulus of higher grain prices is very similar to that in the periods of expansion in the sixteenth century, the Napoleonic Wars, the 1850s and 1860s and during the two World Wars. Indeed, some recent reclamation is of land

22 James Caird, *English Agriculture in 1850–51* (London, 1852), frontispiece.
23 H. Chew, 'The post-war land use of the former grasslands of Eastern Leicestershire', *Geography*, 38 (1953), pp. 287–95.

Table 4.8   Tillage in the major regions, 1875–1985

*(a)*
*Changes in the area in tillage in major regions (percentage change)*

| Region | 1875–1913 | 1913–19 | 1919–38 | 1938–45 | 1945–61 | 1961–85 |
|--------|-----------|---------|---------|---------|---------|---------|
| East | − 20.2 | 10.3 | − 20.1 | 32.1 | − 6.2 | 22.8 |
| Midlands | − 37.3 | 18.5 | − 40.0 | 107.5 | − 22.9 | 45.5 |
| West | − 31.4 | 35.5 | − 46.7 | 103.3 | − 44.3 | − 4.0 |

*(b)*
*Percentage share of each major region in the national tillage total*

| Region | 1875 | 1913 | 1919 | 1939 | 1945 | 1961 | 1973 | 1985 |
|--------|------|------|------|------|------|------|------|------|
| East[a] | 54.8 | 59.4 | 55.8 | 64.3 | 53.6 | 62.2 | 62.4 | 61.9 |
| Midlands[b] | 23.1 | 19.7 | 19.9 | 17.0 | 22.4 | 21.3 | 23.7 | 25.2 |
| West[c] | 22.1 | 20.9 | 24.3 | 18.7 | 24.0 | 16.5 | 13.9 | 12.9 |
| | 100.0 | 100.0 | 100.0 | 100.0 | 100.0 | 100.0 | 100.0 | 100.0 |

[a] 1875–1973: North Riding, Durham, Northumberland, Lincolnshire, Isle of Ely, Huntingdonshire, West Riding, East Riding, Soke of Peterborough, Cambridgeshire, Norfolk, Suffolk, Bedfordshire, Hertfordshire, Essex, London, Middlesex, Hampshire, Surrey, Kent, Isle of Wight, Sussex; 1985 as 1877–1973, but including Tyne, Cleveland, South Yorkshire.
[b] 1875–1973: Nottinghamshire, Rutland, Leicestershire, Northamptonshire, Warwickshire, Oxfordshire, Berkshire, Buckinghamshire, Wiltshire, Gloucestershire, Shropshire, Herefordshire, Worcestershire; 1985 as 1875–1973, but including Avon.
[c] 1875–1973: Cumberland, Westmorland, Lancashire, Cheshire, Derbyshire, Staffordshire, Isles of Scilly, Cornwall, Devon, Somerset, Dorset, Wales; 1985 as 1875–1973, but including Merseyside, West Midlands, Manchester.
*Sources*: Board of Agriculture, *Agricultural Statistics, England and Wales* (London, 1875); Ministry of Agriculture, *Agricultural Statistics, England and Wales*.

abandoned during the fall of agricultural prices after the 1870s. The area of improved land is now less than it was in the 1870s, as is the arable area and the area in tillage, while the current percentage of improved land in arable is only a little more than it was in the 1870s. Nor has the post-war period shown any *great* increase in arable land or tillage. It was the Second World War plough-up that partially restored the arable acreage of the Victorian period after the long decline from the 1870s to the 1930s.

# 5
# The Changing Distribution of Crops

In the 1980s the profit margins on many of the crops grown in England and Wales have fallen, as costs have risen faster than prices; this and the ever-rising cereal surpluses have suggested to many farmers that the time has come to look at alternative crops; and a variety of new crops, such as lupins and flax, have been promoted.

This is reminiscent of a much earlier period. In the sixteenth and the early part of the seventeenth century cereal prices were rising, and farmers did not have to experiment to make money; but from the 1620s until well into the eighteenth century cereal prices were stagnant and a variety of new crops were tried, although never on a large scale. The most exotic was tobacco, surprisingly successful until suppressed by the government in the 1670s to ensure that Virginia had a market in England. Hemp and flax were produced in small quantities until the nineteenth century, and crops such as woad, madder, weld, and safflower, grown for dyes, persisted until replaced by aniline dyes in the nineteenth century.[1]

But there were far more important changes underway in the mid-seventeenth century. Between the 1630s and the 1870s a system of farming was established in lowland England that integrated the growing of crops and the raising of livestock, and produced for sale wheat, barley, wool, beef and mutton. It reached its zenith in the High Farming of mid-Victorian times, and then slowly disintegrated, receiving its *coup de grâce* only in the 1960s. It was based on the adoption of two new crops, turnips and clover.

1 Joan Thirsk, 'The agricultural landscape: fads and fashion', in S. R. J. Woodell (ed.), *The English Landscape Past Present and Future* (Oxford, 1985), pp. 129–47; 'Farming techniques' in J. Thirsk (ed.), *Agrarian History of England and Wales*, vol. IV: *1500–1640* (Cambridge, 1967), pp. 168–77; 'Seventeenth century agriculture and social change', *Agricultural History Review*, 18 (1970), Supplement, pp. 148–77; A. Harris, 'Chicory and woad: a comment', *Lincolnshire History and Archaeology*, 21 (1986), pp. 19–22.

## THE RISE OF FODDER CROPS

In the early seventeenth century a substantial proportion of the arable area was in fallow each year, and of the sown area probably four-fifths was in cereals – barley, wheat, rye and oats. The only other crops of significance were peas and beans, although small amounts of vetch, tares, flax and hemp were cultivated. Some of the oats were grown to feed animals, especially horses, but the other grains were rarely used for livestock unless spoilt. Peas and beans were sometimes ground and mixed in with wheat or barley to make flour, but most of the output was fed to livestock. However, the greater part of the feed of sheep and cattle came from the semi-natural vegetation of the common land that surrounded the open arable fields.[2] In addition livestock fed upon the straw left in the fields after harvest, but, except where well-watered meadows were available, livestock were very poorly fed, matured very slowly and gave little milk.

The key to the great changes of the next 200 years was the adoption of two crops, rotational (or artificial or temporary) grasses and fodder roots – initially turnips. Both crops could be grown upon the bare fallow; together they served the same purposes as the fallow. A year in fallow had three functions. First, it rested the land, and nitrogen from rainfall and the action of free-living bacteria was added to the soil. Second, it provided a break between crops and, if the land was cultivated during the fallow, reduced soil-borne disease. Third, and perhaps most important, it allowed the land to be thoroughly weeded. As long as crops were broadcast – as most of them were until the nineteenth century – crops could not be weeded while the crop was growing; thus a fallow was essential if land was to be properly cleared of weeds.[3]

The growth of turnips and rotational grasses carried out these functions. The rotational grasses were fodder legumes – clover, lucerne and sainfoin – and bacteria associated with the nodules on their roots fixed nitrogen at a higher rate than did those of peas and at a rate comparable with those of beans. Turnips, if drilled in rows, could be hand- or horse-hoed during growth. Most of the mature turnip is above the ground and therefore can be eaten *in situ* by sheep, which added their dung to the soil. Confining sheep with hurdles to part of a turnip field was described as folding. Alternatively the roots were lifted and fed to cattle kept in

2 Thirsk, *op. cit.* (1985), p. 169; Thirsk, *op. cit.* (1967), p. 171; Carolina Lane, 'The development of pastures and meadows during the sixteenth and seventeenth centuries', *Agricultural History Review*, 28 (1980), pp. 18–31.

3 R. S. Loomis, 'Ecological dimensions of medieval agrarian systems: an ecologist responds', *Agricultural History*, 52 (1978), pp. 478–83; Viscount Astor and B. Seebohm Rowntree, *Mixed Farming and Muddled Thinking: an analysis of current agricultural policy* (London, no date [*c.*1946]), pp. 44–52, 67–74.

stalls; their dung and urine mixed with the straw from earlier cereal crops formed farmyard manure.

The new crops were the basis of two new farming systems. In the Midlands and the west rotational grasses were sown and left down as grazing for four to six years. Nitrogen accumulated, as did organic matter; the land was then ploughed up and sown to crops for four to six years before being planted with clover and grass again. This system has been variously described as convertible, alternate and ley farming, and by one historian as 'up and down' husbandry. In the eastern and southern lowlands wheat and barley alternated with clover and turnips; livestock were fed on the fodder crops and their manure maintained crop yields. This system of mixed farming was best developed in Norfolk and Lincolnshire.[4]

The introduction of the new crops replaced the fallow, increased the fodder supply for livestock and integrated crop and livestock production.

### THE SPREAD OF THE NEW CROPS

The adoption of clover and turnips was once seen by historians as being the heart of the Agricultural Revolution, taking place after 1760 and associated – indeed dependent upon – the progress of Parliamentary enclosure. There is little doubt, however, that the new crops were grown much earlier than 1760. Turnips were cultivated in market gardens in the later sixteenth century and possibly as a field crop for livestock in the 1620s, certainly by about 1650; they then spread from Norfolk and Suffolk to the rest of the country. They were first grown in Northumberland between 1710 and 1730, and had reached Cornwall at much the same time. The crop was adopted most rapidly on the light limestone and sandy soils; it was less easily grown on heavy clays, where the roots went 'fangy', sheep poached the wet soils and the sheep themselves were susceptible to foot-rot. In East Anglia the proportion of a sample of farmers growing turnips rose from only 5 per cent before 1660 to half in the early eighteenth century. But in the 1740s most farmers were growing only a small acreage of roots, and the crop was not integrated into a rotational system. The spread of the Norfolk four-course, with its alternation of cereals, roots and clover, was to come later. Even in 1801 the turnip occupied a tenth of the recorded arable only in eastern England, and was little grown elsewhere. But its acreage greatly expanded during the nineteenth century (see table 5.1) and by the 1870s it was a major crop everywhere but Wales, the north-west and on the clay soils in the south and east. The turnip was supplemented by two other fodder root crops: the swede, introduced in the 1760s, which was more winter

---

4  Eric Kerridge, *The Agricultural Revolution* (London, 1967).

Table 5.1  Area under fodder crops and temporary grasses in England and Wales, 1801–1875

(a)
thousand acres

| Date | Turnips, Swedes and Mangolds | Peas and Beans | Rotational grasses |
|------|------------------------------|----------------|--------------------|
| 1801 | 668   | 779   | –     |
| 1812 | 1,150 | –     | 1,149 |
| 1836 | 1,300 | 600   | 2,600 |
| 1846 | 2,000 | 500   | 1,300 |
| 1851 | 2,117 | 1,139 | 2,278 |
| 1854 | 2,445 | 698   | 2,820 |
| 1875 | 1,998 | 891   | 2,969 |

(b)
percentage of sown area

|      | Cereals | Turnips | Temporary grasses | Other crops |
|------|---------|---------|-------------------|-------------|
| 1812 | 67.6    | 11.3    | 11.2              | 9.8         |
| 1854 | 55.3    | 17.8    | 20.5              | 6.4         |
| 1875 | 51.9    | 14.5    | 21.6              | 12.1        |

Sources: M. Turner, 'Arable in England and Wales: estimates from the 1801 returns', Journal of Historical Geography, 7 (1981), pp. 291–302; L. Drescher, 'The development of agricultural production in Great Britain and Ireland from the early nineteenth century', Manchester School, 23 (1985), pp. 155–75; R. J. P. Kain, An Atlas and Index of the Tithe Files of Mid-nineteenth Century England and Wales (Cambridge, 1986), p. 460; H. Prince, 'England circa 1800', in H. C. Darby (ed.), A New Historical Geography of England after 1600 (Cambridge, 1976), p. 103.

hardy, and the mangold, grown from the 1780s, which gave a higher yield.[5]

The fodder legumes – clover, sainfoin and lucerne – were first grown in the 1640s and the 1650s in various parts of southern England, and

5 M. Overton, 'The diffusion of agricultural innovation in early modern England: turnips and clover in Norfolk and Suffolk, 1580–1740', Transactions of the Institute of British Geographers, 10 (1985), pp. 205–21; Joan Thirsk, 'The South West Midlands', in J. Thirsk (ed.), Agrarian History of England and Wales, vol. VI: 1640–1750, pt. 1: Regional Farming Systems (Cambridge, 1984), p. 178; J. R. Wordie, 'The South' in Thirsk, op. cit. (1984), pp. 322, 331; M. Turner, 'Arable in England and Wales: estimates from the 1801 crop returns', Journal of Historical Geography, 7 (1981), pp. 291–302; E. Kerridge, 'Turnip husbandry in High Suffolk', Economic History Review, 6 (1954), pp. 390–2; F. R. Horne, 'British fodder crops excluding maize', Outlook on Agriculture, 5 (1966), pp. 95–103; N. Harvey, 'The coming of the swede to Great Britain', Agricultural History, 23 (1949), pp. 286–8; P. Grimshaw, T. O. Ockwell, H. Daybell and J. Parry, 'Fodder roots: signs point to revival of interest', British Farmer and Stockbreeder, 5 (1975), pp. 34–43; G. V. Harrison, 'The South-West', in Thirsk, op. cit. (1984), pp. 363–5.

spread rapidly; they are recorded in Cornwall, Anglesey and Gower in the first two decades of the eighteenth century, although not in the Lake District until 1750. The number of farmers cultivating them slowly increased. In a sample in Sussex, 6 to 7 per cent grew clover in the 1660s, by 1740, 66 per cent; in East Anglia more than half of farmers had adopted the crop by the early eighteenth century. Improved clovers were imported from Europe and Egypt in the late eighteenth century; indeed much of the clover seed since the time of its earliest use had been imported from the Netherlands. As with the turnip, the diffusion of clover was far from complete when the first statistics become available, and the area at least doubled between 1812 and 1875 (see table 5.1).[6]

The importance of peas and beans as fodder crops was overshadowed by the rise of the fodder roots and legumes, but in the 1870s they occupied not far short of a million acres; beans were the prime fodder crop on the heavy clays of the Midlands and the south-east; wheat, beans and fallow had been a common rotation on the clays in the seventeenth and eighteenth centuries, and even persisted long after enclosure, well into the Victorian period. By the 1870s fodder crops – roots, pulses and other crops such as kohl rabi, cabbage and rape – together with rotational grasses, occupied 40 per cent of the arable, a far cry from the mid-seventeenth century, when only a small fraction of the arable was used to grow crops to feed livestock. These crops integrated livestock and crop production. Folded sheep fed on turnips fertilized the arable; cattle bedded on straw from the wheat crop made the farmyard manure that raised cereal yields. Turnips were hoed to free the land from weeds and rotational grass gave grazing and hay and also added nitrogen to the soil.

Table 5.2  Percentage of the population of England and Wales dependent upon various crops

| Crop | 1695 | 1763 | 1800 | 1850 | 1900 |
|---|---|---|---|---|---|
| Wheat | 38 | 63 | 66 | 88 | 97 |
| Rye | 27 | 15 | 2 | 0 | 0 |
| Barley | 19 | 12 | 17 | 3 | 1 |
| Oats | 16 | 10 | 15 | 9 | 3 |

*Source*: E. J. T. Collins, 'Dietary change and cereal consumption in Britain in the nineteenth century', *Agricultural History Review*, 23 (1975), pp. 97–115.

6 Kerridge, *op. cit.* (1967), pp. 278, 280; Harrison, *op. cit.* (1984), p. 411; E. J. Evans and J. V. Beckett, 'Cumberland, Westmorland and Furness', in Thirsk, *op. cit.* (1984), p. 22; B. Holderness, 'East Anglia and the Fens', in Thirsk, *op. cit.* (1984), p. 223; Brian Short, 'The South-East', in Thirsk, *op. cit.* (1984), p. 287; R. C. Richardson, 'Metropolitan Counties', in Thirsk, *op. cit.* (1984), p. 254; F. Emery, 'Wales', in Thirsk, *op. cit.* (1984), p. 416; J. R. Walton, 'Agriculture 1730–1900', in R. A. Dodgshon and R. A. Butlin (eds), *An Historical Geography of England and Wales* (London, 1978), p. 246.

Table 5.3   Crops as a percentage of arable

|  | 1801 | 1836 | 1875 | 1938 | 1945 | 1961 | 1985 |
|---|---|---|---|---|---|---|---|
| Wheat | 22.7 | 26.8 | 22.4 | 21.2 | 15.0 | 12.7 | 32.5 |
| Barley | 13.6 | 15.7 | 15.5 | 10.3 | 13.7 | 24.9 | 26.8 |
| Oats | 18.8 | 12.6 | 11.5 | 15.1 | 15.9 | 6.7 | 1.8 |
| Cereals[a] | 55.1 | 55.1 | 49.4 | 47.9 | 48.0 | 45.5 | 61.3 |
| Cereals as a % of sown area | 79.3 | 78.7 | 66.1 | 55.9 | 64.6 | 70.2 | 76.5 |
| Potatoes | 1.6 | – | 2.5 | 5.5 | 6.8 | 3.6 | 2.6 |
| Sugar-beet | – | – | – | 3.8 | 2.8 | 3.0 | 3.8 |
| Oilseed rape | – | – | – | – | – | – | 4.9 |
| Horticulture | – | – | 1.1 | 3.7 | 5.6 | 4.9 | 3.7 |
| Fodder roots[b] | 5.9 | 10.2 | 13.8 | 7.4 | 5.3 | 2.1 | 0.7 |
| Peas and Beans | 6.9 | 4.7 | 6.2 | 2.0 | 1.7 | 0.6 | 0.8 |
| All fodder[c] | 12.8 | 14.9 | 20.0 | 12.0 | 9.8 | 6.3 | 3.6 |
| Fallow[d] | 20.3 | 9.4 | 3.6 | 4.1 | 2.3 | 2.1 | 0.6 |
| Other crops | n.d. | n.d. | 2.8 | 0.6 | 0.8 | 0.2 | 0.0 |
| Tillage | 89.8 | 79.5 | 79.4 | 77.5 | 76.1 | 65.5 | 80.5 |
| Temp. grasses[e] | 10.2 | 20.5 | 20.6 | 22.5 | 23.9 | 34.5 | 19.5 |
| Arable | 100.0 | 100.0 | 100.0 | 100.0 | 100.0 | 100.0 | 100.0 |

n.d. no data.
[a] Includes rye and mixed corn.
[b] Turnips, swedes, mangolds and fodder beet.
[c] Includes rape, kohl rabi, kale, cabbages, maize, etc.
[d] No data on fallow in 1801 returns. Assumed to be 2.3 million acres.
[e] No data on temporary grasses in 1801 returns. Assumed to be 1.15 million acres.
*Sources*: As for table 4.4.

THE RISE OF WHEAT

Wheat occupies a larger area than any other crop at present (see table 5.3), and was for long the major cash crop; but it has had some remarkable changes of fortune.

In the early seventeenth century wheat was grown primarily for bread flour and was little cultivated outside the south-east. Rye, which had probably been the leading bread grain in the sixteenth century, was in decline and by the early nineteenth century was found only on a few poor sandy soils. Barley was grown for malt and was sometimes fed to poultry, but it was also produced as a bread grain. Oats was the only cereal grown as a livestock feed, but, as porridge and oatmeal, it was also a staple food in the upland areas of the south-west and north. Although there are no figures on the area in each of the cereals in the seventeenth century, wheat was not the leading crop and no one crop dominated output.[7]

7  P. Mathias, *The Brewing Industry in England 1700–1830* (Cambridge, 1959), p. 392.

Table 5.4  Estimates of the cereal acreage (thousand acres)

| Date | Wheat | Barley | Oats | Total |
|------|-------|--------|------|-------|
| 1801 | 2,572 | 1,534 | 2,125 | 6,231 |
| 1812 | 3,160 | 860 | 2,872 | 6,893 |
| 1836 | 3,400 | 2,000 | 1,600 | 7,000 |
| 1846 | 3,800 | 1,500 | 2,500 | 7,800 |
| 1854 | 3,661 | 2,668 | 1,303 | 7,766 |
| 1875 | 3,240 | 2,245 | 1,659 | 7,144 |

*Sources*: As for table 4.4.

In the eighteenth century rye declined; the number of people eating wheaten bread increased, mainly at the expense of rye eaters (see table 5.2), and of course the population grew after 1740. Beer consumption rose, and the replacement on farms of oxen by horses increased the demand for oats. The first estimates of the cereal acreage (see table 5.4) show that wheat was the leading crop, oats the second; but by the 1870s barley had replaced oats as the second crop. Wheat, however, was the leading cereal nearly everywhere except in Wales, Lancashire and the Lake District and was an important part of most farmers' incomes.[8]

## THE COLLAPSE OF HIGH FARMING: THE FALL OF FODDER CROPS

Although by the 1870s there were farmers specializing in milk production or vegetables, the mixed farming of the lowlands, producing wheat, barley, mutton, wool and beef, was the heart of English farming. The fall of agricultural prices from the 1870s to the 1930s hit this system hard and led to major changes in the crops grown. The fall was greatest in wheat and wool; meat prices dropped as well, less than cereal prices but more than that for milk (see figure 3.2 and table 3.4).

Perhaps the most striking consequence of the collapse of prices was the decline in the area in fodder crops, which has continued uninterruptedly to the present (see figure 5.1). Two-thirds of the area in fodder crops was in roots, which were fed on arable farms to sheep and cattle. This was expensive, particularly compared with feeding based on grass or imported grains. Sheep needed shepherds, folding was expensive, and so was the cultivation, lifting and carting of turnips; to some extent the decline of root crops is exaggerated, for in the 1920s and 1930s the tops and pulp of the new crop sugar-beet were used as fodder. Since the 1950s the traditional functions of the turnip crop have been superseded. Herbicides remove weeds, and the cereal crop has become the cleaning crop –

8 Turner, *op. cit.* (1981), pp. 291–302.

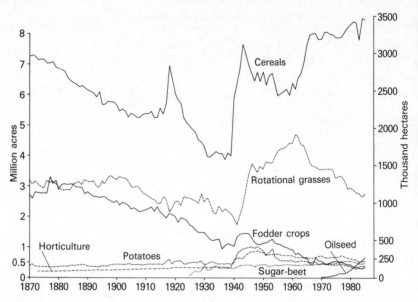

Figure 5.1   Changes in the area in crops, England and Wales, 1870–1985.
*Source*: Ministry of Agriculture, *Agricultural Statistics, England and Wales 1866 to 1985* (London, 1986).

although even earlier the potato and sugar-beet had replaced the turnip. Nor are cattle any longer fed turnips in stalls to produce farmyard manure; chemical fertilizers have replaced dung.[9]

It is not only turnips and the other fodder roots that have declined; peas and beans have fallen to an almost insignificant acreage in the 1980s. As with the roots, the demise of peas and beans has been due mainly to the import of cheaper foods, but there have been other factors. Beans have always given very variable yields and are particularly prone to drought. Neither crop has been of much interest to plant breeders, and yields have not greatly increased in the last half century. In 1978 an EEC subsidy on peas and beans brought an increase in acreage, but they remain, as do all fodder crops, insignificant. In the 1870s they were one-fifth of the arable acreage, in the 1980s less than one twenty-fifth (see table 5.3).[10]

9 E. R. Bullen, 'Break crops on heavy land', *Agriculture*, 73 (1966), pp. 125–30; J. B. Page, 'Arable crop rotation', *Journal of the Royal Agricultural Society of England*, 33 (1972), pp. 98–105.

10 D. A. Bond, 'Recent history of varieties and of the culture of field beans (vicia faba, equina and minor) in the UK', *Journal of the Royal Agricultural Society of England and Wales*, 146 (1985), pp. 144–59; M. C. Heath, 'Grain legumes in UK agriculture', *Outlook on Agriculture*, 16 (1987), pp. 2–7; H. T. Williams, *Principles for British Agricultural Policy* (London, 1960), p. 112.

Although the area devoted to fodder crops has declined dramatically since the 1870s the number of livestock has increased. These have been fed partly by a greater area in grass and by higher hay yields, but most of the extra fodder has come from cereals, which – apart from oats – were rarely fed to livestock in the 1870s. However, from the 1880s imported cheap grain replaced home-grown fodder roots; in the period since 1945 home-grown grain has provided much of the feed of an increasing animal population (see below, pp. 90–2).

### THE FALL AND REVIVAL IN THE CEREAL ACREAGE

The cereal acreage in England and Wales fell by 42 per cent between 1875 and 1938; it had revived briefly during the First World War, but for the rest of the period the trend was downwards. Wheat and barley experienced the greatest decline, their area falling by two-thirds (see figure 5.2). Not only was imported grain cheaper, but brewers were expressing a preference for the malting quality of imported barley – particularly Californian – while the English preference for flour made from hard wheat ensured that most British flour was made from imports. The area in oats, by contrast, increased until 1919, and only then declined: even so, in the late 1930s it was not greatly below the 1870s figure. This was because until the 1920s there was a rising market for oats from the urban horse population.[11]

Although the cereal acreage fell in every county, the decline was smallest in the east. Here it was difficult to establish good pastures, and

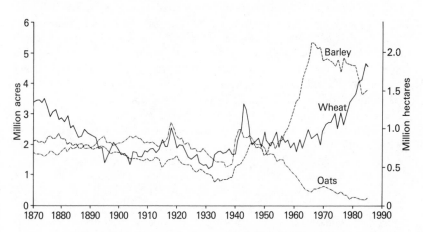

Figure 5.2  Changes in the area in cereals, 1870–1985.
*Source:* Ministry of Agriculture, *Agricultural Statistics, England and Wales 1866 to 1985* (London, 1986).

11 P. J. Perry, *British Farming in the Great Depression 1870–1914* (Newton Abbot, 1974), p. 108.

the cereal acreage held up better than in the Midlands, where good pastures could be easily sown and a living made by switching from cereals to livestock.

The Second World War saw a remarkable rise in the cereal acreage; wheat, barley and oats increased substantially and much old grassland and rough grazing was ploughed up, so that by 1944 the cereal acreage was not far short of the level of the 1870s. But the end of the war saw a reversion towards earlier conditions, despite the system of guaranteed prices, and by 1961 the cereal acreage was below the war-time peak, although still well above the nadir of 1939. The post-war trend of the three cereals was very different (see figure 5.2). As the farm-horse was replaced by the tractor, and the remaining urban work-horses gave way to the lorry, the oats acreage greatly declined. In contrast barley, then wheat, have experienced extraordinary increases until their acreage is well above any previous level, as is the total cereal acreage (see figure 5.1). There are a number of reasons for this remarkable expansion.

First, cereals have been favoured in the post-war pricing policies of both the British government and later the EEC. Second, plant breeders have been remarkably successful in producing varieties that give higher yields and thus greater profits. The adoption of Scandinavian barleys after the war led to the much wider distribution of the crop, which had hitherto been confined largely to the lowlands. However, the new varieties would grow in wetter and cooler districts, and thus replaced oats as it declined in the west and the north. Breeding new wheat varieties has been equally important, not only to obtain higher yields but to produce different varieties for feeding stuffs and for flour. British flour has in the past been made principally from imported high-protein wheats from semi-arid areas. But since the 1950s the proportion of home-grown wheat used has risen substantially, initially because the Chorley Wood process of making dough allowed the use of softer British wheat, more recently because of the breeding of high-protein wheat varieties which can be grown in England. As British wheat is now used for making flour as well as biscuits and cakes, the import of hard wheats from North America has declined.[12]

But there are other reasons for the expansion of the cereal acreage. The rising real cost of labour prompted many farmers to choose enterprises that could easily be mechanized, and this was particularly so of cereal production as the combine harvester spread in the 1950s. By the late 1950s it was apparent that the use of herbicides, pesticides

12  D. K. Britton, *Cereals in the United Kingdom: production, marketing and utilisation* (Oxford, 1969), pp. 23–5, 37, 456; W. Connold, 'Cereal growing in the South-West', *Agriculture*, 73 (1966), pp. 437–43; A. J. Brown, 'Barley growing in Devon', *Agriculture*, 72 (1965), pp. 544–8; B. Holderness, *British Agriculture since 1945* (Manchester, 1985), pp. 50–1; J. T. Coppock, *An Agricultural Atlas of England and Wales* (London, 1976), p. 80; G. A. H. Elton and E. N. Greer, 'The use of home grown wheat for flour milling', *ADAS Quarterly Review*, 2 (1971), pp. 85–94.

and fertilizers could greatly simplify farming systems, making rotations, leys and root crops, as well as livestock, less necessary. Barley proved less susceptible to disease than wheat if grown continuously, and was favoured by cereal specialists in the 1960s. But the primary reason for the rapid expansion first of barley and later of wheat was the increasing use of cereals to feed livestock. Before the war most feed grains were imported; after the 1950s home-grown grain provided much of the feed. The expansion of intensive pig and poultry production provided a market, while later barley began to be fed to young cattle. The dramatic rise of the barley acreage long preceded Britain's entry to the EEC, but the expansion of the wheat acreage owes much to the EEC's pricing policy and the existence of markets in Europe for British feed grains. The great increase in the cereal acreage of the post-war period has restored the crops to the position they occupied in the early nineteenth century, before the rise of vegetables, fruit, potatoes and sugar-beet (see table 5.3).

The distribution of cereals has not, however, changed radically. In 1875 cereals occupied over half the arable area in the eastern counties, less than half in much of the Midlands, the west and Wales. With the fall in cereal prices every county experienced a decline in cereals, though smallest in the east, greatest in the Midlands and the west, so that by 1938 the contrast between east and west was more pronounced. The decline in cereals continued in the immediate post-war period, particularly in the west and Wales. Since the late 1950s the great increase in cereals has come mainly in the Midlands and parts of the east, while the acreage in Wales, the south-west and the north-west has continued a decline that began a century ago. Hence, by the 1980s, the contrast between east and west is far greater than it was in the 1870s.

## POTATOES

Cereals and fodder crops dominated the use of arable in England until the 1870s, but since then the fodder crops have almost disappeared and other crops have taken their place. The rise of horticultural crops is dealt with elsewhere (see below, pp. 197–211). Oilseed rape, sugar-beet and potatoes, the third, fourth and fifth crops in terms of area in the 1980s, (see table 5.3) merit some attention here.

The potato is indigenous to the Americas and was introduced into Europe in the sixteenth century. It was grown in market gardens near London in the early seventeenth century. More important, it was introduced into Lancashire north of the Ribble, probably from Ireland, in the mid-seventeenth century, and from there spread into south Lancashire and Cheshire and north to the Solway plains. It was introduced into the south-west peninsular and into Wales at the same time, where it was grown, as in Lancashire, for human and animal

Table 5.5 Percentage of national potato acreage in selected regions

| | Lancashire and Cheshire | Wales | Lake District | South-west | All West | West Riding | Middlesex and London | Eastern Counties | Others |
|---|---|---|---|---|---|---|---|---|---|
| 1801 | 7.6 | 14.4 | 7.0 | 11.8 | 40.8 | 7.8 | 0.8 | 7.1 | 43.5 |
| 1875 | 11.8 | 12.3 | 3.0 | 9.0 | 36.1 | 6.8 | 0.8 | 17.0 | 39.3 |
| 1919 | 14.1 | 6.1 | 2.1 | 5.2 | 27.5 | 5.7 | 0.4 | 29.3 | 37.1 |
| 1938 | 8.2 | 3.7 | 1.3 | 2.9 | 16.1 | 5.8 | 0.2 | 41.1 | 36.8 |
| 1948 | 5.4 | 6.5 | 2.1 | 6.2 | 20.2 | 5.1 | 0.2 | 27.4 | 47.1 |
| 1961 | 6.0 | 4.2 | 1.0 | 4.0 | 15.2 | 5.6 | 0.1 | 40.1 | 39.0 |
| 1973 | 4.2 | 3.2 | 0.5 | 3.2 | 11.1 | 5.7 | 0.1 | 37.4 | 45.7 |
| 1983 | 6.3 | 3.8 | 0.5 | 4.9 | 15.3 | 2.4[a] | 0.1 | 35.7[b] | 46.5 |

[a] West Yorkshire and South Yorkshire, part of former West Riding, excluded.
[b] Including Humberside.
Source: Ministry of Agriculture, Agricultural Statistics of England and Wales; see also table 4.4.

consumption. In 1801 it was produced mainly in these westerly districts, and to a lesser extent around London and in the Fens. The high grain prices of the Napoleonic Wars encouraged its rapid expansion, and the rest of the century saw a continued increase, the acreage at least doubling between 1801 and 1875. It became an important supplement of the diet of the poor, and in the 1830s and 1840s it may have replaced bread. The crop was grown in small amounts, on small farms, and cultivated with a spade; it was also very important in allotments and gardens.[13]

By the 1840s it was being grown by farmers as well as market gardeners. A special plough for potatoes had been invented in the Napoleonic Wars and in the 1860s a spinner for harvesting the crop was developed. In the 1870s the potato acreage was still located mainly in the west, although there were also considerable acreages in the industrial districts, where potatoes were important on small holdings and allotments. By the 1870s the trade in early potatoes from Cornwall, Pembrokeshire and Kent was developing, and the Fens were emerging – mainly after 1840 – as a major producer, although still well behind the west. The national acreage in potatoes reached a peak in the First World War, but thereafter showed little change, as rising incomes began to reduce per capita potato consumption (see figure 5.1). But the Second World War led to a dramatic increase. Potatoes gave a far higher calorific yield per acre than wheat – or indeed any other staple food – and during the food shortages of the 1940s the area in potatoes soared, to over one million acres in 1948.

Since then the area has declined equally dramatically, because yields have risen but per capita consumption has fallen. Since 1934 – with the exception of 1940–55 – potato production and marketing has been under the direction of the Potato Marketing Board, which has encouraged the growth of alternative outlets for potatoes – mainly in processing – and has also operated a quota system; potatoes can be cultivated only by registered growers. Over the last half century there have been two major trends in potato production. First, as the harvesting of potatoes has been mechanized – only since the 1950s – smaller growers have abandoned production and output has increasingly been found not on small holdings with much hand labour, but on large mechanized arable farms. Second, and as a consequence, output has increasingly become concentrated in eastern England not only in the nineteenth-century centre of the Fens, but on large farms on a variety of soils. The eastern counties – from the East Riding to Suffolk – account for over a third of the country's potato

13 R. Salaman, *The History and Social Influence of the Potato* (Cambridge, 1985), pp. 453–76; Evans and Beckett, *op. cit.*, p. 24; Harrison, *op. cit.* (1984), p. 373; W. G. Burton, *The Potato: a survey of its history and of factors influencing its yield, nutritive value, quality and storage* (London, 1966), p. 21; D. Hey, 'Yorkshire and Lancashire', in Thirsk, *op. cit.* (1984), p. 64; E. L. Jones, *Agriculture and the Industrial Revolution* (Oxford, 1974), p. 52; Turner, *op. cit.* (1981), pp. 291–302.

acreage, compared with only 17 per cent in 1875. The share of the west, once dominant, has fallen from over a third in 1875 to only 15 per cent in 1983 (see table 5.5).[14]

SUGAR-BEET

The late nineteenth century saw a steady increase in the consumption of sugar. In Europe most of this came from the expansion of the sugar-beet acreage and a sugar-refining industry protected by duties from imported cane-sugar. In Britain, by contrast, cheap cane-sugar came from the colonies – the West Indies, Mauritius, Fiji and Natal – and it occurred to few to grow sugar-beet, although there were abortive attempts in Essex in 1832 and Suffolk in 1868. The first sugar-beet factory was established by Dutch interests at Cantley, near Norwich, in 1912, the second at Kelham, near Newark, in 1923, but it was not until the government subsidized sugar made from beet in the Act of 1925 that there was much progress; it was then remarkably rapid. By 1934 a further 16 factories had opened and the area grown rose from 57,750 acres in 1925 to 396,348 acres in 1934. Most of the factories were in eastern England; farmers paid the cost of transporting the beet to the factory and were paid on the basis of weight and sugar content. Factories relied mainly upon local production; in the 1930s 90 per cent of all the sugar-beet processed came from within a radius of 25 miles of the factory.[15]

By 1935 the factories, which were started by several private companies, were united as the British Sugar Corporation. The subsidizing of sugar-beet met government aims. It provided a reliable source of income for arable farmers, who were suffering in the 1920s, and, together with the 1932 Wheat Act, began the revival of farming prosperity in England. It was less successful in halting the downward trend of agricultural employment, although the crop certainly required considerable labour in singling, weeding and lifting. It fitted easily into the crop rotations of eastern England, replacing the fodder roots. Until the 1960s the tops and the pulp were used for feeding livestock.

The area in sugar-beet reached a peak in the 1940s, remained little changed until the 1960s and has since slowly increased (see figure 5.1). Yields of both weight and sugar content have risen, the former doubling between the 1930s and the 1960s. There have been major changes in

---

14 J. D. Sykes and J. B. Hardaker, *The Potato Crop: policy and practices* (Wye, 1962), pp. 10, 29.

15 Ministry of Agriculture and Fisheries, *Report on the Sugar Beet Industry at Home and Abroad*, Economic Series no. 27 (London, 1931), pp. 29, 32, 37, 39, 41; H. D. Watts, 'The Location of the beet-sugar industry in England and Wales, 1912–36', *Transactions of the Institute of British Geographers*, 53 (1971), pp. 95–116.

the way the crop is grown. The original sugar-beet seed gave clusters of seedlings on emergence, which had to be singled. The breeding of monogerm seed in the United States and its adoption in England, combined with precision drilling and the use of herbicides, has greatly reduced the labour input. The mechanization of the harvest, also previously highly labour-intensive, was complete by the late 1960s. Between 1954 and 1980 the time required to cultivate one acre of sugar-beet fell by 84 per cent. The changes in production have not been matched by changes in location. The eastern counties accounted for four-fifths of the acreage in 1938 and still do so (see table 5.6).[16]

Table 5.6    Location of the sugar-beet acreage

|  | 1938 | 1945 | 1961 | 1973 | 1983 |
|---|---|---|---|---|---|
|  |  |  | (a) |  |  |
|  |  |  | thousand acres |  |  |
| Eastern Counties[a] | 266 | 293 | 315 | 380 | 390 |
| West Midlands[b] | 21 | 33 | 29 | 38 | 41 |
| Other | 42 | 79 | 67 | 62 | 60 |
| England and Wales | 329 | 405 | 411 | 480 | 491 |
|  |  |  | (b) |  |  |
|  |  | regions as a percentage of England and Wales | | | |
| Eastern Counties[a] | 80.9 | 72.3 | 76.6 | 79.2 | 79.4 |
| West Midlands[b] | 6.4 | 8.2 | 7.1 | 7.9 | 8.4 |
| Other | 12.7 | 19.5 | 16.3 | 12.9 | 12.2 |
| England and Wales | 100 | 100 | 100 | 100 | 100 |

[a] East Riding, Nottinghamshire, Lincolnshire, Soke of Peterborough, Huntingdonshire, Isle of Ely, Cambridgeshire, Norfolk and Suffolk.
[b] Shropshire, Herefordshire, Staffordshire, Worcestershire.
*Source*: Ministry of Agriculture, *Agricultural Statistics of England and Wales*.

OILSEED RAPE

If sugar-beet provided a remarkable instance of the rapid diffusion of a new crop in the 1920s and 1930s, oilseed rape provided an equally dramatic expansion in the 1970s (see figure 5.1). Most of the crops from which vegetable oils are derived are tropical, and these were the source

16 O. S. Rose, 'The development of sugar beet growing in the United Kingdom', in A. H. Bunting (ed.), *Change in Agriculture* (London, 1976), pp. 147–54; 'The British sugar beet industry', *Journal of the Royal Agricultural Society of England*, 133 (1972), pp. 106–18; C. R. W. Spedding, ed., *Fream's Agriculture* (London, 1983), pp. 508–13; Bullen, *op. cit.* (1966), pp. 125–30.

of the oils used in Britain from the mid-nineteenth century to the 1970s. The only temperate crop that yields a suitable oil is *brassica napus*. Oilseed crops described as coleseed or turnip-rape were grown in the Fens in the late sixteenth century, and an oilseed-crushing industry was established in the early seventeenth century. The residual after extracting oil was used to make oil-cake for cattle. The oilseed-crushing industry ceased to use home-grown oilseeds from the early nineteenth century and rape was by then hardly grown.[17] When Britain entered the EEC oilseed rape was quickly adopted by English farmers, for the EEC subsidies on oils from indigenous plants made the crop highly profitable. It also made an excellent break crop for farmers growing continuous cereals. It was first adopted on large cereal farms on the chalk lands of Hampshire. Since the early 1970s it has spread north-east and has become essentially a crop of eastern arable England, for in Hampshire the build-up of disease has led to a decline in the acreage there. By the mid-1980s it occupied 5 per cent of the country's arable area, more than any crop other than wheat or barley.[18]

SUMMARY

In the early seventeenth century four-fifths of the country's sown area was occupied by cereals, and the only other crops of significance were the pulses. But from 1650 to 1870 lowland farming was transformed by the adoption of fodder roots and rotational grasses, grown to feed livestock and to maintain soil fertility and cereal yields. From the 1870s fodder crops declined and were replaced by imported grain; new cash crops occupied this area, initially potatoes, vegetables, and fruit, then sugar-beet and more recently oilseed rape. Since 1950 cereals have been grown increasingly as livestock feed; crops are no longer used in rotations to maintain soil fertility or to rid the land of disease or weeds.

17 Thirsk, *op. cit.* (1985); G. E. Fussell, 'History of Cole (Brassica sp.)', *Nature*, 176 (1955), pp. 48–51; E. S. Bunting, 'New arable crops: retrospect and prospects', *Journal of the Royal Agricultural Society of England*, 135 (1974), pp. 107–21.

18 A. B. Lane, 'Benefits and hazards of new crops: oilseed rape in the UK', *Agricultural Ecosystems and Environment*, 10 (1983), pp. 299–309; J. E. Wrathall, 'The oilseed rape revolution in England and Wales', *Geography*, 63 (1978), pp. 42–5; J. E. Wrathall and R. Moore, 'Oilseed rape in Great Britain: the end of a revolution', *Geography*, 71 (1986), pp. 351–4.

# 6
# The Productivity of the Land: Crop Yields

INTRODUCTION

The great increase in output since the 1930s has come not from a greater area in crops but from a dramatic increase in crop yields. However, not all crop yields have increased at the same rate. The largest increase in the 50 years has been of the cereals, particularly wheat, the average yield of which is now three times what it was in the 1930s (see table 6.1). Sugar-beet and hay have experienced far less notable increases. But in all cases the rate of increase since the 1930s has been greater than in the preceding half century; indeed the yield of both fodder roots and hay declined between the 1880s and the 1930s (see table 6.1).

## CROP YIELDS IN THE PAST

The agricultural census did not collect information on the yield of crops until 1884; before that there were estimates only at irregular intervals and generally only for wheat. There seems little doubt, however, that medieval yields were low, probably averaging 10 bushels (see figure 6.1). Thereafter there is little or no evidence until the late sixteenth century, when wheat yielded no more than 8 bushels on a sample of East Anglian farms. It seems reasonable to suppose that there was little increase between medieval times and the early seventeenth century. But by 1800 there had been a substantial increase; then the national average was 20 to 21 bushels. There was little increase in the early decades of the nineteenth century, but from the 1830s to the 1880s the yield rose from 20 to 30 bushels, a very substantial increase over half a century. From the 1880s to the 1930s the yield of the cereal crops again rose, but slowly, only 10 per cent for wheat, although more for oats and barley (see table 6.1). Thereafter the increase in yields was precipitous. By the early 1980s wheat yields were twice the level of the 1950s, three

Table 6.1  Average yield of selected crops, England and Wales (hundredweight per acre)

| Crop | 1885–9 | 1921–5 | 1933–7 | 1950–4 | 1970–4 | 1980–4 | % increase | |
|---|---|---|---|---|---|---|---|---|
| | | | | | | | 1885–9 to 1933–7 | 1933–7 to 1980–4 |
| Wheat | 16.2 | 18.6 | 17.8 | 22.7 | 35.6 | 52.7 | 10 | 195 |
| Barley | 13.0 | 14.6 | 16.2 | 21.1 | 30.0 | 38.9 | 25 | 140 |
| Oats | 13.8 | 13.8 | 16.2 | 19.4 | 30.8 | 37.3 | 18 | 130 |
| Potatoes | 119.9 | 126.4 | 136.1 | 162.8 | 254.3 | 290.0 | 14 | 113[a] |
| Sugar-beet | n.d | 148.2 | 188.7 | 231.7 | 277.0 | 330.5 | n.d | 75 |
| Turnips and Swedes | 238.1 | 238.1 | 213.0 | 321.6 | 386.4 | 491.7[b] | − 10 | 131 |
| Hay | 27.5 | 22.7 | 21.1 | 20.3 | 34.8 | n.d. | − 24 | 65[c] |

n.d. no data.
[a] Data for 1980–3.
[b] Fodder beet.
[c] 1933–7 to 1970–4; no statistics after 1977.

Sources: Ministry of Agriculture, Fisheries and Food, A Century of Agricultural Statistics: Great Britain, 1866–1966 (London, 1967); Agricultural Statistics, England and Wales, 1974 (London, 1975); Agricultural Statistics, United Kingdom, 1984 (London, 1985).

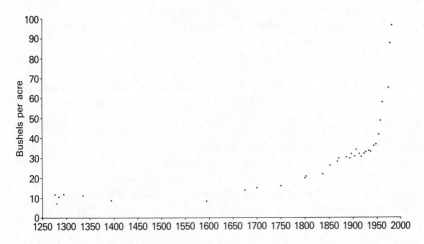

Figure 6.1 The yield of wheat in England 1250–1980s.

times that of the 1930s, three and a half times that of the 1880s, five times that of the 1830s and ten times the level of the yields obtained before 1650.[1]

### WHAT DETERMINES CROP YIELDS?

The yield of a crop is a direct function of the quantity of solar radiation received.[2] It can also be affected by temperature, over which the farmer

1 M. Turner, 'Agricultural productivity in England in the eighteenth century: evidence from crop yields', *Economic History Review*, 35 (1982), pp. 489–510; B. M. S. Campbell, 'Arable productivity in medieval England: some evidence from Norfolk', *Journal of Economic History*, 43 (1983), pp. 379–404; J. Z. Titow, *Winchester Yields: a study in medieval agricultural productivity* (Cambridge, 1972), p. 31; M. K. Bennett, 'British wheat yield for seven centuries', *Economic History*, 3 (1935), pp. 12–29; M. Mate, 'Profit and productivity on the estates of Isabella de Foz (1260–92)', *Economic History Review*, 33 (1980), pp. 326–34; M. Overton, 'Estimating crop yields from probate inventories: an example from East Anglia, 1585–1735', *Journal of Economic History*, 39 (1979), pp. 363–78; J. B. Lawes and J. H. Gilbert, 'On the home produce, imports, consumption and price of wheat over twenty eight (or twenty seven) harvest years, 1852–53 to 1879–80 inclusive', *Statistical Journal*, 43 (1880), pp. 313–51; P. Craigie, 'On statistics of agricultural production', *Journal of the Statistical Society*, 46 (1883), pp. 1–58; R. J. P. Kain, *An Atlas and Index of the Tithe files of Mid-nineteenth Century England and Wales* (Cambridge, 1986), p. 460; M. J. R. Healey and E. L. Jones, 'Wheat yields in England, 1815–59', *Journal of the Royal Statistical Society*, 125A (1962), pp. 574–9; G. Stanhill, 'Trends and deviations in the yield of the English wheat crop during the last 750 years', *Agro-Ecosystems*, 3 (1976), pp. 1–10.

2 J. L. Monteith, 'Climate and the efficiency of crop production in Britain', *Philosophic Transactions of the Royal Society*, 281B (1977), pp. 277–94.

has little control; an excess or absence of soil moisture, which can be modified by underdrainage or irrigation; the leaf area of the plant, which can be altered by the plant breeder; and soil acidity, which can be reduced by applying lime. But to the farmer the most obvious determinant of crop yield is the amount of plant nutrients in the soil, and a great deal of his time is spent trying to maintain or increase this quantity.

Under climax vegetation the plant nutrients – nitrogen, potassium and phosphorus, with traces of other elements – in the soil and the vegetation are in equilibrium. When vegetation dies it decays and nutrients pass back into the soil. Small additions of phosphorus and potassium are released from the decomposition of minerals in the regolith, and nitrogen is fixed both in the atmosphere, by lightning, from whence it reaches the soil in rain, and in the soil itself, by free-living bacteria. It is the constant return of decomposing vegetation that keeps the cycle in equilibrium. But when the vegetation is cleared and the land farmed, nutrients are removed in every harvest of both crops or animals, and there is no vegetation decay to maintain soil fertility. Hence crop yields will fall. The farmer's art is to avoid this decline and, if possible, to increase the flow of nutrients and hence crop yields.[3]

There are a number of ways in which plant nutrients can be returned to the soil. The most important is in the dung of livestock, which contains nitrogen, phosporus and potassium. Grazing livestock return dung directly to grassland, but it is less easy to get dung to cropland. In the open-field system cattle grazed the arable only during the fallow and on the stubble after the harvest. But from the late eighteenth century the principal method was by preparing farmyard manure. Cattle were kept in stalls on straw litter, and their dung, mixed with the straw, was carted to the fields. This remained the main means of maintaining soil fertility until it was superseded by chemical fertilizers in the 1950s and 1960s. In some arable areas this method was supplemented by the folding of sheep. Sheep were confined to a small part of a turnip field by wooden hurdles; they ate the turnips and dunged the land, and when the turnips had been eaten the sheep were moved to another part of the field. Their dung benefited the next crop.

These were the principal ways of manuring the land, but medieval and early modern farmers had discovered a variety of other manures. Near coasts seaweed was used, and sea sand was carted inland in Devon; pigeon droppings were highly regarded, and near a few towns – Norwich and Newcastle are examples – night soil was used. Down to the 1930s horse droppings from London were valued by market gardeners in Sandy. Chalk and marl were also applied, although their main function

3 J. Tivy, 'Nutrient cycling in agro-ecosystems', *Applied Geography*, 7 (1987), pp. 93–114; J. L. Jollans, *Fertilizers in UK Farming*, CAS Report no. 9 (Reading, 1985), pp. 30–5.

was to reduce soil acidity and hence to release plant nutrients already in the soil rather than adding them.[4]

Another important way of adding plant nutrients is to grow leguminous crops. Before the mid-seventeenth century the main legumes were peas and beans; both have nodules on their roots, which, together with bacteria in the soil, can fix nitrogen. From the mid-seventeenth century clover, a fodder legume, was widely grown both in the rotations of eastern England and in the convertible husbandry of the Midlands and the west; in both systems the following crops benefited from the accumulated nitrogen and, in the case of convertible husbandry, where land was in grass and clover for four to five years, from organic matter.[5]

Liming, as already noted, does not add plant nutrients to the soil but it does make existing nutrients more easily available. Acid soils, which are common in higher altitudes and the wetter areas of England and Wales, reduce the capacity of bacteria – whether free-living or associated with legumes – to fix nitrogen and reduce the plant's capacity to take up nutrients. Liming, then, indirectly increases soil fertility, and has long been practised.[6]

WEEDS

Conditions that favour crop growth will also favour the growth of weeds, which will use plant nutrients that could be going to the crop, thus reducing yields. Traditionally the most important means of weeding the land were the mouldboard plough, which cut through the roots of the weed as the land was ploughed in autumn or spring in preparation for sowing, or the hoe, during the growth of the crop. As long as crops were broadcast, weeding was possible only during the fallow. When crops were sown with a drill in rows it was possible to hand-hoe or horse-hoe during growth; more accurately it was possible to do this with root crops such as turnips, swedes, mangolds, potatoes and sugar-beet, which were known as 'cleaning' crops and were an indispensible part of the rotation.

4 G. E. Fussell, 'The early days of chemical fertilizers', *Nature*, 195 (1962), pp. 750–4; 'Crop nutrition in the late Stuart age, 1660–1714', *Annals of Science*, 14 (1958), pp. 173–84; 'Early eighteenth century crop nutrition theory and practice', *Proceedings of the Chemical Society* (June 1960), pp. 193–8; Joan Thirsk, 'Farming techniques', in Thirsk (ed.), *The Agrarian History of England and Wales*, vol. IV: *1500–1640* (Cambridge, 1967), pp. 167, 168; M. Havinden, 'Agricultural history in the South-west', in M. Havinden and C. M. King (eds), *The South West and the Land*, Exeter Papers in Economic History no. 2 (1969), pp. 7–18.

5 G. W. Cooke, 'Soils and fertilizers', in G. W. Cooke (ed.), *Agricultural Research 1931–1981: a history of the Agricultural Research Council* (London, 1981), pp. 183–202.

6 I. G. Burns, 'Nitrate movement in soil and its agricultural significance', *Outlook on Agriculture*, 9 (1976), pp. 144–8.

Cereals, in contrast, with rows much nearer together, could not be hoed for long after growth got underway.[7]

### PESTS

Just as a fertile soil allows weeds to thrive, so crops provide food for a variety of animals. Crops are eaten by higher mammals such as rabbits, and by birds, while insects also eat some and carry diseases that destroy others; fungi are parasites that obtain their food from the plant tissue of crops. Traditional farmers had very limited means of controlling these pests. Birds could be scared off with scarecrows or by small boys with rattles, while mammals could be snared; both birds and mammals could be shot, and in the eighteenth and nineteenth centuries many parish councils would pay headage for birds. Insects were less easy to deal with. Indeed the only control was what is now called biological control: some insects ate other insects and some birds ate some insects. Fungi could be dealt with only by ploughing the fallow or crop rotations. During the fallow the vectors of disease could be destroyed by the plough, while rotating crops prevented the build up of soil-borne disease, for most disease is specific to one crop.[8]

### TECHNICAL CHANGE AND THE PROGRESS OF CROP YIELDS UNTIL THE 1930s

During the Middle Ages crop yields showed very little change; yields were low, perhaps little more than 10 bushels. Hence relatively small amounts of plant nutrients were removed from the soil: a crop of 15 bushels per acre would have removed only about 18 pounds of nitrogen, and the return of sufficient nitrogen was accomplished by the small amount of manure received after harvest or during the fallow, from rain and from free-living bacteria in the soil, and from growing peas and beans (see table 6.2). This nutrient cycle would have allowed yields of about 15 bushels, but weeding was highly ineffective and it was this that reduced the average from 15 to 10 bushels. Implements were cumbersome and inadequate, oxen weak; livestock were few per acre, and relied largely on the waste of the commons for feed, for little land was set aside to grow crops for them. The supply of farmyard manure

7 J. G. Elliot, 'Weed control: past, present and future – a historical perspective', in R. G. Hurd, P. V. Biscoe and C. Dennis (eds), *Opportunities for Increasing Crop Yields* (London, 1980), pp. 285–95.

8 E. L. Jones, 'The bird pests of British agriculture in recent centuries', *Agricultural History Review*, 20 (1972), pp. 107–25.

Table 6.2 Estimates of the nitrogen cycle in pre-nineteenth century farming systems

|  | *lbs per acre* | |
|---|---|---|
|  | *Loomis* | *Chorley* |
| From rain, etc. | 7.0–10.7 | 2.2–3.6 |
| Seed | 3.5 | 2.5–3.1 |
| Manure | 4.5 | 9.9–16.3 |
| Free-living bacteria | 1.8–4.5 | 2.1 |
| Legumes as 10% of arable | 1.8–8.9 | – |
| Total | 18.8–32.1 | 16.9–22.6 |

*Source*: R. S. Loomis, 'Ecological dimensions of medieval agrarian systems: an ecologist responds', *Agricultural History*, 52 (1978), pp. 478–83; G. P. H. Chorley, 'The agricultural revolution in northern Europe, 1750–1880; nitrogen, legumes and crop productivity', *Economic History Review*, 34 (1981), pp. 71–93.

was thus poor in quality and small in quantity, and most of the dung was wasted upon the common.[9]

Between 1650 and 1800 wheat yields possibly doubled, from about 10 bushels per acre in 1650 to 15 bushels in 1700, and from then to 20 to 21 bushels in the very early nineteenth century. The major cause of this increase was the growing proportion of the agricultural area sown with legumes and the effect upon the nitrogen content of soils. There are no statistics of the area in peas and beans until the early nineteenth century, but there is no reason to suppose that they had declined in the preceding two centuries. To these were added clover, sainfoin and lucerne, crops which fixed nitrogen in the soil at a rate well above that of peas and comparable with that of beans. By the early nineteenth century legumes, a very small proportion of the arable in 1650, were nearly one-fifth; they continued to expand, and by the 1870s pulses and rotational grasses were one-quarter of the arable of England and Wales.[10]

9 G. P. H. Chorley, 'The agricultural revolution in northern Europe, 1750–1880: nitrogen, legumes and crop productivity', *Economic History Review*, 34 (1981), pp. 71–93; R. S. Loomis, 'Ecological dimensions of medieval agrarian systems; an ecologist responds', *Agricultural History*, 52 (1978), pp. 478–83; W. Harwood Long, 'The low yields of corn in medieval England', *Economic History Review*, 32 (1979), pp. 459–69.

10 Overton, *op. cit.* (1979), pp. 363–78; Turner, *op. cit.* (1982), pp. 489–510; Bennett, *op. cit.* (1935), pp. 12–29; Craigie, *op. cit.* (1883), pp. 1–58; P. S. Nutman, 'Alternative sources of nitrogen for crops', *Journal of the Royal Agricultural Society of England*, 137 (1976), pp. 16–24.

## THE CONTROL OF PESTS AND WEEDS BEFORE 1830

Any improvements in the preparation of the seed bed would have reduced the number of weeds; in the eighteenth century the design of ploughs improved so that they became less cumbersome and lighter, while from 1730 an increasing number were made entirely from iron, whereas earlier this had been used simply for the share and coulter. But the major contribution to weeding was the adoption of the turnip after 1650, supplemented by the mangold and the swede in the later eighteenth century. These crops, together with the potato, allowed both hand-hoeing and the use of the horse-hoe. Invented in the early eighteenth century by Tull, the drill, which gave the straight, widely spaced and parallel rows of seeds that allowed hoeing during the crop's growth, was not a practical implement until improvements made in the 1780s. It was little used even in the first decade of the nineteenth century, however, and did not finally oust broadcasting until the 1850s. The first half of the nineteenth century saw the invention and improvement of a great number of implements and machines such as clod-crushers, better harrows and rollers, which increased the efficiency with which the seed bed was prepared and weeding carried out.[11]

One final cause of the rise in crop yields between the mid-seventeenth century and the early nineteenth century was the increased number of livestock, their better feeding and thus the increased supply of farmyard manure. This was particularly noticeable with sheep, which increased substantially between 1700 and 1800 (see table 7.2, p. 82); much of this increase came on the limestone hills of the south and east, where sheep were folded on turnips; indeed, without this these soils could not have been used for growing cereals.[12]

## THE BEGINNINGS OF MODERN AGRICULTURE

In the first few decades of the nineteenth century wheat yields rose little, but from the 1830s to the 1880s by between 40 and 50 per cent;[13] from then until the 1930s the rate of increase of wheat was low, although that of oats and barley was more substantial (see table 6.1). The nineteenth-century acceleration was due to a number of factors, but of most significance was that farmers began to buy fertilizers and feeding stuffs; this might be said to signal the beginning of modern agriculture.

11 R. Wilkes, 'The diffusion of drill husbandry', in W. E. Minchinton (ed.), *Agricultural Improvement, Medieval and Modern*, Exeter Papers in Economic History (1981), pp. 65–94.

12 G. E. Fussell and Constance Goodman, 'Eighteenth century estimates of British sheep and wool production', *Agricultural History*, 4 (1930), pp. 131–51.

13 Healey and Jones, *op. cit.* (1962), pp. 574–9.

The eighteenth century saw a great increase in the number of sheep, and their dung contributed to the maintenance of soil fertility. In the nineteenth century sheep continued to be important but it was cattle that played the primary role. Numbers increased, but it was not this that was paramount. More significant was the introduction of stall feeding and the increased purchases of oil-cake; dung mixed with straw provided large quantities of farmyard manure. Stall feeding, which required investment in new buildings, developed in the later eighteenth century but reached its apogee in the 1850s and 1860s. High Farming, as has been frequently noted, meant high feeding. In the 1840s many farmers in the better-farmed areas of eastern England kept cattle as much for their dung as for their beef. In the eighteenth century oil-cake, which not only fattened beast but provided a rich manure, came from British oilseeds, but in the nineteenth century linseed and other crops were imported, and oil-cake consumption rose sixfold between the 1830s and the 1860s.[14]

But it was not only the supply of farmyard manure that increased in this period. The first chemical fertilizers were produced in the 1840s. Bones had been spread on fields in Yorkshire and Lincolnshire in the late eighteenth century; later they were ground to dust before being spread. Finally, J. B. Lawes dissolved bones in sulphuric acid and his factory at Deptford, opened in 1842, was soon copied by others, notably by Packards at Ipswich – later to be Fisons. By 1870 there were 70 superphosphate works in Britain. As the supply of bones waned manufacturers turned to Norwegian apatite, Cambridgeshire coprolites and phosphates from Belgium and America; by 1900 North Africa had become, as it remains, the major source. In the 1880s basic slag, a byproduct of the processing of phosphoric iron ores, became an important source of phosphorus, and remained so until the demise of phosphoric ores in the steel process in the 1960s. Potassium came only from farmyard manure until the opening of the potash mines at Stassfurt in 1851, but imports were not significant until the end of the century. In the early nineteenth century the major source of nitrogen was farmyard manure; however, this began to be augmented from elsewhere in the 1840s. Initially it was obtained from imports of guano, the droppings of seabirds on islands off the Peruvian coast, and between the 1840s and the 1870s lavish imports supplemented the nitrogen obtained from farmyard manure. However, the Peruvian government eventually priced their main export out of the market and in the 1870s nitrates from Chile replaced Peruvian guano. Later in the century home-produced ammonium sulphate, a byproduct of the gas industry, began to be used by farmers.[15]

14 F. M. L. Thompson, 'The Second Agricultural Revolution 1815–1880', *Economic History Review*, 21 (1968), pp. 62–77.

15 L. F. Haber, *The Chemical Industry during the Nineteenth Century: a study of the economic aspect of applied industry in Europe and North America* (Oxford, 1958), pp. 49, 57, 60, 61, 62,

Table 6.3   The amounts of fertilizer used in the
United Kingdom, 1837–1934 (thousand tons)

| Date | N | $P_2O_5$ | $K_2O$ |
|------|-----|-----|-----|
| 1837 | – | 15 | – |
| 1841 | 0.2 | 20 | – |
| 1845 | 33 | 46 | – |
| 1855 | 33 | 45 | – |
| 1874 | 34 | 90 | 3 |
| 1896 | 33 | 122 | 5 |
| 1913 | 29 | 180 | 23 |
| 1929 | 48 | 198 | 53 |
| 1934 | 54 | 139 | 50 |

*Source*: G. W. Cooke, 'The Nation's Plant Food Larder',
*Journal of Science of Food and Agriculture*, 9 (1958), pp.
761–2.

From the 1830s to the 1930s farmyard manure remained the main
source of plant nutrients in British farming. Nitrogen fertilizers showed
little long-term increase in use and only phosphorus was applied in large
amounts (see table 6.3 and figure 6.2). By the 1930s applications of
chemical fertilizers per acre were still very low and confined mainly to

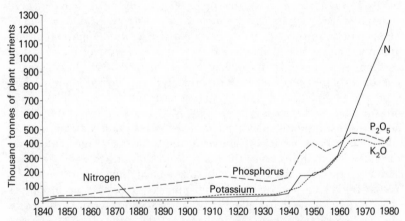

Figure 6.2   Fertilizer consumption in the United Kingdom, 1840–1977.
*Sources*: G. W. Cooke, 'The nation's plant food larder', *Journal of the Science of Food and
Agriculture*, 9 (1958), pp. 761–2; G. W. Cooke, 'Changes in fertilizer use in the UK from 1950 to
1980', *Proceedings of the Fertilizer Society*, 190 (1980), pp. 1–29.

66, 106; G. W. Cooke, 'The Nation's Plant Food Larder', *Journal of the Science of Food and
Agriculture*, 9 (1958), pp. 761–72; J. L. Jollans, *op. cit.* (1985), pp. 75, 135; R. Grove,
'Coprolite mining in Cambridgeshire', *Agricultural History Review*, 24 (1976), pp. 36–43;
W. M. Mathew, 'Peru and the British guano market, 1840–1870, *Economic History Review*,
23 (1970), pp. 112–28; J. P. Olinger, 'The guano age in Peru', *History Today*, 30 (1980),
pp. 13–16.

potatoes, sugar-beet and some horticultural products. Indeed in the 1930s many farmers were still doubtful of the value of 'artificials', and in many cases very ignorant of their properties; lime, for example, was thought by some to contain plant nutrients. The relatively limited use of chemical fertilizers after the 1880s was due partly to the lack of profitability of many crops, but also to the great decline in the area in arable; few applied fertilizers to grass.

THE CONTROL OF PESTS

Farmers had long sought to protect their crops against insects and fungi, and were familiar with the symptoms if not the causes of disease. Steeping – soaking seed in some supposedly protective liquid before sowing – and attempts to protect crops by putting soot on leaves were both ancient practices. But the beginnings of chemical protection date from the second half of the nineteenth century, when there were attempts to prevent vine mildew and phylloxera by chemical spraying in France, while in the United States the depredations of the Colorado beetle in 1868 also prompted experiments with spraying. In England such experiments were largely limited to garden sprays, and the only significant advance was W. Cooper's dressings for wheat, first produced in 1856. By the late nineteenth century pesticides derived from plants – nicotine, derris and pyrethrum – were in use. The early sprays were used mainly on the more valuable plants such as fruit, hops and some vegetables. However, in the 1920s the chemical industry began to take a greater interest in pesticides as their potential profitability became apparent. By the 1930s over a million acres of land were being sprayed.[16]

However, the major growth in the use of chemical protection has come only since the 1950s. Unfortunately there are no reliable figures on the use of either herbicides or pesticides, only on the value of British manufacturers' output, which includes exports (see figure 6.3). Although selective herbicides were known in the 1890s and used in France at that time, they were not widely employed in England until after the Second World War. ICI had marketed DNOC in 1932, but the major technical advances came with the discovery of MCPA and 2,4-D during the war. These and later herbicides were rapidly adopted by farmers from the late 1940s, but were used initially only on cereals. By the late 1960s

16 W. C. Moore, 'Some modern developments in crop protection', *Journal of the Royal Agricultural Society of England*, 116 (1955), pp. 20–8; G. Ordish, *The Constant Pest: a short history of pests and their control* (London, 1976), pp. 111–12, 150–1, 152, 167, 186, 187, 189; *Biological Methods in Crop Pest Control: an introductory study* (London, 1967), pp. 20, 65, 95, 171, 174, 175; E. S. E. Southcombe, 'Developments in herbicide application', in Hurd et al., *op. cit.* (1980), pp. 323–33; A. E. Smith and D. M. Secoy, 'Organic material used in European crop protection before 1850', *Chemistry and Industry* (5 November 1977), pp. 863–9.

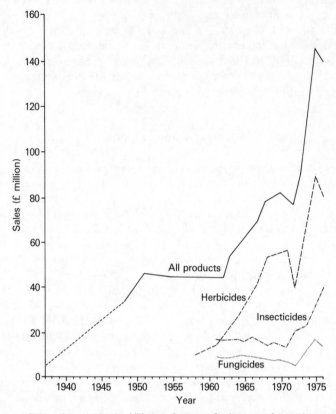

Figure 6.3    Sales of pesticides by UK manufacturers for home and export use, at 1976 values.
*Source*: Sir Hans Kornberg, *Royal Commission on Environmental Pollution: seventh report, agriculture and pollution* (London, Cmnd. 7644 (1979), p. 131.

65 per cent of the United Kingdom's cereal acreage was treated with herbicides, by 1975, 94 per cent. From the 1960s the use of weed-killers spread to other crops; by 1977 virtually all sugar-beet and two-thirds of the potato acreage was treated. In contrast, grassland remained largely untouched by the use of herbicides even in the later 1970s.[17]

Herbicides were rapidly adopted by farmers because of their very obvious labour savings. Weeding crops by hand with the hoe or even with tractor-drawn hoes is expensive. The use of herbicides initiated some other changes. Research in the United States showed that the only

17 J. Sheail, *Pesticides and Nature Conservation: the British experience 1950–1975* (Oxford, 1985), pp. 16, 19, 22, 58, 83, 123, 162; J. D. Fryer, 'Recent developments in the agricultural use of herbicides in relation to ecological effects', in F. H. Perring and K. Mellanby (eds), *Ecological Effects of Pesticides* (London, 1977), pp. 27–45; D. W. Robinson, 'The impact of herbicides on crop production', in Hurd et al., *op cit.* (1980), pp. 297–312; R. J. Makepeace, 'Herbicides: past, present and future', in Hurd et al., *op. cit.* (1980), pp. 335–46.

agronomic value of ploughing is to destroy weeds. Farmers, who since Tull's time had been vigorously ploughing land to obtain a fine tilth, were told that ploughing reduced soil fertility. Once herbicides could deal effectively with weeds there was little need for the frequent and deep cultivations with a mouldboard plough, and in the 1960s and 1970s some farmers have turned to minimum-cultivation techniques, where only tines or discs are used to turn the upper soil before the direct drilling of seed and fertilizer.[18]

In the 1930s pesticides were confined largely to protection for fruit and outbreaks of potato blight; the most widespread form of chemical protection was seed dressing, effectively begun in the 1850s. By 1942, 70 per cent of wheat seed was disinfected before sowing. However, the war led to some major advances in pesticides as it had in herbicides, most notably with the discovery and exploitation of DDT. The number of pesticides available to farmers increased greatly in the post-war years. In 1950, 15 chemical ingredients were used to produce 352 products, by 1975, 200 to give over 800 products. From 1950 organophosphorus insecticides discovered in Germany began to replace organochlorine sprays such as DDT. From the late 1960s the principal advance was the increasing use of fungicides.[19]

However, neither insecticides, herbicides nor fungicides have been entirely successful, and some have had unfortunate side-effects. First, there is evidence that some insecticides kill birds and thin egg-shells; as a consequence a number, including DDT, have been withdrawn from use. Second, some insects have become immune to sprays. Although further chemicals can be developed, the cost of new pesticides has been rising rapidly. Nor have herbicides been entirely successful in eliminating weeds nor fungicides in dealing with soil-borne disease; there is good evidence that farmers using chemical protection *and* rotations get better yields than those using only chemical protection.[20]

18 R. Q. Cannell, D. B. Davies, D. Mackney and J. D. Pigeon, 'The suitability of soils for sequential direct drilling of combined-harvested crops in Britain: a provisional classification', *Outlook on Agriculture*, 9 (1977), pp. 306–17; P. Allen, 'ICI plant protection division experience with direct drilling systems, 1961–1974', *Outlook on Agriculture*, 8 (1976), pp. 213–15.

19 H. C. Gough, 'Pesticides on crops – some benefits and problems', in Perring and Mellanby, *op. cit.* (1977), pp. 7–26; Moore, *op. cit.* (1955); J. M. A. Sly, 'Changes in use of pesticides since 1945', in Perring and Mellanby, *op. cit.* (1977), pp. 1–6.

20 Joyce Tait, 'The flow of pesticides: industrial and farming perspectives', in T. O'Riordan and R. Kerry Turner (eds), *Progress in Resource Management and Environmental Planning*, 3 (1981), pp. 219–50; R. L. Metcalfe, 'Changing role of insecticides in crop protection', *Annual Review of Entomology*, 25 (1980), pp. 219–56; R. J. Chancellor, 'The manipulation of weed behaviour for control purposes', *Philosophic Transactions of the Royal Society*, 295B (1981), pp. 103–10; J. D. Fryer, 'Weed management: fact or fable?', *Philosophic Transactions of the Royal Society*, 295B (1981), pp. 185–99; Fryer, *op. cit.* (1977), pp. 27–45; Sheail, *op. cit.* (1985), pp. 54, 58, 83, 86, 123; P. Stanley and P. J. Bunyan, 'Agricultural chemicals and the environment: a review of the impact of agricultural chemical usage on flora and fauna', *ADAS Quarterly Review*, 33 (1979), pp. 115–28.

### THE USE OF FERTILIZERS SINCE 1945

Although chemical fertilizers have been used by British farmers since the 1840s, the growth in their consumption since the 1930s has been dramatic (see figure 6.2). The reason for this has been their falling real cost. The major cost in fertilizer production, particularly for nitrogen, is not the raw material but the petroleum used to provide the large amounts of energy needed, and until the 1970s petroleum was cheap. Over most of the post-war period the increasing use of fertilizers has also brought increases in farm profits; the point of decreasing returns in fertilizer application has not yet been reached. Since 1945 the concentration of nutrients in the fertilizer has increased, so that the physical handling has become easier; modern granular fertilizers can be applied in drills that combine the actions of sowing seed and applying fertilizer. In contrast, using farmyard manure means keeping large cattle herds, which in turn need much labour to feed, and until the mechanization of muck-spreading the moving and applying of farmyard manure was time-consuming and unpleasant. One ton of chemical fertilizer contains as much plant nutrient as 25 tons of farmyard manure.[21]

There have been important changes in fertilizer use since 1945. Until then greater amounts of phosphorus and potassium than of nitrogen had been applied to English soils (see figure 6.2), and by the 1940s the soil reserves of these two elements were considerable. Thus while from 1945 to the early 1960s the application of all three nutrients was raised, thereafter it was that of nitrogen alone that was increased. The application of fertilizers to different crops has also changed. In the 1940s potatoes and sugar-beet received the most per acre, cereals and grass very little (see table 7.4, p. 87). Since then, as cereal prices became more favourable, applications of fertilizers to wheat and barley approached the level of those used on cash root crops. Perhaps more surprising has been the steady growth of fertilizer usage on grass, particularly temporary grass (see table 6.4). Indeed in the late 1970s half all the fertilizer used in England and Wales went onto grass.[22]

Because of the far greater ease of application and the low cost of chemical fertilizers, the use of farmyard manure declined after 1945; indeed in some parts of England the disposal of dung has become a problem, particularly on the farms of intensive livestock producers. However, some writers have exaggerated the decline in the role of animal dung in providing plant nutrients. Although the relative importance of

21 G. W. Cooke, 'Changes in fertilizer use in the UK from 1950 to 1980', *Proceedings of the Fertilizer Society*, 190 (1980), pp. 1–29.

22 K. G. Gostick, 'Agricultural Development and Advisory Service recommendations to farmers on manure disposal and recycling', *Philosophic Transactions of the Royal Society*, 296B (1981), pp. 329–32; B. M. Church, 'Use of fertilizers in England and Wales, 1980', *Report of Rothamsted Experiments for 1980*, pt. 2 (1981), p. 115.

Table 6.4 Percentage of area in sample of farms receiving fertilizers and farmyard manure, 1980

| | % of area receiving | | | |
|---|---|---|---|---|
| | N | P | K | FYM |
| Tillage | 95 | 88 | 83 | 18 |
| 1-year leys | 98 | 58 | 55 | 20 |
| 2 to 7-year leys | 93 | 70 | 70 | 43 |
| Permanent grass | 73 | 52 | 51 | 36 |
| All crops and grass | 87 | 73 | 70 | 28 |

*Source*: B. M. Church, 'Use of fertilizers in England and Wales, 1980', *Report of Rothamsted Experiments for 1980* (1981), p. 12.

Table 6.5 Fertilizers and farmyard manure usage, 1979 (thousand tons of plant nutrients)

| | N | % | P | % | K | % |
|---|---|---|---|---|---|---|
| Animal manures | 368 | 24.4 | 74 | 29.2 | 235 | 41.0 |
| Chemical fertilizers | 1156 | 75.6 | 178 | 70.8 | 338 | 59.0 |
| Total | 1524 | 100.0 | 252 | 100.0 | 573 | 100.0 |

*Source*: C. R. W. Spedding, ed., *Fream's Agriculture* (London, 1983), p. 179.

manure and chemical fertilizers is difficult to estimate, the former probably supplies a quarter of all the nitrogen used in England and Wales, rather more of the phosphorus and 41 per cent of the potassium (see table 6.5). Much of this is of course applied to grass; of the 170 million tons voided each year by cattle in the United Kingdom, nearly two-thirds goes directly onto grass. However, less farmyard manure is used on crops; in 1980 only one-fifth of the area in tillage received farmyard manure (see table 6.4).[23]

## THE ROLE OF THE PLANT BREEDER

In the post-war increase in crop yields the importance of chemical fertilizers and chemical protection has often been stressed, but the role of the plant breeder has been little emphasized; yet the introduction of new varieties has been the single most important cause of the increase in yields. Until the rediscovery of Mendel's principles of genetics in 1900, breeding for specific characteristics was impossible, and the

23 Sir Hans Kornberg, *Royal Commission on Environmental Pollution: Seventh Report, Agriculture and Pollution*, HMSO Cmnd. 7644 (1979), p. 131.

selection of better plants could proceed only by observing plants with the wanted character and using them for seed. However, after 1900 plant-breeding institutes were established in England and other parts of Western Europe. In England the Cambridge Institute very rapidly produced new varieties of practical importance for the farmer. Little Joss, a wheat resistant to rust, was marketed in 1912, whilst Plumage Archer and Spratt Archer dominated English barleys until after 1945. Imported Scandinavian barleys crossed with English varieties gave rise in 1933 to Proctor, which spread rapidly, particularly into cold and wet areas where oats was in decline and where existing varieties of barley could not be grown.[24]

In the post-war period breeders have produced cereal varieties that give much higher yields. These are responsive to nitrogen fertilizer and have much shorter stalks, and can thus support the much larger grain heads. Modern wheats do not have a greater biomass than earlier varieties, but a far greater proportion is in the head. Farmers have been remarkably quick to adopt new varieties. Thus Capelle-Desprez, a French wheat, was introduced into England in 1954, and by 1965, 88 per cent of the acreage of winter wheat was in this variety. Its demise was equally rapid. Maris Huntsman, introduced in 1972, gave a yield 20 per cent greater than did Capelle-Desprez; by 1975 Huntsman occupied 34 per cent of the acreage and Capelle-Desprez only 3 per cent.[25]

The impact of plant breeding on crops other than the cereals has been limited. But on the cereals it has been dramatic. Experiments growing new and old varieties with the same inputs suggests that 60 per cent of the increase in wheat yield and 45 per cent in that of barley between 1947 and 1975 was due to the new varieties. In contrast, new varieties are thought to be responsible for only 10 per cent of post-war potato yield increases.[26]

SUMMARY

The use of chemical technology has changed not only yields but also land use since the 1950s; however, the history of fertilizers and pesticides

24 R. Riley, 'Plant breeding', in Cooke, *op. cit.* (1981), pp. 115–38; T. J. Riggs, P. R. Hanson, N. D. Start, D. M. Miles, C. L. Morgan and M. A. Ford, 'Comparison of spring barley varieties grown in England and Wales between 1880 and 1980', *Journal of Agricultural Science*, 97 (1981), pp. 599–610; J. D. Palmer, 'Plant breeding today', *Journal of the Royal Agricultural Society of England*, 131 (1970), pp. 7–17.

25 K. Dexter, 'The impact of technology on the political economy of agriculture', *Journal of Agricultural Economics*, 28 (1977), pp. 211–19; P. W. Russell Eggitt, 'Choosing between crops: aspects that affect the user', *Philosophic Transactions of the Royal Society*, 281B (1977), pp. 93–100.

26 V. Silvey, 'The contribution of new varieties to increasing cereal yield in England and Wales', *Journal of the National Institute of Agricultural Botany*, 14 (1978), pp. 367–384; Riley, *op. cit.* (1981); F. G. H. Lupton, 'Recent advances in cereal breeding', *Netherlands Journal of Agricultural Science*, 30 (1982), pp. 11–24.

goes back, in the former case to the 1840s, in the latter to the early part of the century. The greater use of these techniques after 1945 has been due to the increasing sophistication of the chemical industries and the continued subsidy and protection of agriculture, which has allowed the farmer to continue using these expensive techniques. The adoption of chemical methods has made older techniques for maintaining yields and reducing disease less necessary. However, the rising protest at the misuse of chemicals and the prospect of falling profit may lead to a return to traditional methods.

# 7
# Land Use, Livestock and Densities

Livestock are ubiquitous in England, being found on the higher slopes of Snowdonia in the west and at sea level in the Fens in the east. Livestock production provides the British farmer with 61 per cent of his income – and the percentage was higher before entry into the EEC. Since then higher grain prices have had adverse effects on poultry and pig producers, while dairy farmers have suffered from cuts in quota, but between the beginning of the twentieth century and the 1970s two-thirds of British farm income was derived from livestock output (see table 2.7).

Before the eighteenth century the relative importance of livestock products was different from the present. Wool was probably the single most important product, both for the home textile industry and for export, until the latter was banned in 1614. In the eighteenth century a growing demand for mutton led to the breeding of sheep for meat rather than for wool; as a result the quality of English wool declined and in the nineteenth century it was undercut by imports of cheaper and finer wool from Australia. Although British wool output rose in the nineteenth century, by the 1870s it was a small fraction of farm income and much less important than mutton (see table 7.1). Cattle, until the eighteenth century, were valued as much for their draught capacity as for meat and milk, while their hides were also an important product.[1]

Since the 1870s cattle have provided 55 to 60 per cent of the income from livestock, with milk of increasing importance from the 1870s to the 1950s; beef, however, has recently gained the primacy it once had (see table 7.1). In contrast, the value of sheep has fallen from over one-

---

1 G. G. S. Bowie, 'New sheep for old – changes in sheep farming in Hampshire, 1792–1879', *Agricultural History Review*, 35 (1987), pp. 15–24; J. Thirsk, 'Agricultural policy: public debate and legislation', in J. Thirsk (ed.), *The Agrarian History of England and Wales*, vol. V: *1640–1750*, pt. 2 (Cambridge, 1984), pp. 198–388; J. D. Chambers and G. E. Mingay, *The Agricultural Revolution 1750–1880* (London, 1966), p. 66.

Table 7.1   Livestock output in the United Kingdom (as a percentage of the value of gross output)

|  | 1870–6 | 1904–10 | 1924–9 | 1935–9 | 1969–72 | 1982–4 |
|---|---|---|---|---|---|---|
| Cattle | 55.6 | 60.1 | 59.2 | 57.3 | 55.0 | 59.9 |
| Milk and dairy | 26.9 | 31.4 | 32.2 | 32.8 | 31.8 | 25.7 |
| Meat | 28.7 | 28.7 | 27.0 | 24.5 | 23.2 | 34.2 |
| Sheep | 22.5 | 17.3 | 16.0 | 13.1 | 6.7 | 8.3 |
| Meat | 19.3 | 14.9 | 13.7 | 11.1 | 5.8 | 7.8 |
| Wool | 3.2 | 2.4 | 2.3 | 2.0 | 0.9 | 0.5 |
| Pigs | 15.2 | 12.9 | 12.3 | 12.4 | 16.8 | 13.4 |
| Meat | 15.2 | 12.9 | 12.3 | 12.4 | 16.8 | 13.4 |
| Poultry | 5.6 | 8.0 | 11.6 | 16.0 | 20.5 | 16.5 |
| Eggs | 4.2 | 6.0 | 8.7 | 12.1 | 12.0 | 7.5 |
| Meat | 1.4 | 2.0 | 2.9 | 3.9 | 8.5 | 9.0 |
| Others | 1.1 | 1.7 | 0.9 | 1.1 | 1.0 | 1.9 |
| Total | 100.0 | 100.0 | 100.0 | 100.0 | 100.0 | 100.0 |

*Sources*: E. M. Ojala, *Agriculture and Economic Progress* (Oxford, 1952), p. 209; Ministry of Agriculture, *Annual Reviews of Agriculture*.

fifth to less than one-tenth of livestock output; nearly all of this is now accounted for by meat, which is now mainly lamb rather than mutton. Pigs, like cattle, have shown little change in relative importance over the last century. It is poultry that has seen the most dramatic increase, mainly from the 1920s; in the same period poultry-meat has overtaken eggs, which once formed three-quarters of all income from poultry.

LIVESTOCK NUMBERS

Estimates of livestock numbers before the beginning of the agricultural census are not very reliable, particularly those of poultry and pigs. However, it seems likely that there was a substantial increase in sheep numbers in the eighteenth century, and a less dramatic rise in cattle in the first three-quarters of the nineteenth century (see table 7.2). Since the 1870s cattle have shown a steady increase, not quite doubling by the 1980s (see figure 7.1). Sheep, in contrast, fell without check until the dreadful winter of 1947, but have since more than doubled so that their numbers now exceed those in the 1870s. It must be said, however, that these numbers include more lambs and fewer adults than they did in and before the 1870s. Poultry, which were for long the concern only of the farmer's wife, began to be organized on a large scale in the 1920s. But when advances in heating, ventilation and vaccination made factory-like production possible numbers soared, and by the 1970s had increased

Table 7.2  Livestock numbers in England and Wales, 1700–1985 (millions)

| Date | Cattle | Sheep | Pigs | Poultry |
|------|--------|-------|------|---------|
| 1700 | 4.5 | 12.0 | 2.0 | n.d |
| c.1800 | 3.4 | 26.7 | n.d | n.d |
| 1875 | 4.8 | 22.0 | 2.1 | 10.8[a] |
| 1895 | 5.1 | 18.6 | 2.7 | 28.8[b] |
| 1913 | 5.7 | 17.1 | 2.1 | 29.7 |
| 1919 | 6.2 | 15.1 | 1.8 | 25.3[c] |
| 1938 | 6.7 | 17.9 | 3.6 | 53.3 |
| 1949 | 7.7 | 11.7 | 2.1 | 57.8 |
| 1961 | 8.8 | 19.1 | 4.6 | 93.2 |
| 1973 | 10.3 | 19.4 | 7.3 | 116.7 |
| 1985 | 9.06 | 25.6 | 6.8 | 96.2 |

[a] 1885.
[b] 1908.
[c] 1921.
n.d. no data.
*Source*: H. Prince, 'England circa 1800', in H. C. Darby (ed.), *A New Historical Geography of England and Wales* (Cambridge, 1973), pp. 403, 417; G. E. Fussell and C. Goodman, 'Eighteenth century estimates of British sheep and wool production', *Agricultural History*, 4 (1930), pp. 131–51; Ministry of Agriculture, *Agricultural Statistics of England and Wales*.

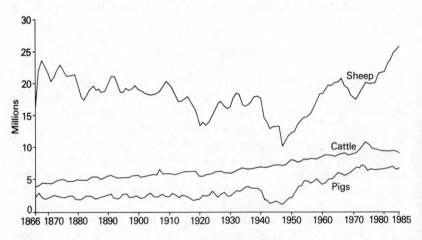

Figure 7.1  Changes in the total number of sheep, cattle and pigs in England and Wales, 1866–1985.
*Source:* Ministry of Agriculture, *Agricultural Statistics, England and Wales 1866 to 1985* (London, 1986).

fivefold, although rising feed costs have led to a decline since then (see figure 15.1, p. 192, and table 7.2). Pigs, like poultry, have shown a considerable increase since the 1920s, the numbers more than tripling, and, as with poultry, are increasingly organized on a large scale.

However, the increase in the number of animals needs to be qualified for three reasons. First, between the 1870s and the 1980s the age structure of the livestock population has changed; there are now more lambs than wethers and proportionally more piglets than sows, while chickens are slaughtered much earlier. If the livestock population is measured in livestock units – where allowances are made for the difference between a steer and a chicken, and for the different weights of young and old animals – then rather different increases in livestock are obtained.[2] Whereas the *number* of cattle doubled between the 1870s and the 1980s, the number of cattle expressed in livestock units increased by only four-fifths; the difference for sheep was 21 per cent as against 11 per cent, for poultry 667 per cent and 612 per cent, and for pigs a much greater increase in numbers than units, 191 per cent to 62 per cent. The increase in the total number of livestock units between 1877 and 1985 was 83 per cent. Second, it should be remembered that since the 1870s there has been a great decline in the number of farm-horses, and if they are included then the number of livestock units has increased by only 52 per cent. If the non-farm-horse population is included, then the increase in all livestock units since 1877 is only one-third. However, a third qualification needs consideration. Although the increase in the number of livestock units since 1877 is less than at first sight would appear, livestock *densities* have increased considerably since the 1870s because of the decline – by about 4 million acres – of the agricultural area. Hence the *density* of livestock *units* has doubled, though if farm-horses are excluded the density has risen by only three-quarters.[3]

THE CHANGING DENSITY AND DISTRIBUTION OF LIVESTOCK

The changing distribution of dairy cattle, sheep, pigs and poultry are dealt with in later chapters. Here it suffices to note some of the broader changes over the last century. In 1875 there was a clear distinction between the east and west of the country (see figure 7.2); densities were greater in Wales, the Midlands and the west, with a notable outlier of high densities on the summer fattening pastures of Northamptonshire and Leicestershire. In 1875, as at present, stock were rarely bred, fattened and sold for slaughter from the same farm. The uplands of

2 J. T. Coppock, *An Agricultural Atlas of England and Wales* (London, 1976): the livestock conversion units are on p. 226.
3 F. M. L. Thompson, 'Nineteenth century horse sense', *Economic History Review*, 29 (1976), pp. 60–81.

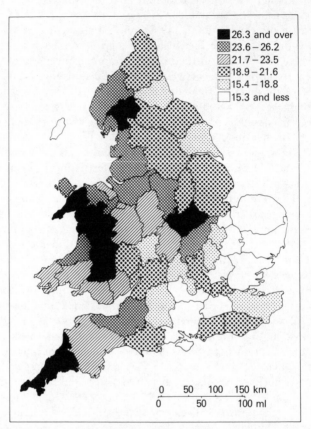

Figure 7.2   Livestock units per 100 acres of crops and grass, 1875.
*Source*: Board of Agriculture, *Agricultural Statistics, England and Wales 1875* (London, 1876).

Wales, the Pennines and the Lake District had large flocks of breeding
ewes, and to a lesser extent of cows, that produced lambs and store
cattle, which were sold to be fattened on the lowlands of the east and
south-east. Nor were the uplands the only source of stores. Cattle bred
in Scotland and Ireland were also imported for fattening in the south
and east. They were fattened on two types of farm. First were arable
farms, where stores were fed on turnips in winter and temporary grasses
in summer. Second were specialized grazing districts, most notably the
pastures on the heavy clays of Northamptonshire and Leicestershire, to
a lesser degree in the clay vale of Buckinghamshire, and on the good
summer pastures where water-tables were too high for crop production,
such as the Lincolnshire marshes.[4]

4  W. Smith, *An Economic Geography of Great Britain* (London, 1959), pp. 58–60.

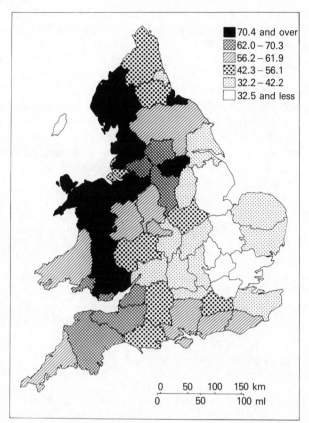

Figure 7.3  Livestock units per 100 acres of crops and grass, 1985 (cattle, pigs, sheep and poultry.
*Source*: Ministry of Agriculture, *Agricultural Statistics, United Kingdom 1985* (London, 1986); Welsh Office, *Welsh Agricultural Statistics, no. 8, 1986* (Cardiff, 1986).

Although livestock densities are now much higher than they were in 1875, the difference between east and west persists (see figure 7.3); the pastures ploughed up in Leicestershire and Northamptonshire during the Second World War have never returned to grass. Sheep in the 1870s were found in the uplands and the lowlands, but the decline of sheep from 1875 to 1947 was greatest in the lowlands of the east and south, where feeding sheep on turnips became too expensive. Although sheep densities recovered after 1947, there are few counties in the east or south-east where densities are now more than one-fifth of those in 1875. Cattle increased in the east between 1875 and 1938 as milk production became profitable, particularly in the counties immediately to the south, east and west of London; but since 1949 the number of cattle in some parts of eastern England has declined as farmers in Lincolnshire, Norfolk,

Cambridgeshire and Essex have specialized in grain and dropped their beef and dairy herds. Nevertheless cattle densities in most of eastern England are much the same as they were in the 1870s and the 1930s (see table 14.1, p. 180).[5]

GRAZING

Livestock numbers and densities in the rest of England and Wales are higher than they were 40, 50 or indeed 100 years ago. As the area in crops and grass has declined, how have the extra animals been fed?

Grass remains, as it always has been, the most important source of food for animals in England and Wales, providing 62 per cent of the dry matter (see table 7.3), while cereals provide one-quarter. There have been, however, major changes in the way cattle are fed since the 1870s. Then crops grown to feed animals – turnips, swedes, mangolds, kohl rabi, cabbages, peas and beans – occupied one-fifth of the arable area, but now they are less than one-twentieth. Although there was a substantial increase in the area in grass before the First World War, the area in temporary and permanent grass changed little until the Second World War and has since declined; in the 1870s there were 14 million acres in grass, in 1910, 18 million, but now there are only 12 million, so that the area in grass has not compensated for the decline in fodder crops.

Table 7.3 Supply of animal feeds in the United Kingdom, 1981

| | Dry matter (million tons) | (%) | Value (£ million) | (%) |
|---|---|---|---|---|
| Pasture | | | | |
| Grazed | 20.0 | 38.3 | 500 | 14.9 |
| Conserved | 12.5 | 23.9 | 625 | 18.7 |
| Other fodder crops | | | | |
| Roots | 1.7 | 3.3 | 150 | 4.5 |
| Kale | 0.6 | 1.2 | 40 | 1.2 |
| Straw | 1.5 | 2.9 | 35 | 1.0 |
| Cereals | | | | |
| Home-grown | 8.5 | 16.3 | 850 | 25.4 |
| Imported | 3.0 | 5.7 | 400 | 11.9 |
| Byproducts | 2.0 | 3.8 | 250 | 7.5 |
| Protein concentrates | | | | |
| Oilseed residues | 1.8 | 3.4 | 350 | 10.4 |
| Fish and meat meal | 0.6 | 1.2 | 150 | 4.5 |
| Total | 52.2 | 100.0 | 3350 | 100.0 |

*Source*: C. R. W. Spedding, ed., *Fream's Agriculture* (London, 1983), p. 364.

5 J. F. Hart, 'The changing distribution of sheep in Britain', *Economic Geography*, 32 (1956), pp. 260–74; Ministry of Agriculture, *Agricultural Statistics, England and Wales*.

## FERTILIZERS AND GRASS VARIETIES

Although the grass area is now less than it was a century ago, the output is greater. Hay yields, which declined from the 1870s until the 1930s, have since substantially increased (see table 6.1) for a number of reasons. Although the adoption of legumes had transformed pastures in the seventeenth and eighteenth centuries, grassland management in the late nineteenth century was poor. Permanent grassland was rapidly invaded by inferior species – pastures often included 20 or more species – and the only fertilizer used, apart of course from animal dung, was basic slag. Things were little better in the 1930s, when a national survey showed how much grassland was of poor quality or, indeed, derelict. Since 1945 this has changed, due partly to the work of Sir George Stapledon in the 1930s. Swards now consist of carefully selected varieties; three or fewer are grown in a pasture. Rye grass is the leading variety; first-class rye grass made up only 10 per cent of all swards in the 1930s but 40 per cent in the 1970s, and currently four-fifths of all seed sown is rye grass. Fertilizer, once rarely applied to grass, is now widely used (see table 6.4 and 7.4), particularly on temporary grass, although one-quarter of all grass still receives none at all.[6]

One notable change in the composition of pastures since 1945 has been the decline of clover, a major crop in the eighteenth and nineteenth centuries. It has a shorter growing season than does grass, it is liable to disease, and cows suffer if they eat too much of it. Farmers have replaced clover, with its ability to fix nitrogen, with rye grass and nitrogen fertilizers.[7]

Table 7.4   Nitrogen fertilizer usage, England and Wales (pounds per acre)

| Date | Winter wheat | Spring barley | Potatoes | Sugar-beet | Temporary grass | Permanent grass |
|------|------|------|------|------|------|------|
| 1943–5 | 17.0 | 18.7 | 70.5 | 82.1 | 3.6 | 3.6 |
| 1980 | 129.4 | 77.6 | 161.5 | 120.0 | 149.0 | 83.0 |

Source: A. E. M. Hood, 'Fertilizer trends in relation to biological productivity within the UK', Philosophical Transactions of the Royal Society, 296B (1982), pp. 315–28.

6 A. Hopkins, 'The botanical composition of grassland in England and Wales', Journal of the Royal Agricultural Society of England, 140 (1977), pp. 140–50; W. F. Raymond, 'Grassland Research', in Agricultural Research 1931–1981: a history of the Agricultural Research Council, ed. G. W. Cooke (London, 1981), pp. 311–24; G. W. Cooke, 'Soils and fertilizers,' in Cooke, op. cit. (1981), pp. 183–202; B. M. Church, 'Use of fertilizers in England and Wales, 1980', Report of Rothamsted Experiments for 1980, pt. 1 (1981).

7 John Frame, 'The role of white clover in United Kingdom pastures', Outlook on Agriculture, 16 (1987), pp. 28–34.

*Grass being cut for silage, a way of conserving grass that is replacing hay-making. A Hereford bull watches in anticipation.* (Author)

### MANAGING GRASSLAND

Managing grassland has always been difficult. Grass growth increases rapidly in the spring, reaches a peak in June, and then declines to very little in autumn, so that farmers have always aimed to conserve some of the early summer growth to feed their cattle in the winter. Until recently this was done by cutting the grass in July, drying it in the field – not easy to do because of the weather – and storing it in stacks as hay. The alternative, which has now overtaken hay-making, is to make grass into silage. Grass is cut and taken immediately to silos, where it is sealed off from the air. Under these conditions protein content is preserved better than in hay-making; nor is silage-making dependent on three or four days of sunshine. Silage-making is not a new method. Advocated by a French farmer in a book published in 1877, it was taken up rapidly in France and the United States and was tried in England, but did not prove successful. Some 57 silos were built in Westmorland, for example, but all were abandoned by 1913. No interest was shown in silage-making until after 1945; even in 1968 no more than 15 per cent of the conserved grass area was converted to silage, but by 1973, 28 per cent, in 1980, 45 per cent, and now over half is ensiled.[8]

8 P. J. Perry, *British Farming in the Great Depression 1870–1914: an historical geography* (Newton Abbot, 1974), p. 112; D. C. Thomas, N. C. Kelley and D. G. Chamberlain, 'Silage', *Proceedings of the Nutrition Society*, 39 (1980), pp. 257–64.

## THE DISTRIBUTION OF GRASS

The rate of grass growth and the length of the growing season depend upon temperature and evapotranspiration. In the uplands of England and Wales low temperatures and rainfall substantially in excess of evapotranspiration requirements give a poor grass and low yields, while in the east high summer temperatures and a low summer rainfall provide too little moisture for good grass growth. In the western lowlands, however, both temperatures and rainfall favour grass growth and hay yields are some 40 per cent higher than in the east of the country.[9] In the east and south grass is found mainly on the heavier clays, which retain soil moisture in the summer, areas with high water-tables such as Romney Marsh or the Norfolk river valleys, or very poor sandy soils where few other crops will grow.

Not surprisingly Wales, the north-west and the south-west have always had a higher proportion of their improved land in grass than has the

*The plough-up in the Second World War. Land Girls harvest a large wheat field on the Sussex Downs, August 1941.* (BBC Hulton Picture Library)

9 J. P. Green and R. D. Baker, 'Classification, distribution and production of UK grasslands', in J. L. Jollans (ed.), *Grassland in the British Economy*, CAS Paper no. 10 (Reading, 1981), pp. 237–60.

east. In 1875, however, only 51 per cent of the national improved area was in temporary and permanent grass. By 1938 the area in grass had risen by 4 million acres to 72 per cent of the improved area, and only a handful of counties in the east had less than half their area in grass (see figure 4.5). In the war there was of course a great plough-up of grassland, but perhaps the most notable post-war feature has been the decline since 1960 of temporary grass, particularly in arable rotations (see figure 4.3). The use of chemical fertilizers, herbicides and pesticides has reduced the need for rotations, and hence for temporary grass.

ARABLE FEEDS

Greater grass yields have not been sufficient to make up for the decline of fodder crops, and since the 1870s there has been an increase in the amount of grain and other concentrates fed to livestock (see table 7.5). Little is known of the use of grain as a livestock feed before the modern period. Spoilt barley and wheat were fed to cattle, most commonly to poultry and pigs, in the seventeenth and eighteenth centuries, but only oats was grown primarily as a cattle and horse feed. In the late eighteenth century oil-cake began to be an important feed in eastern England. Oil-cake was the residue when oil was crushed from coleseed and later from linseed. In the nineteenth century there were substantial increases in the import of oilseeds, initially linseed from Europe, later a variety of tropical oilseeds, and they were fed to cattle in stalls to fatten them and to make a rich farmyard manure.[10]

Table 7.5   Imports of concentrated feeding stuffs (thousand tons)

| 1867–9 | 1,171 | 1938–9 | 5,179 | 1961–2 | 6,900 | 1973–4 | 4,700 |
|---|---|---|---|---|---|---|---|
| 1870–6 | 1,782 | 1952–3 | 2,800 | 1962–3 | 6,200 | 1974–5 | 4,300 |
| 1877–85 | 2,479 | 1953–4 | 4,500 | 1963–4 | 5,900 | 1975–6 | 5,400 |
| 1886–94 | 2,728 | 1954–5 | 5,300 | 1964–5 | 5,700 | 1977 | 6,060 |
| 1984–1903 | 3,823 | 1955–6 | 4,700 | 1966–7 | 5,500 | 1978 | 4,370 |
| 1904–10 | 3,895 | 1956–7 | 4,700 | 1967–8 | 5,500 | 1979 | 4,535 |
| 1911–15 | 4,132 | 1957–8 | 5,300 | 1969–70 | 6,000 | 1980 | 4,227 |
| 1920–2 | 3,762 | 1958–9 | 6,800 | 1970–1 | 6,200 | 1981 | 5,860 |
| 1924–9 | 4,342 | 1959–60 | 6,200 | 1971–2 | 5,100 | 1982 | 5,306 |
| 1930–4 | 5,291 | 1960–1 | 6,100 | 1972–3 | 5,700 | 1983 | 4,765 |

*Source*: E. M. Ojala, *Agriculture and Economic Progress* (Oxford, 1952); Ministry of Agriculture, *Output and Utilization of Farm Produce in the UK 1977 to 1983* (London, 1984) *Annual Reviews of Agriculture*.

10 Joan Thirsk, 'The Farming Regions of England', in J. Thirsk (ed.), *The Agrarian History of England and Wales*, vol. IV, *1500–1640*, (Cambridge, 1967), p. 51; B. A. Holderness, 'East Anglia and the Fens', in J. Thirsk (ed.), *The Agrarian History of England and Wales*, vol. V, *1640–1750*, pt. 2, (Cambridge, 1984), pp. 197–238; F. M. L. Thompson, 'The Second Agricultural Revolution', *Economic History Review*, 21 (1968), pp. 62–77.

After 1845 the fall in grain prices led to some wheat and barley being fed to livestock; in the 1880s, however, less than 10 per cent of total wheat output was so used, although rather more of barley and oats.[11] But from the 1860s imported grains began to play a major role in feeding English and Welsh livestock (see table 7.5), and imports of concentrates quadrupled between the 1870s and the eve of the First World War. Most of these imports were grain, especially maize, but they also included tropical oilseeds and protein feeds such as soya and fish-meat. Imports further increased in the inter-war period, with a growing market among poultry and pig farmers, but then were greatly reduced in the Second World War. Since the 1950s imports have grown again, but have not, in spite of the post-war increase in livestock numbers, greatly exceeded the post-war level. This has been because of the great rise since 1945 in home-grown wheat and barley and its use for livestock feed (see table 7.6). Concentrates now provide one-quarter of the metabolic energy needs of UK livestock (see table 7.7) and have replaced

Table 7.6 Percentage of United Kingdom home-grown grains fed to livestock

| Crop | 1922 | 1930 | 1967 | 1976 | 1982 |
|---|---|---|---|---|---|
| Wheat | 30 | 33 | 45 | 43 | 49 |
| Barley | 30 | 25 | 66 | 65 | 49 |
| Oats | 80 | 60 | 81 | 66 | 56 |

*Sources*: D. K. Britton, *Cereals in the United Kingdom: production, marketing and utilisation (Oxford, 1969)*, p. 389: Ministry of Agriculture, *Output and Utilization of Farm Produce in the UK 1977 to 1983* (London, 1984); E. H. Whetham, *Agrarian History of England and Wales*, vol. VIII: *1914–1939* (Cambridge, 1978), p. 232; Ministry of Agriculture, *Departmental Committee on Distribution and Prices of Agricultural Produce: interim and final reports* (London, 1924), pp. 12, 17.

Table 7.7 Metabolic energy requirements for United Kingdom livestock (percentages)

| Source | 1951 | 1961 | 1971 | 1976 |
|---|---|---|---|---|
| Concentrates[a] | 16 | 19 | 22 | 24 |
| Bulk feeds[b] | 12 | 8 | 6 | 5 |
| Grass[c] | 72 | 73 | 72 | 71 |
| | 100 | 100 | 100 | 100 |

[a] Including grain.
[b] Forage crops, byproducts.
[c] Including rough grazing.
*Source*: J. O. Green and R. D. Baker, 'Classification, distribution and productivity of UK grasslands', in *Grassland in the British Economy*, ed. J. L. Jollans, CAS Paper no. 10 (Reading, 1981), pp. 237–47.

11 Chambers and Mingay, *op. cit.* (1966), pp. 183–4; W. Vamplew, 'A grain of truth: the nineteenth century corn averages', *Agricultural History Review*, 28 (1980), pp. 1–17.

the oilseed-cake, fodder roots and legumes used in the Victorian period. Grass, however, remains the main source of animal food.

The art of feeding livestock has become a science in the last half century. The ideas on the difference between maintenance and fattening rations were put forward by German agriculturists in the nineteenth century and schemes for controlled rations were adopted in England in the 1920s. Now compounders can mix rations according to age and need, while the feeding of animals on the farm has been increasingly automated.[12]

LIVESTOCK BREEDS AND PERFORMANCE

Part of the greater productivity of livestock – in milk yields, for example, or in the number of piglets per sow – is due to better management and better feeding. But genetic improvement of animals has also been important. Thus, for example, it has been estimated that half the post-war increase in milk yield in western countries has been due to better breeding. Attempts to improve livestock productivity by breeding dates back to the eighteenth century, although in much of the nineteenth century it was based upon appearance rather than performance. In the eighteenth century Robert Bakewell publicized his new breeds and the art of breeding but his Longhorn cattle were never important, and his New Leicester sheep, which gave better and earlier mutton, were most significant when cross-bred with other types. The major new breed was the Southdown, bred in Sussex by John Ellman in the 1780s, from which were derived the Hampshire, the Oxford Down and the Cotswold. The Southdown and its variants became the dominant lowland sheep in the nineteenth century.[13]

Of cattle, the Shorthorn, bred by the Collings brothers near Darlington in the 1780s, spread slowly south until by the 1850s it was the dominant breed in lowland England – except in the far south, where the Sussex and South Devon breeds persisted. Originally a dual-purpose animal, it was increasingly bred for beef alone. There were few specialist dairy cattle in the nineteenth century. Channel Island cattle were first imported in the early eighteenth century but were confined to squirarchal parks, while the first Friesians were not imported until the 1870s – the British Friesian herd-book dating only from 1911. Most British cattle remained

12 R. Trow-Smith, *A History of British Livestock Husbandry 1700–1900* (London, 1959), pp. 300–4; K. Baxter, 'Animal nutrition', in Cooke, *op. cit.* (1981), pp. 237–54; P. N. Wilson and T. Brigstoke, 'Animal nutrition over twenty years', *Span*, 21 (1978), pp. 66–8.

13 T. B. Mepham, 'Changing prospects and perspectives in dairy research', *Outlook on Agriculture*, 16 (1987), pp. 182–8; Chambers and Mingay, *op. cit.* (1966), pp. 68–9; Bowie, *op. cit.* (1987); J. R. Walton, 'The diffusion of improved sheep breeds in eighteenth and nineteenth century Oxfordshire', *Journal of Historical Geography*, 9 (1983), pp. 175–95; Juliet Clutton-Brook, 'British cattle in the 18th century', *Ark*, 9 (1982), pp. 55–9.

dual-purpose animals. The Aberdeen Angus and the Hereford, like the dairy cattle, were of small importance in the national herd in the early twentieth century (see table 7.8).[14]

Nor were there any great changes in breed structure before the second World War, except for a slight increase in the importance of specialist dairy cows. The dominance of the Friesian among dairy breeds and its pre-eminence among all cattle has come only since 1945, and reached a peak in the late 1960s. Most British beef is derived from the dairy herds, and of beef breeds only Herefords are of much significance (see table 7.8). However, since 1970 there has been an important change in

Table 7.8 Cattle breeds in Great Britain, 1908–1985 (as a percentage of all cattle in sample)

| Breed | 1908[a] | 1937–8[b] | 1984–5[c] |
|---|---|---|---|
| Shorthorn | 64.0 | 64.8 | 0.2 |
| Devon | 6.5 | 2.9 | 0.2 |
| Ayrshire | 6.3 | 1.3 | 0.7 |
| Hereford | 5.5 | 5.8 | 17.4 |
| Welsh | 3.5 | 0.9 | 0.2 |
| Aberdeen Angus | 2.8 | 2.1 | 2.7 |
| Lincoln Red | 2.4 | 3.6 | – |
| Highland | 1.4 | – | – |
| South Devon | 1.4 | 1.2 | – |
| Red Poll | 0.4 | 1.6 | – |
| Sussex | 0.3 | 0.6 | 0.1 |
| Jersey | – | 1.5 | 1.3 |
| Guernsey | – | 5.2 | 0.7 |
| Friesian | – | 7.3 | 54.2 |
| Charolais | – | – | 8.5 |
| Limousin | – | – | 10.5 |
| Simmental | – | – | 1.6 |
| Others | 5.5 | 1.2 | 1.7 |
| Total | 100.0 | 100.0 | 100.0 |

[a] Census of Agriculture 1980: all cattle included. *Source*: E. S. Simpson, 'The cattle population of England and Wales: its breed, structure and distribution', *Geographical Studies*, 5 (1958), pp. 45–60.
[b] Proportion of licensed bulls, total 37,485. *Source*: L. D. Stamp, *The Land of Britain: its use and misuse* (London, 1950), p. 399.
[c] As a percentage of number of inseminations – 1,605,000 – from Milk Marketing Boards in England, Scotland and Wales. *Source*: Federation of UK Milk Marketing Boards, *UK Dairy Facts and Figures, 1985* (Thames Ditton, 1985).

14 J. R. Walton, 'The diffusion of the improved Shorthorn breed of cattle in Britain during the eighteenth and nineteenth centuries', *Transactions of the Institute of British Geographers* (new series), 9 (1984), pp. 22–35; 'Pedigree and the national cattle herd circa 1750–1950', *Agricultural History Review*, 34 (1986), pp. 149–70; C. S. Orwin and E. H. Whetham, *History of British Agriculture 1846–1914* (London, 1964), pp. 13–14, 131, 133–4; P. J. Perry, 'The Shorthorn comes of age 1822–1843: agricultural history from the herdbook', *Agricultural History*, 56 (1982), pp. 560–6.

the structure of the national herd. From the 1890s to the 1940s health regulations limited the import of live cattle from abroad, but since 1960 the Charolais and Limousin have made great advances, and together with the Simmental account for one-fifth of all the inseminations carried out annually by the Milk Marketing Board (see table 7.8). Artificial insemination has been a major advance in the post-war period. The first station was established in Cambridge in 1942 and AI is now almost universal among dairy cattle, but it has had rather less impact upon beef cattle and none at all among sheep.[15]

Sheep breeds in Britain have always shown a greater diversity than have cattle breeds. In the nineteenth century there were three major upland breeds – the Blackface, the Cheviot and the Welsh – while lowland areas were dominated by the Southdown and its several variants. Statistics on sheep breeds are even less accurate than those for cattle. However, in the first half of the twentieth century lowland sheep farming, based on turnips and folding, greatly declined and so did the lowland breeds such as the Lincoln and Hampshire Down (see table 7.9), while upland breeds and upland crosses such as the Half-bred, the Clun, the

Table 7.9   Sheep breeds in Great Britain, 1908 and 1962 (percentage)

| Breed | 1908 | 1962 |
|---|---|---|
| Blackfaced Mountain | 20.7 | 25.0 |
| Cheviot | 10.0 | 5.0 |
| Welsh Mountain | 9.6 | 15.0 |
| Lincoln | 9.2 | 5.0 |
| Hampshire Down | 6.3 | – |
| Shropshire | 5.9 | 5.0 |
| 'Scotch' | 4.4 | – |
| Oxford Down | 4.1 | – |
| Kent or Romney | 3.7 | – |
| Suffolk | 3.3 | – |
| Half-bred[a] | – | 15.0 |
| Clun | – | 5.0 |
| Kerry Hill | – | 5.0 |
| Masham | – | 5.0 |
| Others | 22.8 | 15.0 |
| Total | 100.0 | 100.0 |

[a] Border-Leicester/Cheviot cross.
*Sources*: J. T. Coppock, *An Agricultural Geography of Great Britain* (London, 1971), pp. 204–5; C. S. Orwin and E. H. Whetham, *History of British Agriculture 1846–1914* (London, 1964), p. 360.

15 J. W. B. King, 'Animal breeding research in Britain 1931–1981', in Cooke *op. cit.* (1981), pp. 277–88; J. C. Bowman, 'Developments in animal breeding', *Agricultural Progress*, 49 (1974), pp. 17–30.

Kerry and the Masham increased in relative importance. European sheep such as the Ile de France and Texel have been imported, but there is no reliable guide to their current importance.[16]

British livestock are subject to some 400 different diseases; this has dramatically reduced the number of animals and their output in the past. Disease still remains a major problem, but it has been slowly reduced by limiting the movement of infected livestock, improving hygiene and, since 1945, using vaccines and antibiotics. Rinderpest outbreaks in the eighteenth century were dealt with by the slaughter of infected animals, for which compensation was paid, by quarantine and isolation, and by the regulation of imports. The repeal of duties on imported livestock in 1842 and 1846 led to a revival of the import of cattle and in 1865 to the great outbreak of pleuropneumonia. Slowly the movement of cattle was again brought under control and in 1896 imported live cattle were excluded altogether; only since the late 1950s have live cattle been allowed into Britain in any number.[17]

Since the late 1930s a number of diseases, including bovine TB, foot-and-mouth, brucellosis and mastitis, have been eliminated or greatly reduced by the use of antibiotics and vaccines, while among pigs swine fever has been eliminated. Better hygiene greatly improved the health of dairy cattle in the 1920s and 1930s, and especially that of pigs and poultry in the post-war period. Indeed neither of these animals could be kept on a large scale until disease had been brought under control.[18]

The increases in meat and milk output achieved since the 1930s (see table 7.10) have been due to a considerable extent to an increase in the numbers of livestock kept; the number of livestock units rose by 50 per cent between 1938 and 1973. But an increase in output per animal has also been achieved due to a combination of better feeding, health, management and breeding. Thus milk per cow has risen 120 per cent

---

16 Bowman, *op. cit.* (1974), pp. 17–30.

17 K. N. Burns, 'Disease of farm animals', in Cooke *op. cit.* (1981), pp. 255–76; J. R. Fisher, 'The economic effects of cattle disease in Britain and its containment 1850–1900', *Agricultural History*, 57 (1983), pp. 104–15.

18 Burns, *op. cit.* (1981), pp. 255–76; W. M. Henderson, 'An historical review of the control of foot and mouth disease', *British Veterinary Journal*, 134 (1978), pp. 3–9; A. C. L. Brown, 'Animal health, present and future', *Philosophical Transactions of the Royal Society*, 281B (1977), pp. 181–91; J. B. Brooksby, 'Advances in animal health', *Span*, 21 (1978), pp. 69–70.

Table 7.10　Increases in livestock productivity and production in the United Kingdom (meat output in thousand tonnes)

|  | 1930s | 1950s | 1960s | 1970s |
|---|---|---|---|---|
| Beef and Veal | 550 | – | – | 1048 |
| Mutton and Lamb | 190 | – | – | 238 |
| Pork | 210 | – | – | 634 |
| Poultry | 89 | – | – | 726 |
| Milk (million litres) | 4500 | – | – | 15093 |
| Milk yield (litres) | 2100 | – | – | 4626 |
| Beef output per livestock unit (Kg) | – | 165 | – | 254 |
| Eggs per hen | 150 | 172 | 185 | 272 |
| Piglets per sow | 11 | – | 14 | 17 |

Sources: W. Holmes, 'Animal husbandry 1931–80', in G. W. Cooke (ed.), *Agricultural Research 1931–1981* (London, 1981), pp. 289–310; Anon, 'Pigment in the United Kingdom', *Retail Business*, 180 (1973), pp. 19–31; A. Brown, 'Animal Health: present and future', *Philosophical Transactions of the Royal Society*, 281B (1977), pp. 181–91; J. T. Coppock, *An Agricultural Geography of Great Britain* (London, 1971), p. 240; S. R. Wragg, 'A note on long term trends in the grassland and ruminant livestock sector of farming', in J. Jollans (ed.), *Grassland in the British Economy* (Reading, 1981), pp. 261–7.

since the 1920s, eggs per hen by 81 per cent, piglets per sow by 55 per cent and beef output per livestock unit by 54 per cent between the 1950s and the 1970s (see table 7.10). Only sheep-meat output per ewe has remained little changed. Although the number of lambs born per ewe has risen, 15 to 25 per cent of all lambs still die at or near birth.[19]

One tendency common to all livestock has been earlier slaughter, and thus a greater turnover of animals. In the eighteenth century cattle were slaughtered at 5 to 7 years old, by 1850 at $3\frac{1}{2}$ to $4\frac{1}{2}$ years, a century later at $2\frac{1}{2}$ to 3 years, and the average age has fallen since. This is because animals have been bred that will mature earlier, but also because of greatly improved feeding and changing demand. From the end of the nineteenth century there was an increasing demand for smaller joints, and leaner meat rather than fat, the joy of the nineteenth century show-judge. This has altered the age-structure of both sheep and cattle populations. In the 1890s sheep under one year old were 38.5 per cent of all sheep in England and Wales, whereas now they are 50 per cent and lamb has replaced mutton; cattle under two years were only one-third of all cattle in the 1860s, but now they are one-half.[20]

19 S. R. Wragg, 'A note on long term trends in the grassland and ruminant livestock sector of farming', in J. L. Jollans (ed.), *Grassland in the British Economy*, CAS Paper no. 10, (Reading, 1981), pp. 261–7.

20 Orwin and Whetham, *op. cit.* (1964), p. 131; H. K. Baker, 'Beef production', *Journal of the Royal Agricultural Society of England*, 130 (1969), pp. 7–19.

SUMMARY

Livestock output has been two-thirds of the value of British agricultural output for approximately a century. Since the 1870s the numbers of livestock have increased considerably. This has been achieved by replacing fodder roots with imported and home-grown grain and by increasing the productivity of grassland. Output per animal of milk and meat has been increased by better management, better health, better feeding and, since 1942, greatly improved breeding. Over the last half century cattle and pigs have retained their relative positions as a proportion of livestock output, sheep have declined, and poultry have risen. But in terms of absolute output, all animal products except wool have increased substantially in the last 50 years.

# 8

# The Ownership of Farmland

CHANGING LANDLORDS

The ownership of agricultural land is not currently a major political issue in Britain; in the past, however, it has been central to economic and political life. In the Middle Ages the occupancy of land was essential for the means of subsistence, and ownership provided military power. With the decline of feudalism ownership still gave great economic and political power. Although the 1832 Reform Act did away with rotten boroughs, it was not until the introduction of the secret ballot of 1872 that the direct control of the landlord over the tenant's vote was ended. Until the middle of the nineteenth century great landlords were the richest as well as the most powerful men in England.

Currently about 70 per cent of the farmers in England and Wales own their farms, 30 per cent rent them either from private landlords or from institutions such as the Crown, insurance companies or university colleges (see table 8.4). In this the country is not greatly different from the rest of Western Europe. In 1975 35 to 40 per cent of the agricultural area of England and Wales was farmed by tenants, the rest by occupier-owners. Comparable figures for other countries were: the Netherlands 44 per cent, France 47 per cent and West Germany 29 per cent.[1] But in the past England *was* very different from the rest of Europe. Until the 1920s most English agricultural land was rented by a small number of landlords to tenant farmers, and no more than 10 to 15 per cent of farmers owned their land. The rise and decline of this system is explored here.

## LAND-OWNERSHIP IN THE PAST

There is no register of land-ownership in Britain at present, and except for one year, 1877, there has been no national record in the past. Hence

---

1 G. H. Peters and A. H. Maunder, 'Efficiency, equity and agricultural change with special reference to land tenure in Western Europe', in A. H. Maunder and K. Ohkawa (eds), *Growth and Equity in Agricultural Development* (London, 1983), pp. 429–42.

Table 8.1    Distribution of land in England and Wales, 1436–1873

| Percentage of land owned by | | 1436 | c.1690 | c.1790 | 1873[a] |
|---|---|---|---|---|---|
| I | Great owners | 15–20 | 15–20 | 20–5 | 24 |
| II | Gentry | 25 | 45–50 | 50 | 55 |
| III | Yeomen freeholders | 20 | 25–33 | 15 | 10 |
| IV | Church and Crown | 25–35 | 5–10 | 10 | 10 |

[a] England only.
*Source*: G. E. Mingay, *The Gentry: the rise and fall of a ruling class* (London, 1976), p. 59.

any discussion of national trends relies upon the studies by historians of rather limited areas or small samples of land-owners; and the subject has given rise to much disagreement, not least because of the very differing ways of classifying land-owners. However, the broader trends do not seem to be in dispute.

In the fifteenth century it was not the Crown that was the leading owner of land, but the Church (see table 8.1). Next were the great land-owners, mainly peers, who possessed less than one-fifth of the country; of more importance were the owners of rather smaller estates than the peers, the gentry, who retained a quarter of the country. They and the great land-owners rented out their estates to tenant farmers. In contrast, the freeholders owned the land they farmed and were far more numerous than the members of other classes, but they enjoyed only slightly more than the great land-owners.[2]

After 1436 there are no estimates of the relative importance of these types of land-owners until the end of the seventeenth century; but by then there had been major changes. Possession of land in the fifteenth century was a means of raising soldiers as well as obtaining food. In the sixteenth century farming was rapidly commercialized so that the prime purpose of occupying and owning land became profit. In the middle of the sixteenth century Henry VIII tried to pay off his debts by dissolving the monasteries (1531–40) and disposing of their land; by 1558 three-quarters had been sold. This, and other events, changed the standing of the different groups. The Church obviously declined. However, little of the land that came on the market was bought by the traditional landlords of feudal origin, and the main purchasers were the gentry and the freeholders. The former became the dominant land-owning class, a major influence in government not only at the county level but also in Parliament. The inter-relationships of the Crown, the gentry and the old

2 J. P. Cooper, 'The social distribution of land and men in England, 1436–1700', *Economic History Review*, 20 (1967), pp. 419–40.

aristocracy have been seen by some historians as the key to the changes of the sixteenth and seventeenth centuries, and a cause of the Civil War. Be that as it may, the Commonwealth saw further changes in land-ownership, as the property of many of Charles I's supporters was confiscated, as was the land of the Crown and the bishops. This was reversed in a fairly equable way at the restoration of Charles II; he very rapidly disposed of much of his own land to supporters of his cause. By the end of the century the Crown's land holdings were very small indeed.[3]

After the Restoration there were two major trends. First, the great landowners – those with over 5,000 acres – began to increase their share of the country's farmland at the expense of the smaller squires and yeomen. This seems to have occurred mainly in the late seventeenth and early eighteenth centuries, when low and uncertain prices impoverished many smaller land-owners, while the introduction of the Land Tax in 1692, borne by land-owners, hit some hard. It was also in the early eighteenth century that the distinction between landlord and tenant responsibilities became clear. Annual rents, based upon economic realities, rather than quit rents, became the norm. The difference between landlord and tenant capital emerged, with the landlord being responsible for the maintenance and improvement of land and buildings, tenants for the provision of livestock, seed and implements.[4]

The second major trend was the decline of the small land-owner, for the most part farmers who owned their land, but including artisans, shopkeepers and others who owned small amounts of land but rented it to others to farm. Their numbers were much reduced before the great age of Parliamentary enclosure; but enclosure, with its high costs, particularly of fencing the land, accelerated their decline. After a revival in the Napoleonic Wars, the depression after 1815 led to the final demise of the small land-owner (see table 8.1). By the beginning of Victoria's reign – and of the period of High Farming – nine-tenths of the farmland of England and Wales was farmed by tenants. The owners of this land were few. The great landlords held one-quarter, the gentry over one-half. The Crown had ceased to be of much significance when in 1760 George III exchanged most of the Crown's land for a Civil list award voted annually by Parliament.[5]

3 I. Gentiles, 'The sale of Crown lands during the English Revolution', *Economic History Review*, 26 (1973), pp. 614–35; 'The sale of bishop's lands in the English Revolution, 1646–1660', *English Historical Review*, 90 (1980), pp. 573–96; G. E. Mingay, *The Gentry: the rise and fall of a ruling class* (London, 1976), p. 48; D. C. Coleman, 'The "gentry" controversy and the aristocracy in crisis 1558–1641', *History*, 51 (1966), pp. 165–78.

4 H. J. Habakkuk, 'English landownership 1680–1740', *Economic History Review*, 10 (1940), pp. 2–17; C. Clay, 'Marriages, inheritance and the rise of large estates in England, 1660–1815', *Economic History Review*, 21 (1968), pp. 503–18; F. M. L. Thompson, *English Landed Society in the Eighteenth Century* (London, 1963), pp. 15, 25, 32, 50.

5 J. V. Beckett, 'The decline of the small landowner in eighteenth and nineteenth century England: some regional considerations', *Agricultural History Review*, 30 (1982), pp. 97–111.

In the eighteenth and nineteenth centuries the great landlords and the gentry increased their share of the farmland; they ensured that estates were rarely broken up by the strict settlement of estates which prevented an owner selling land before his heir came of age, and by careful marriages. However, estates were not occupied by the same families *in perpetuum*. Debt – for various reasons – often led to the dissolution of a family estate, as did a succession of daughters. But there was never any shortage of purchasers of land by those who had made money elsewhere, particularly in the City. In the early eighteenth century merchants and lawyers bought land, in the nineteenth century it was financiers, while in the 1970s it was insurance companies.[6]

The land-ownership of Victorian England is known with some accuracy; indeed the 1870s is the only time in English history when it is known who owned England. An account of the ownership of land was published based on the parish rate-books of 1874–5. These were full of defects: some owners were double-counted, woodland was excluded, waste and common were not included, and the records do not cover London, but all other towns have records. Long leases were counted as freehold, while glebe land was described as being owned by the parish clergy. This data was corrected by J. Bateman and revised up to 1877 (see table 8.2). The collection of the data had originally been proposed by the Earl of Derby to counter the arguments of radicals who claimed there was an excessive concentration of land in a few hands. In this it singularly failed. Although there were admittedly 269,722 owners of over one acre of land, 1.4 per cent of these – just over 4,000 men and women – owned 56 per cent of the area, and 4.2 per cent of all owners owned all but 4.4 per cent of the land. If anything, this underestimated the degree of concentration, for the return excluded waste and rough grazing, much of which was in the hands of great land-owners.[7]

### THE DECLINE OF THE LANDED CLASSES

The great estate reached its peak in late Victorian times; since then, and particularly since the 1920s, the large estates have declined, being sold mainly to the sitting tenants, so that England is now a country where the occupier-owner is the rule rather than the exception. The causes of this decline go back well before the 1920s and are as much political as economic. Indeed the change reflects, with a considerable lag, the change from a country where power and wealth derived from the ownership of land to one where industry and commerce provided the most powerful sources of money and political power.

6 L. Binfield, 'Marriage settlements and the "Rise of Great Estates": the demographic aspect', *Economic History Review*, 32 (1979), pp. 483–93; J. V. Beckett, 'The pattern of landownership in England and Wales, 1660–1880", *Economic History Review*, 37 (1984), pp. 1–22.
7 G. C. Brodrick, *English Land and Landlords* (London, 1881), pp. 157–96.

Table 8.2   Distribution of land in England and Wales, 1877

| Class | Number of owners | % | Area owned (acres) | % |
|---|---|---|---|---|
| Peers[a] | 400 | 0.1 | 5,728,979 | 17.4 |
| Great landowners[b] | 1,288 | 0.5 | 8,497,694 | 25.9 |
| Squires[c] | 2,529 | 0.9 | 4,319,271 | 13.1 |
| Greater yeomen[d] | 9,585 | 3.6 | 4,782,627 | 14.6 |
| Lesser yeomen[e] | 24,412 | 9.1 | 4,144,272 | 12.6 |
| Small properties[f] | 217,049 | 80.5 | 3,931,806 | 12.0 |
| The Crown and state | | | 165,427 | 0.5 |
| Religious, educational philanthropic etc. | 14,459 | 5.3 | 947,655 | 2.9 |
| Commercial and miscellaneous | | | 330,466 | 1.0 |
| Total[g] | 269,722 | 100.0 | 32,848,197 | 100.0 |

[a] Peers includes peeresses and eldest sons of peers.
[b] All commoners owning at least 3,000 acres if rental exceeds £3,000.
[c] Estates of between 1,000 and 3,000 acres.
[d] Estates of between 300 and 1,000 acres.
[e] Estates of between 100 and 300 acres.
[f] Over 1 acres and under 100 acres.
[g] Cottagers excluded from table.
Source: G. C. Brodrick, *English Land and Landlords* (London, 1881), p. 187.

The political influence of the peers and the gentry was at its height in the eighteenth century, and the beginning of its long decline was signalled by the abolition of rotten boroughs in the 1832 Reform Act. While this gave the vote to the larger tenants, who until the introduction of the secret ballot in 1872 could be persuaded to vote for the right candidate, the 1867 Reform Act gave the urban working class the vote, and in 1883 the agricultural labourer was enfranchized.

Perhaps more significantly, in the late nineteenth century radicals began to question the fairness of excessive land concentration; this view was most forcibly expressed in Ireland, but in Britain radicals doubted the validity of landlordism, most notably in Wales, where the tenantry was mainly nonconformist and often Welsh speaking while the landlords were Anglican and English speaking. Lloyd George had an early interest in land reform, and unleashed a series of onslaughts on the landed interest, culminating in the budget of 1909. Few of the fiscal threats therein actually materialized, but the right to own land was no longer so easily accepted. Threats of land nationalization have rumbled on to the present day.[8]

8 J. Davies, 'The end of great estates and the rise of freehold farming in Wales', *Welsh Historical Review*, 7 (1974), pp. 186–212; D. W. Howell, *Land and People in Nineteenth Century Wales* (London, 1977), pp. 23, 28; B. B. Gilbert, 'David Lloyd George: the reform of British landholding and the budget of 1914', *Historical Journal*, 21 (1978), pp. 107–41.

The early nineteenth-century landlord had considerable power over his tenants, although, in contrast to Ireland, this was rarely exercised. He could evict, except where the land was held on a long lease, direct the tenant to follow particular agricultural practices, and hunt and shoot over the tenant's farm. These rights were slowly eroded. Tenant right to compensation for improvement to land and buildings had become customary in parts of England after 1815 and was slowly established on an obligatory basis in a series of Acts that began in 1875. Tenants slowly gained more security of tenure; since 1941 they have had lifetime security, and an Act of 1976 gave security not only to the sitting tenant but to the following two generations, though this was limited to one generation in 1984. In 1881 the Ground Game Act allowed tenants the right to shoot rabbits, thus to some extent reducing the amenity value of an estate.[9]

The slow loss of control over tenants combined with the decline of political power would not alone have led to the decline of the estate, but economic factors began to run against the landed interest. For much of the nineteenth century interest on landlord's capital was low, and returns were much poorer than on investment in government bonds or industrial enterprises. But from 1880 both the rent and the sale price of land fell as the British farmer was undercut by imports. Between 1877–8 and 1901 the average rent per acre in England and Wales fell by 29 per cent; the return of a subdued prosperity in the first two decades of the twentieth century saw little increase in rents, and between 1921 and 1936 rents fell by 25 per cent. While landlord income was falling, there were extra costs. The budget of 1894 introduced Estate Duty, which was initially low but by 1919 had reached 40 per cent on estates valued at £2 million or over; the death of sons in the First World War increased the problems of many landlords.[10]

Thus for a variety of reasons the ownership of agricultural land became less worthwhile, and there began the break-up of estates; most farms were sold to sitting tenants, so the number of occupier-owners steadily increased (see table 8.3).

The sale of land began just before the First World War; tenants bought, somewhat reluctantly, for fear that new landlords might evict them. But the real explosion came after the end of the war. Between 1919 and 1927 the proportion of the farmland of England and Wales farmed by occupier-owners rose from 12 per cent to 36 per cent (see table 8.3), a change of land-ownership unparalleled since the mid-

9 R. Douglas, *Land, People and Politics: a history of the land question in the United Kingdom, 1878–1952* (London, 1976), pp. 17, 42, 43, 46–7, 50, 53, 96–7; D. Grigg, 'The development of tenant right in South Lincolnshire', *The Lincolnshire Historian*, 2 (1962), pp. 41–9.

10 P. Perry, *British Farming in the Great Depression 1870–1914* (Newton Abbot, 1974), p. 76; D. Spring, 'Land and politics in Edwardian England', *Agricultural History*, 58 (1984), pp. 17–42; F. M. L. Thompson, *English Landed Society in the Nineteenth Century* (London, 1963), pp. 303–24, 327, 338.

Table 8.3    Owner-occupiers in England and Wales

| Date | % of holdings | % of area |
|------|---------------|-----------|
| 1887[a] | 14.4[d] | 15.2[d] |
| 1891[a] | 14.6[d] | 15.0[d] |
| 1908[a] | 12.8[e] | 12.2[e] |
| 1914[a] | 11.3[e] | 10.9[e] |
| 1919[a] | 11.7[e] | 12.1[e] |
| 1922[a] | 15.1[e] | 17.8[e] |
| 1927[a] | 36.6[e] | 36.0[e] |
| 1941 | 34.6 | 32.7 |
| 1950[b] | 39.0[e] | 38.0[e] |
| 1960[c] | 56.7[e] | 49.2[e] |
| 1970 | 60.0[e] | 53.1[e] |
| 1975 | 62.9[e] | 53.7[e] |
| 1983[c] | 70.4[e] | 60.2[e] |

[a] Area of crops and grass only.
[b] Area of crops and grass and rough grazing.
[c] Total area on agricultural holdings.
[d] Excluding holdings partly rented or partly owned.
[e] Including holdings 'owned' and 'mainly owned'.
Sources: Ministry of Agriculture, Fisheries and Food, *A Century of Agricultural Statistics, Great Britain 1866–1966* (London, 1968); S. G. Sturmey, 'Owner farming in England and Wales 1900–1950', in W. E. Minchinton (ed.), *Essays in Agrarian History*, 2 (London, 1968), pp. 283–306; Ministry of Agriculture, *Agricultural Statistics United Kingdom 1983* (London, 1984).

sixteenth century when monastery land was being sold. The consequences of land purchase were not always happy for the new owners, for they were now responsible for maintenance as well as for paying substantial mortgages at a time when agricultural prices were falling. The 1930s thus saw little change, but since 1945 the purchase of farms by their tenants has revived. The 1948 Agricultural Act confirmed the lifetime security of a tenant, freed him from all restrictions on cropping, and until 1958 controlled rents, which rose less than farm incomes. Landlords, however, were faced with rapidly rising maintenance costs but income from rents that until 1984 was treated by the Inland Revenue as unearned. The maintenance of estates from generation to generation was eased by the gifting of estates to the heir, although this ceased after the 1975 Capital Transfer Tax.[11]

Thus in the 1920s and in the period since the end of the Second World War there has been a substantial decline in the area owned by the traditional land-owning classes. There is no modern equivalent of the 1877 return of land-owners, but some estimates suggest a considerable fall. R. Perrott compared the area owned by 40 peers in 1877 and in

11 Thompson, *op. cit.* (1963), pp. 329–38.

the 1960s and estimated a decline in area of 76 per cent. Others believe that the decline has been least among the great land-owners; it is the greater gentry – those who owned from 3,000 to 10,000 acres – who have suffered the largest proportional decline. Between 1920 and 1960 some 40 per cent of the cultivated area of England and Wales passed from the hands of the great land-owners and the gentry to the farmers themselves.[12]

LAND-OWNERSHIP IN THE 1970s

In the 1970s the sale price of agricultural land rose dramatically, and considerable amounts of land were purchased by financial institutions and by foreigners. The alarm this provoked led to the appointment of a Select Committee to inquire into the ownership of agricultural land in Great Britain; this provided the only modern figures of ownership, although it produced no evidence on the individual owners of land (see table 8.4). Most of Britain's farmland is owned by private individuals; indeed most of the companies owning land have been formed as arrangements to reduce the tax obligations of farming families and are not conventional companies. Of the private individuals, foreigners own at the most 1 per cent of Britain. There is no way of recording the size

Table 8.4   The ownership of agricultural land in Great Britain, 1978

|  | Thousand acres | % of agricultural area | |
| --- | --- | --- | --- |
| Private individuals, companies, trusts | 39,520 | 90.3 | |
| overseas owners | – | | 1.0 |
| Institutions | 4,272 | 9.7 | |
| Central government | 1,142 | | 2.6 |
| Local authorities | 902 | | 2.05 |
| Statutory agencies and nationalized industries | 556 | | 1.25 |
| The Crown | 404 | | 0.9 |
| Religious institutions | 172 | | 0.4 |
| Universities and schools | 241 | | 0.55 |
| Conservation authorities | 327 | | 0.75 |
| Financial institutions | 530 | | 1.2 |
| Total | 43,794 | 100.0 | |

*Source*: Report of the Committee of Inquiry into the Acquisition and Occupancy of Agricultural Land, HMSO, Cmnd. 7599 (1979), Chairman Lord Northfield, pp. 63, 119.

12 F. M. L. Thompson, 'The social distribution of landed property in England since the sixteenth century', *Economic History Review*, 19 (1966), pp. 505–17; P. Perrott, *The Aristocrats* (London, 1968), pp. 180–2; H. A. Clemenson, *English Country Houses and Landed Estates* (London, 1982), pp. 119, 127.

of estates owned by individuals, although some lists of large holdings by peers have been compiled. But 95 per cent of all private owners of land of fewer than 1,000 acres are probably farmers who own their land.[13]

Institutions own only one-tenth of Britain. The Crown estates surrendered by George III in 1760 consist of only 350,000 acres scattered through 25 counties. The Royal family own directly at least 278,000 acres – the Duchy of Lancaster, Balmoral and Sandringham, and the Duchy of Cornwall. An approximately similar area is owned by the Church, universities and schools together. Much more important are the holdings of central and local government, including the nationalized industries. The Ministry of Defence is by far the largest government owner of land, and temporarily during the Second World War retained over one-fifth of the country. Half the land owned by local authorities is as a result of the Small Holdings Act of 1892 and subsequent legislation that authorized local authorities to buy agricultural land to let as small holdings. This area has declined since 1970 as many county councils have sold their land.[14]

The rising price of agricultural land in the 1970s prompted property trusts, insurance companies and pension funds to buy land as a long-term investment; there were worries that these institutions would not farm in accordance with traditional values. In the event the area they purchased was not great, and further acquisitions were few in the 1980s as land prices began to fall. However, purchases in eastern England were certainly substantial, and 12 per cent of Lincolnshire's farmland and 10 per cent of Norfolk passed into the hands of financial institutions in the 1970s. In the early 1980s, however, only 2.25 per cent of the farmland of England and Wales was so owned.[15]

NEW FORMS OF TENURE

The traditional land-owning pattern in England and Wales has been of the landlord and tenant or of the occupier-owner. In the 1970s there were fears that the increasing importance of land-ownership by City institutions would lead to company farming, with large farms run by managers for short-term profit and without regard to local interests or the long-term condition of the land. Certainly post-war conditions have given rise to some new tenurial arrangements. Some land-owners have

13 Doreen Massey and A. Catalano, *Capital and Land: landownership by capital in Great Britain* (London, 1978), p. 60.

14 R. Norton-Taylor, *Whose Land is it Anyway? Agriculture, planning and land use in the British countryside* (London, 1982), pp. 35, 41; Lord Northfield, *Report of the Committee of Inquiry into the Acquisition and Occupancy of Agricultural Land*, HMSO, Cmnd. 7599 (1979), p. 146; A. Harrison, R. B. Tranter and R. D. Gibbs, *Landownership by Public and Semi-public Institutions in the U.K.*, Centre for Agricultural Strategy Paper no. 3 (Reading, 1977), pp. 15, 23, 26.

15 R. Munton, 'Investment in British agriculture by the financial institutions', *Sociologia ruralis*, 25 (1985), pp. 155–73; 'Financial institutions: their ownership of agricultural land in Great Britain', *Area*, 9 (1977), pp. 29–37.

Table 8.5   The mixed-tenure farm in England and Wales, 1891–1983

| | Percentage of all holdings | | | Percentage of total area | | |
|---|---|---|---|---|---|---|
| Date | Entirely rented | Mixed | Entirely owner-occupied | Entirely rented | Mixed | Entirely owned |
| 1891 | 81.8 | 4.3 | 13.9 | n.a. | n.a. | n.a. |
| 1950 | 48.7 | 14.8 | 36.5 | – | – | – |
| 1960 | 37.1 | 15.6 | 47.3 | 41.6 | 21.7 | 36.7 |
| 1970 | 30.7 | 23.1 | 46.2 | 32.6 | 32.8 | 34.6 |
| 1975 | 25.5 | 30.5 | 44.0 | 27.2 | 40.8 | 32.0 |
| 1980 | 23.3 | 22.7 | 53.9 | 26.8 | 33.9 | 39.4 |
| 1983 | 20.4 | 22.3 | 57.4 | 24.4 | 34.4 | 41.3 |

n.a. not available.
Source: Berkeley Hill, 'Farm tenancy in the United Kingdom', *Agricultural Administration*, 19 (1985), pp. 189–207.

taken more farms in hand for tax reasons and run them with the aid of farm managers. In many such relationships there is a profit-sharing element in the partnership between landlord and manager. Further, many farmers no longer either exclusively rent or own their farms; since the 1940s many have tried to increase the size of their farms, both to raise gross income and to benefit from economies of scale. Extra land conveniently near to hand is not always available; where it becomes so it has to be acquired, whether by renting or by purchasing. By 1983 one-fifth of all the agricultural holdings in England and Wales were of mixed tenure and they occupied one-third of the area (see table 8.5); they are of particular importance in the east of England, where most of the increase in large farms has taken place.[16]

SUMMARY

For most of the eighteenth century English agriculture was characterized by a tripartite structure: a small number of land-owners rented land to tenant farmers, who employed agricultural labourers. Freeholders were few, and the occupier-owner declined in importance from 1700 to 1880, while the great land-owners and the gentry increased their share of the land. But for a variety of political and economic reasons many of the larger estates were sold to sitting tenants in the early 1920s and again in the 1950s and 1960s, so that the typical English farmer is now an occupier-owner. Corporate farming has made little progress, although many family farms have formed themselves into companies for tax and other reasons.

16 P. Derrick, 'Common ownership in British agriculture', *Land Reform, Land Settlement and Co-operation*, 1 (1977), pp. 46–54; B. Hill, 'The rise of the mixed-tenure farm: an examination of official statistics', *Journal of Agricultural Economics*, 25 (1974), pp. 177–82.

# 9

# Farmers and their Farms

PART-TIME FARMERS IN THE PAST

The last 20 years have seen a revival of the rural population of England and Wales. However, over the previous century many parishes in rural England had been in decline or stagnating. This was not due simply to the fall in the agricultural population; other occupations decreased as the attraction of the towns grew greater and the trades of the countryside were threatened by the railway and the factory. The traditional country trades that supported farming declined and services locally supplied were centralized in nearby towns. The railway, the bus and the private car have transformed country life in the last century. Modern rural England has a less complex social and occupational structure than that of mid- or late Victorian England. The idea of villages consisting solely of land-owners (living outside the village), farmers and landless labourers has always been a simplification. In particular the sharp distinction between farmer and non-farmer becomes blurred if examined closely.

An analysis of villages in nineteenth-century England shows that many agricultural holdings were occupied and farmed by men who had another job; for them farming was not the sole or indeed the most important occupation. This distinction between full-time and part-time farming cannot be traced for the country as a whole before the mid-nineteenth century but the population censuses of mid-Victorian times show how important part-time farming then was. In 1851, 1861 and 1871 the census asked everyone their occupation, and those who described themselves as a farmer were asked to state the size of their farm. In 1871, 245,907 men and women described themselves as farmers or graziers, but the agricultural census of the same year recorded 481,422 holdings of agricultural land of 1/4 acre or over, of which 309,708 were over 5 acres.[1] This discrepancy was partly because some English farms consisted of two or more separate blocks of agricultural land; partly because a lot of the agricultural holdings were simply of grass or gardens,

---

1 *Census of England and Wales, 1871, General Report,* iv (1873); Board of Agriculture, *Agricultural Statistics England and Wales, 1871.*

and not farms in any sense; but also because many who occupied agricultural land and farmed it in a small way had another and more important job, and it was this, not farming, that they returned as their occupation. In the 1851 census, when 229,318 returned themselves as farmers, there were also doubtless many who farmed land who returned themselves under another and to them more important occupation. But 10 per cent of those who did return themselves as farmers also indicated a second job. On the basis of this it can be estimated that between 10 per cent and 30 per cent of the agricultural holdings in early Victorian England were part-time in the sense that the occupier had another job.[2]

In 1851 these second jobs of farmers were for the most part closely related to village life. First of all, many had jobs as retailers – particularly as innkeepers and publicans, but also as millers or butchers. Second, many craftsmen – carpenters, masons, tailors and bricklayers – had farms. A third category was more closely related to agriculture – higglers, land agents, corn merchants, seed merchants, horse dealers, saddlers and game-keepers. Fourth, in a few parts of the country the use of land was combined with industrial work – in Lancashire and Yorkshire with textiles, in Derbyshire with lead mining, in Cornwall with tin mining and in the north-east with coal mining. There were few white-collar workers and fewer labourers with farms.[3]

There is no subsequent source on the extent and nature of part-time farming as valuable as the 1851 census; however, it seems that the proportion of farmers or holdings which can be defined as part-time has not declined. In 1907 the agricultural census asked occupiers to state if farms were run primarily for or not for business purposes: 25 per cent returned their holdings in this latter category. In 1930 G. T. Garrett estimated that there were 330,000 farmers in England and Wales and that 30 per cent of these were part-time, although they occupied only 4 per cent of the farmland. The National Farm Survey of 1941–3 provided the first comprehensive data since the 1851 census, and defined 25 per cent of the holdings of England and Wales as part-time, spare-time and held by hobby farmers, occupying 12 per cent of the farmland.[4]

It was estimated in 1969 that 30 per cent of the principals on a sample survey of farms in England and Wales had another source of earned income; in 1970 the annual agricultural census began to record the number of farmers, directors and partners working on farms in England and Wales. Those working fewer than 40 hours a week were defined as part-time, and they rose from 20 per cent of the total in 1970

2 *1851 Census, Great Britain, Ages, Civil Condition, Occupations and Birth Places*, 1: *Accounts and Papers*, 88, pt. 1 (1852–3), p. lxxix.

3 *1851 Census, op. cit.* (1852–3), p. cclxxv.

4 Ruth Gasson, *Gainful Occupations of Farm Families* (School of Rural Economics, Wye College, 1983), p. 4; Ministry of Agriculture, *National Farm Survey of England and Wales (1941–1945): a summary report* (London, 1946), p. 11; Viscount Astor and K. A. H. Murray, *The Planning of Agriculture* (Oxford, 1933), p. 9.

to 30 per cent in 1984. Thus for the last 150 years or more about one-quarter of the farmers of England and Wales have had a second job.[5]

## THE CHARACTERISTICS OF MODERN PART-TIME FARMERS

The modern part-time farmer is very different from his nineteenth century predecessor. Most of the off-farm jobs are white-collar, over a third businesses, and in most second jobs the farmer is self-employed. For most part-time farmers the other job provides a majority of their income. In England part-time farming is not a transitional state of those trying to become full-time farmers, or the poor farmer about to leave farming for another full-time job. Few part-time farmers intend to become full-time farmers or to sever their connection with farming.[6]

Nowadays their differences from full-time farmers are diminishing. It is true that they do not choose the most labour-intensive activities – dairying is rare – but on the other hand the most common enterprise is rearing young cattle, and cereals are the most usual crops. Few part-time farmers have more than two enterprises on their farms, which are mainly under 50 acres; the family provides 75 per cent of the labour input.[7]

It seems likely that part-time farming will increase in the future as the Common Agricultural Policy becomes less generous to farmers. At present farmers are being encouraged to diversify, principally by using their farmland to provide a second income – bed and breakfast, campsites and farm shops are all being encouraged, and indeed in some areas have made considerable progress. In the early 1980s one-fifth of the farms in the Less Favoured Areas – the uplands of England and Wales – had some sort of tourist activity.[8]

## CHANGING FARM SIZE

The size of farms has attracted much attention from historians, and the sceptical observer might think that there has been no period when the large farm has not been gobbling up the small farm, from the fourteenth century, when the large sheep farm was the supposed culprit, to the

5 Ministry of Agriculture, *Agricultural Statistics England and Wales*; A. Harrison, *Farmers and Farm Businesses in England*, Department of Agricultural Economics and Management, Miscellaneous Study no. 62 (Reading, 1975), p. 12; B. Hill, 'Plan of work and methodology', in D. Agostini and A. Maunder (eds), *Mixed Income Farms* (Oxford, 1984), pp. 135–64.

6 J. W. Aitchison and P. Aubrey, 'Part-time farming in Wales: a typological study', *Transactions of the Institute of British Geographers*, 7 (1982), pp. 88–97.

7 Gasson, *op. cit.* (1983).

8 K. C. Abercrombie, *Part-time Farming in the Rural Development of Industrialized Countries* (Arkleton Trust, 1976), pp. 8–13.

present, when some fear the spread of farms run by managers and owned by financial institutions or food-processing industries.

In the eighteenth century Parliamentary enclosure was one of the means by which the smaller farms were absorbed by the larger. Small land-owners often found the costs of enclosure, particularly fencing their new farm, to be prohibitive and were forced to sell; they were usually bought out by local landlords and their land added to an existing farm. But enclosure was not a necessary condition for amalgamation. Thus on the estates of the Leveson Gower family between 1714 and 1832 there was a marked decline in small tenancies; they were added to the larger farms. But all this land was already enclosed before 1714. It was the managers of the estate who thought larger farms to be more profitable for the estate and the tenants. This was doubtless how change took place over most of England at this time. There were no sudden changes; slowly small farms declined both in numbers and in the proportion of the area of farmland they occupied, while the larger farms became more numerous and occupied a greater part of the area.[9]

It was not, however, until 1851 that there were any national statistics on farm sizes. In that year the population census asked each householder to state his occupation, and, if farmer, to state the size of his farm. As noted earlier many occupiers of agricultural land had other jobs and so did not describe themselves as farmers. Consequently the number of small holdings is understated. Nonetheless there were 215,615 farms of 5 acres or more (see table 9.1). The small farm had far from disappeared, indeed 40 per cent of holdings were fewer than 50 acres and 62 per cent fewer than 100 acres. But, in terms of the area they occupied, the small farms were far less important, occupying respectively only 8 per cent and 22 per cent of the agricultural area. Farms over 300 acres were not very numerous, although they occupied a third of the area in crops and grass. But it was the medium-sized farms that dominated, for although less than a third of the number of farms they accounted for nearly one-half of the area. During the prosperous years of the 1850s and 1860s the number of small farms continued to fall, those of the large farms to increase. In the counties of arable England between 1851 and 1871 the number of farms of fewer than 300 acres declined, the number over 300 acres increased.[10]

MODERN TRENDS

From 1885 the agricultural census provides information on the size of agricultural *holdings*, not farms; there are, however, some difficulties in

9 J. R. Wordie, 'Social change on the Leveson-Gower estates 1714–1832', *Economic History Review*, 27 (1974), pp. 569–98; G. E. Mingay, 'The size of farms in the eighteenth century', *Economic History Review*, 14 (1961–2), pp. 469–88.

10 *Census of England and Wales 1871, General Report*, iv (London, 1873).

Table 9.1 The size of agricultural holdings in England and Wales, 1851–1975

| Size (acres) | (a) Number of holdings | | | | (b) Area of crops and grass | | | |
|---|---|---|---|---|---|---|---|---|
| | 1851 | % | 1975 | % | 1851 | % | 1975 | % |
| 5–20 | 42,315 | 19.8 | 36,595 | 19.7 | 523,905 | 2.1 | 423,973 | 1.8 |
| 20–50 | 47,829 | 21.9 | 38,883 | 20.9 | 1,598,945 | 6.5 | 1,290,919 | 5.5 |
| 50–100 | 44,558 | 20.7 | 40,780 | 21.9 | 3,206,451 | 13.0 | 2,945,381 | 12.5 |
| 100–150 | 29,020 | 13.5 | 23,453 | 12.6 | 3,627,500 | 14.7 | 2,857,112 | 12.2 |
| 150–300 | 35,133 | 16.3 | 28,671 | 15.4 | 7,388,275 | 30.0 | 5,974,435 | 25.4 |
| 300–500 | 11,646 | 5.4 | 10,646 | 5.7 | 4,360,925 | 17.7 | 4,029,221 | 17.1 |
| 500–700 | 3,076 | 1.4 | 3,560 | 1.9 | 1,802,300 | 7.3 | 2,072,021 | 8.8 |
| 700–1,000 | 1,267 | 0.6 | 2,031 | 1.1 | 1,038,750 | 4.2 | 1,669,514 | 7.0 |
| 1000, and over | 771 | 0.4 | 1,497 | 0.8 | 1,123,300 | 4.5 | 2,273,678 | 9.7 |
| Total | 215,615 | 100.0 | 186,116 | 100.0 | 24,670,351 | 100.0 | 23,536,254 | 100.0 |

Source: 1851 Census, Great Britain, Ages, Civil Condition, Occupations and Birth Places, 1: Accounts and Papers, 88, pt. 1: 1852–3; Ministry of Agriculture, Fisheries and Food, Agricultural Statistics, England and Wales, 1975 (London, 1976).

interpreting the statistics. Holdings include all pieces of land of over a quarter, later one acre of agricultural land, and many of these holdings were not farms in any sense. Further, some English farms consisted of more than one holding; a separate census form was, until 1922, required for each holding, thus exaggerating the number of 'farmers'.

After 1922, however, farmers were encouraged to return only one census form for each farm, while the ministry began to exclude what it defined as part-time holdings from the census in 1968. The continuity of the statistics is thus broken in the late 1960s and early 1970s; in addition to the exclusion of minor holdings, the county boundaries were changed, size classes began to be recorded in hectares and, while the English statistics began to record the total area of holdings, the Welsh statistics continued to measure only the area in crops and grass. Recent trends – and particularly distributions – are thus difficult to decipher. It must also be recalled that between the 1880s and the present some 4 million acres of crops and grass have been lost to urban expansion, afforestation and other uses. This in itself would account for the decline of 50,000 holdings or more since the 1880s. A further diminution occurs because since 1922 farmers have been asked to return fragmented holdings as one. Thus the decline since 1870 in the number of farms due to amalgamation is smaller than might be thought (see table 9.2).[11]

Table 9.2 Total number of and area occupied by agricultural holdings (of 5 acres and over), England and Wales, 1851–1983 (thousand acres)

| Date | Number | Area[a] | Average size of holding |
|------|--------|---------|-------------------------|
| 1851 | 215,615 | 23,082 | 107.1 |
| 1885 | 338,715 | 27,378 | 80.8 |
| 1895 | 342,649 | 27,382 | 80.0 |
| 1915 | 342,710 | 26,773 | 78.1 |
| 1925 | 330,425 | 25,636 | 77.6 |
| 1935 | 312,503 | – | |
| 1944 | 295,247 | 24,136 | 81.7 |
| 1951 | 296,332 | 24,251 | 81.8 |
| 1960 | 273,135 | 24,254 | 88.8 |
| 1966 | 248,636 | 24,154 | 97.1 |
| 1975 | 186,116 | 23,536 | 126.5 |
| 1983 | 173,336[b] | 26,921[c] | 155.3 |

[a] Crops and grass: excludes rough grazing.
[b] Excluding 12,657 holdings of fewer than 2 hectares.
[c] Total farm area.
*Source*: Ministry of Agriculture, *Agricultural Statistics, England and Wales*; Census of Great Britain, *1851 Census, Great Britain, Ages, Civil Condition, Occupations and Birth Places*, 1: *Accounts and Papers*, 88, pt. 1: *1852–3*.

11 David Grigg, 'Farm size in England and Wales, from Early Victorian Times to the Present', *Agricultural History Review*, 35 (1987), pp. 179–89.

Nonetheless there is little doubt that the total number of agricultural
holdings has been in decline since 1870 (see table 9.2); the average size
of holding at first showed little change – a slight decrease until the
1930s, a slight increase from then until 1950, and then a more striking
increase in the 1960s. After 1966 changes in the definition of an
agricultural holding, and later the recording of the *total* area of a farm
rather than simply the area in crops and grass, make it impossible to
trace recent changes in the average size of farms. In any case it is
probably more useful to look at changes in the numbers in each size
class (see figure 9.1). Over most of the period the smallest holdings,
those of 5 to 20 acres, have been in continuous decline; but between
the 1880s and the 1930s the large farms were in slight decline, whilst
the numbers of those of fewer than 300 acres were increasing. From the
1930s to the present day these trends have been reversed. All size classes
below 300 acres have decreased since 1930, steeply since the 1950s,
while the larger classes have increased. The *area* occupied by these
classes (see figure 9.2) has shown the same trend, but the growing

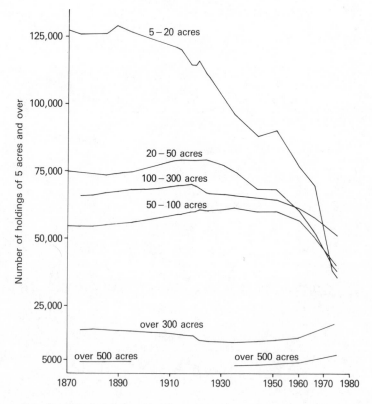

Figure 9.1   Number of agricultural holdings of 5 acres and over in selected size classes
*Source*: Ministry of Agriculture, *Agricultural Statistics, England and Wales.*

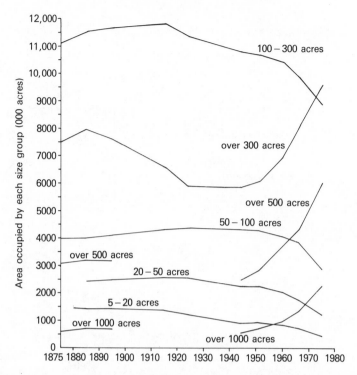

Figure 9.2 Area occupied by agricultural holdings over 5 acres in selected size classes
*Source*: Ministry of Agriculture, *Agricultural Statistics, England and Wales.*

importance of farms over 300 acres is much more apparent. If the *relative* importance of the *numbers* in each class is traced over the last hundred years, then the difference in the proportion of small, medium and large farms showed very little change between 1851 and 1975 (see table 9.3b). On the other hand the *area* occupied by the large farms – over 300 acres – has increased quite dramatically in the post-war period, from 25.2 per cent of the area in crops and grass in 1951, to 42.7 per cent in 1975 and over half of the *total* area on farms in 1985 (see tables 9.3a and 9.4).

Changes in the size of holdings over the last ten years cannot be linked to the long-term statistics because not only has the ministry changed the definition of a holding, so that 50,000 or more have been dropped from the census since 1968, but the size classes are now recorded in hectares; furthermore the area of the holdings includes rough grazings and woodland rather than simply crops and grass. However, the trend to the larger farm continues (see table 9.4). As seen earlier, over half the total area on holdings is now on farms of more than 300 acres. But 300 acres, although thought a large farm in the nineteenth

Table 9.3   The number and area of small, medium and large holdings, England and Wales, 1851–1983

|  | (a) Area of crops and grass occupied by small, medium and large holdings | | | |
|---|---|---|---|---|
|  | Crops and grass[a] (000 acres) | Small (5–100 acres) | Medium (100–300 acres) | Large (over 300 acres) |
| 1851 | 24,660 | 21.6 | 44.7 | 33.7 |
| 1885 | 27,379 | 28.9 | 42.1 | 29.0 |
| 1895 | 27,382 | 29.5 | 42.6 | 27.8 |
| 1915 | 26,773 | 31.1 | 44.1 | 24.7 |
| 1924 | 25,636 | 32.6 | 44.3 | 23.1 |
| 1944 | 24,136 | 31.0 | 44.8 | 24.2 |
| 1951 | 24,251 | 30.8 | 44.0 | 25.2 |
| 1960 | 24,254 | 28.7 | 42.9 | 28.4 |
| 1966 | 24,154 | 25.6 | 40.5 | 33.4 |
| 1975 | 23,537 | 19.8 | 37.5 | 42.7 |
| 1983[b] | 26,954 | 14.4 | 31.8 | 54.3 |

|  | (b) Number of small, medium and large holdings | | | |
|---|---|---|---|---|
|  | Total numbers[a] (000s) | Percentage | | |
| 1851 | 215,615 | 62.5 | 29.7 | 7.8 |
| 1870 | 336,497 | 76.6 | 23.4 |  |
| 1885 | 338,715 | 75.3 | 19.8 | 4.9 |
| 1895 | 342,649 | 75.3 | 19.9 | 4.8 |
| 1915 | 324,710 | 75.5 | 20.3 | 4.2 |
| 1925 | 330,425 | 75.7 | 20.4 | 3.8 |
| 1944 | 295,247 | 73.7 | 22.2 | 4.1 |
| 1951 | 296,332 | 73.9 | 21.8 | 4.3 |
| 1960 | 273,135 | 72.0 | 22.9 | 5.0 |
| 1966 | 248,636 | 70.1 | 23.5 | 6.4 |
| 1975 | 186,116 | 62.5 | 28.0 | 9.5 |
| 1983[b] | 185,993 | 59.6 | 26.7 | 13.7 |

[a] Area and numbers of holdings of 5 acres and over.
[b] Includes all statistically significant holdings and is of total area; figures for over 300 acres are an estimate.
Sources: 1851 Census, Great Britain, Ages, Civil Condition, Occupations, and Birth Places, 1: *Accounts and Papers*, 88, pt. 1: *1852–3*; Ministry of Agriculture and Fisheries, *The Agricultural Output of England and Wales, 1925*, HMSO, Cmnd. 2815 (1927); Ministry of Agriculture, Fisheries and Food, *A Century of Agricultural Statistics, Great Britain, 1866–1966* (London, 1968); *Agricultural Statistics, England and Wales, 1975* (London, 1976); *Agricultural Statistics, United Kingdom, 1983* (London, 1984).

century and indeed down to the 1950s, can hardly be so counted now. Farms of over 500 acres have slowly increased their importance; they occupied one-seventh of the area in crops and grass in the 1850s and one-eighth in the 1950s, but by the mid-1980s one-third of the total area in farms. Numerically, however, the smaller farms still predominate. In 1985 58 per cent of all holdings were fewer than 100 acres although they occupied only 14 per cent of the area (see table 9.4).

WHY HAVE FARMS BECOME LARGER?

Over the last 200 years the general tendency has been for the number of smaller holdings to decline and those of the larger holdings to expand, so that the latter have come to occupy an increasing proportion of the agricultural area. This tendency was halted in the period between 1880 and 1930, but otherwise stretches back to at least the beginning of the eighteenth century. It thus seems to predate the period of mechanization, which can perhaps be determined by the adoption of the reaper and the mower in the 1850s and 1860s.

The most dramatic increases in farm size, however, have come in the post-war period, and particularly since 1960. There are a number of reasons for the growth of large farms. First, by acquiring extra land, farmers have been able to spread their fixed costs and reduce cost per acre. This is particularly true of the use of machinery, assiduously acquired by all but the smallest farmers over the last 30 years; but much of this machinery has not been worked to its capacity and has thus been expensive. Acquiring extra land has ensured that machines are fully utilized. Other economies of scale have been less important. There seem to be few differences between farms of different sizes in the farmer's ability to acquire credit or negotiate favourable terms for the purchase of inputs or the sale of products.[12]

Although economies of scale exist in English farming, they are not perhaps as marked as many believe. The optimum size of farm differs from enterprise to enterprise and ceases to be significant above a certain size, when diseconomies of scale may be more important. Twenty-five years ago it was held that there were no extra economies of scale above 700 acres; somewhat later D. K. Britton and B. Hill suggested that there were few economies above 400 acres. For dairying the upper figure was 150 acres, for mixed farms 200 acres, for cropping farms 250 acres and for livestock-rearing 300 acres. Beyond this there are no scale advantages.[13]

12 D. K. Britton and B. Hill, *Size and Efficiency in Farming* (London, 1975), p. 112.
13 F. G. Sturrock and H. J. Gunn, 'The development of large scale farming', *Westminster Bank Review* (February 1968), pp. 59–65; D. K. Britton, 'Size and efficiency in farming', *Farm Management*, 3 (1979), pp. 560–7.

Table 9.4 Changes in the size of agricultural holdings in England and Wales, 1977–1985

| Date | Number of holdings (hectares) | | | | | | Total |
|---|---|---|---|---|---|---|---|
| | 0 – 19.9 | 20 – 39.9 | 40 – 99.9 | 100 – 299.9 | 300 – 699.9 | 700 and above | |
| 1977 | 84,852 | 37,463 | 47,945 | 24,272 | 3,860 | 649 | 199,041 |
| 1985 | 75,019 | 33,692 | 45,321 | 24,723 | 4,117 | 702 | 183,574 |
| % change 1977–85 | − 11.6 | − 10.1 | − 5.4 | − 1.9 | + 6.2 | + 7.5 | − 7.8 |
| *Number of holdings as a percentage of total* | | | | | | | |
| 1977 | 42.6 | 18.8 | 24.2 | 12.2 | 1.9 | 0.3 | 100.0 |
| 1985 | 40.9 | 18.4 | 24.7 | 13.5 | 2.2 | 0.3 | 100.0 |
| *Area[a] occupied by holdings in each class (hectares)* | | | | | | | |
| 1977 | 61,159 | 1,085,278 | 3,037,281 | 3,859,766 | 1,626,475 | 708,175 | 10,968,134 |
| 1985 | 594,750 | 981,223 | 2,887,658 | 3,966,259 | 1,735,593 | 748,273 | 10,913,756 |
| % change 1977–78 | − 8.7 | − 9.6 | − 4.9 | + 2.7 | + 6.7 | + 5.7 | − 0.5 |
| *Area of each size class as a percentage of total area* | | | | | | | |
| 1977 | 5.9 | 9.9 | 27.7 | 35.2 | 14.8 | 6.5 | 100.0 |
| 1985 | 5.4 | 9.0 | 26.5 | 36.3 | 15.9 | 6.9 | 100.0 |

[a] Total area: it includes crops, grass, woodland and rough grazing.
*Sources:* Ministry of Agriculture, *Agricultural Statistics United Kingdom 1985* (London, 1986); *Agricultural Statistics United Kingdom 1980 and 1981* (London, 1983).

Yet, of course, during this period farms did get larger, and certainly well beyond the point where economies of scale cease to exist. There were – and are – several reasons for this. First, and most important, farmers *believed* they were gaining economies of scale. Second, increasing area is one way of increasing gross income. Third, land was acquired as an investment.[14]

For farms to get larger, land must be available for rent or for purchase, and for this to occur, other farmers must be giving up farming. As seen earlier, there has been a substantial decline in the number of farms in England and Wales over a long period, but particularly since the 1950s, and this decline has been predominantly in the smaller farms. The decline is easily explained. On many small farms the available area and capital has been insufficient to provide an adequate income for the farmer, not simply when compared with bigger farms or other non-agricultural businesses; many small farmers have a net income – when allowances are made for their manual labour on the farm – which is less than the farm-worker's wage. Not only are such farms poor but they are also inefficient, principally because they cannot fully utilize the labour of one man, and thus labour costs per unit of output are disproportionately high. The small family farm has too high a fixed-labour input. Thus while the smaller farms invariably have a higher output per acre than do larger farms, they have a far less favourable output per £100 of labour or of total inputs.[15]

Thus, unless in very intensive enterprises, most farms of fewer than 100 to 150 acres are inefficient and have a low net income, although income per acre may be high; more than half the farms of England and Wales fall into this category. Indeed the small-farm problem is not new, but it has become more acute as the threshold size for an adequate living has constantly risen. Thus it has been estimated that a livestock rearer in 1957 needed 50 acres to earn a satisfactory living, but by 1967 150 acres. In the 1930s, 30 acres was a full-time job for a man and a pair of horses. By the 1950s the same farmer with a tractor would need 90 to 120 acres to keep him occupied.[16]

It is perhaps surprising, then, not that the small farm has declined, but that it has not declined much faster. At times indeed there have been efforts to create new small farms. Acts of 1892 and 1908 empowered county councils to purchase agricultural land for lease as small holdings; by 1913 some 13,000 small farms had been created. At the end of the

14 *Report of the Committee of Inquiry into the Acquisition and Occupancy of Agricultural Land*, HMSO Cmnd. 7599 (1979), pp. 35–9.

15 Britton and Hill, *op. cit.* (1975); M. Bramley, *The Small Farmer: present situation and future prospects* (London, 1961), pp. 14, 17, 27–9, 31; F. G. Sturrock, 'A solution for the small farm problem', *Westminster Bank Quarterly Review* (May 1965), pp. 40–5.

16 Sturrock, *op. cit.* (1965), pp. 40–5; W. G. Owen, 'The one man farm', *Agriculture*, 74 (1967), pp. 111–13.

First World War some thought returning soldiers could be settled on the land. By 1931 there were 27,000 tenants on nearly half a million acres. But there was little further progress, and since 1945 these holdings have been too small to provide an adequate living. But small farmers have proved remarkably tenacious. Even schemes to pension them off, such as the 1967 Act, had little effect on numbers. It would seem that for many a sense of independence and a preference for country life have kept them on the land, while a lack of urban skills, and since 1973 a shortage of urban jobs, have stemmed the rural exodus. Nonetheless the decline of the small farms and the increasing dominance, in terms of land occupied, of the large farm, is the principal structural change of the last 40 years.[17]

SUMMARY

It is one of the curiosities of agricultural statistics that there is no record of the number of farmers in England and Wales, or of the size of farms as distinct from agricultural holdings. But it seems fairly certain that for much of the last two centuries at least a quarter of all the farms have been run by men who combined farming, usually on a small scale, with some other active job. Equally certain has been the long-term decline in the number of small farms, whether full-time or part-time, and the increase in the proportion of all farmland occupied by larger farms. Such a process of change began at least in the early eighteenth century, and continued, with a slight pause from 1880 to 1930, to the present. But while an ever-increasing proportion of the farmland is in a few big farms, the majority of English and Welsh farms remain comparatively small.

17 J. A. Venn, *The Foundations of Agricultural Economics* (Cambridge, 1953), pp. 129–38; J. A. Robson, 'Agricultural structure in England and Wales, 1955–1966: a quantitative analysis', *Farm Economist*, 11 (1970), pp. 460–81.

# 10

# Farm Distribution and Layout

THE GEOGRAPHY OF FARM SIZE

In spite of the great decline in the number of small farms since 1950, the geography of farm size has not greatly changed. In the east and south of the country large farms form a greater proportion of farms – and occupy a greater part of the area – than they do in Wales, the south-west and the north-west (see figure 10.1). Small farms on the other hand form a greater proportion of all farms in the latter regions than they do in the east and south (see figure 10.2). This difference between east and west was noted by Thomas Robertson in his review of the information on farm size in the Board of Agriculture's *General Reports* on the agriculture of the English and Welsh counties in 1796.[1] But it was not until 1851 that there was any statistical evidence upon the distribution of farm sizes. In that year there was a clear distinction between the south-east and the rest of the country. Farms of fewer than 100 acres were rarely more than half of all farms east of a line from the Wash to the Bristol Channel (see figure 10.3), whilst to the west they were invariably so, and in some counties were more than three-quarters of all farms. The map may exaggerate the importance of small farms in Norfolk and Lincolnshire, where there were a remarkable number of small farms in the Fenland, but medium and large farms predominated elsewhere in the two counties.[2]

Thus the essential difference was between the east, the south-east and the south, where small farms were unimportant except in the Fens, and the rest of the country, where small farms predominated. Large farms – 300 acres and over – were of little importance in the south-west, Wales, the Midlands and the north-west. They were a greater – but still not a major – proportion of all farms east of the Pennines and east of a line from Lincolnshire to Somerset (see figure 10.4).

---

[1] Thomas Robertson, *Outline of the General Report on the Size of Farms* (Edinburgh, 1796), pp. 11, 17, 38–9, 47–8.
[2] David Grigg, *The Agricultural Revolution in South Lincolnshire* (Cambridge, 1966), p. 170.

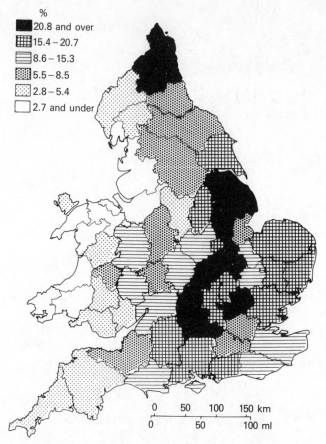

Figure 10.1 Agricultural holdings of 300 acres and above, as a percentage of all holdings of 5 acres and above, 1973).
*Source*: Ministry of Agriculture, *Agricultural Statistics, England and Wales* (London, 1974).

The great changes in the numbers of farms after 1851 did not alter this major difference between east and west. The Fenlands and counties to the south of London were inliers of small farms in 1973 (see figure 10.2). The fact that the counties near London did not appear to have an above-average proportion of small farms in 1851 may be because many part-time farmers did not then record themselves as such and were so missing from the census. Otherwise the pattern of distribution of both large and small farms is little changed.

This clear and persistent regional difference in farm size refers to the differences in the area of crops and grass; in most of lowland England and Wales rough grazing is unimportant and its omission from the statistics of farm size has no significance. In parts of the Pennines and

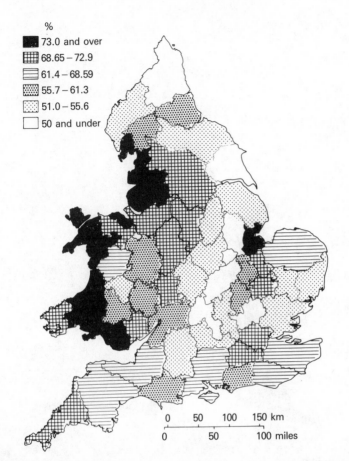

Figure 10.2 Agricultural holdings of 5 acres and above and fewer than 100 acres, as a percentage of all holdings of 5 acres and above, 1973.
*Source*: Ministry of Agriculture, *Agricultural Statistics, England and Wales* (London, 1974).

upland Wales, however, rough grazing is a very substantial part of the land used by hill sheep-farmers. Records of farm size that include rough grazing are available only intermittently in the past; currently farm-size statistics for England do include rough grazing, but those for Wales do not. If rough grazing is included in the size of farms, then the northern Pennines and northern Wales become areas of predominantly large farms.[3]

The regional difference in farm-size structure was apparent in the 1790s and perhaps long before then. The explanation of this enduring difference is not entirely clear. Larger farms appear to be – and have

[3] J. T. Coppock, *An Agricultural Atlas of England and Wales* (London, 1976), pp. 53–7.

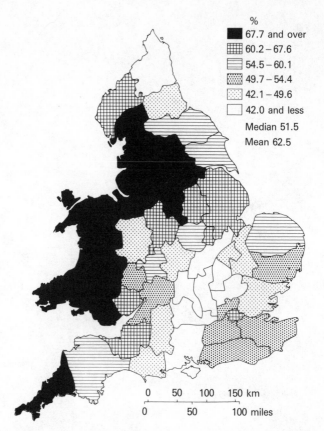

Figure 10.3   Farms of 5 to 100 acres, as a percentage of all farms of 5 acres and above, 1851.
*Source: 1851 Census, Great Britain, Ages, Civil Condition, Occupations and Birth Places,* 1: *Accounts and Papers,* 88 pt. 1 (1852–3).

been – more important in the flat, lowland areas east of the Pennines and east of a line from Nottingham to the mid-Dorset coast. This is also the western limit of the area in which arable – and particularly cereals – predominates. West of this line grass has always played a larger role. It may be that farm sizes have slowly adjusted to the optimum, which has been larger for crop-production than for livestock farms. Since the beginning of modern mechanization in the 1920s the area occupied by small farms – fewer than 100 acres – in England and Wales has fallen by over two-thirds, but the decline has been far greater in the east than in the west. As mechanization has extended from cereals to potatoes, sugar-beet, many vegetables and some fruit, the smaller farms of the east have been less viable and have given way. In the west, although

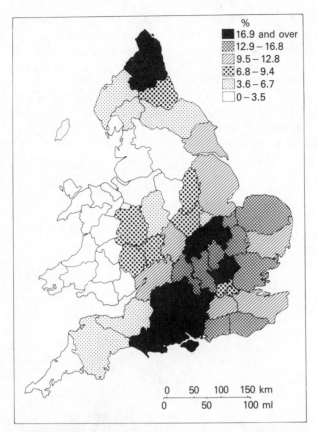

Figure 10.4   Farms of 300 acres and over, as a percentage of all farms of 5 acres and above, 1851.
*Source*: As for Figure 10.3.

small farms have been in decline, it has been less dramatic than the east because a living may be made on a smaller farm, and mechanization on rearing and feeding farms has made less progress.[4]

The pattern of farm sizes has other possible explanations. In much of Wales, the south-west and the north-west, most arable land and grass had been enclosed before the seventeenth century, as it had been in the extreme south-east in the coastal regions of Suffolk, Essex, Kent and parts of Sussex. In between, in a great band that ran from the North Yorkshire moors through Lincolnshire and Nottinghamshire and then south westwards towards the coasts of Dorset and Hampshire, lay a zone where the open fields were not enclosed until the Parliamentary

[4] David Grigg, 'Farm size in England and Wales, from early Victorian times to the present', *Agricultural History Review*, 35 (1987), pp. 179–89.

Acts of the eighteenth and early nineteenth centuries. Thus in the west much land had long been in consolidated farms – not a number of scattered strips – and the fields were hedged, fenced or walled. In contrast, in much of the east and south the unfenced fields, with the characteristic scattering of each man's strips of land throughout the three or four main fields, survived into the eighteenth and nineteenth centuries. Enclosure led not only to the fencing of fields but to the grouping of scattered plots into compact blocks of land. Many small owners sold out, and their land was added to existing farms. Certainly the area of larger farms corresponds fairly closely to the area where the open fields

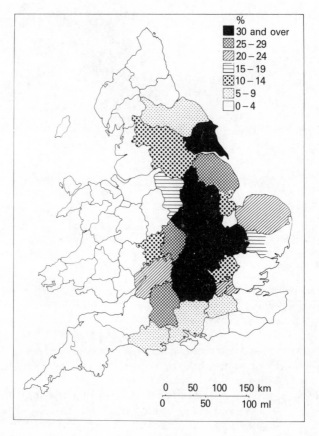

Figure 10.5  Percentage of total area, enclosed by Acts, that contained open field arable.
*Source*: M. Turner, *English Parliamentary Enclosure: its historical geography and economic history* (Folkestone, 1980), pp. 182–3.

survived longest and required Parliamentary Acts to extinguish them (see figures 10.1 and 10.5).[5]

There may be other influences upon farm sizes. Gavelkind or partible inheritance, where land passed not to a single heir but was divided equally among all children, had been common among peasants throughout England and Wales in early medieval times, but was slowly replaced by primogeniture. Gavelkind lasted longest in Wales, where it was not replaced by primogeniture until the sixteenth century. A further factor of importance may be population density. In the nineteenth century the counties of the Midlands and the north all had a very small proportion of their population engaged in agriculture and a very high total population per acre of agricultural land, and, perhaps as a consequence, a very high proportion of small farms. P. G. Craigie also noted the occurrence of small farms on the edge of towns, but whether this predominance of small farms existed before industrialization and population growth in the nineteenth century is unknown.[6]

The growth of large farms since 1950 has been the result of decisions made mainly by farmers. However, in the eighteenth and nineteenth centuries such decisions were made not by farmers – who were mainly tenants – but by landlords, for the most part owners of considerable estates. They and their estate managers preferred large to small farms; having an estate divided into large rather than small farms reduced the number of buildings to be built and maintained. Landlords preferred tenants with capital and enterprise, who in turn preferred the larger farms – except perhaps in the periods of low cereal prices, when indeed the number of large farms in England declined (see figure 9.1). But the distribution of large estates seems to have had no necessary relationship to the distribution of large and small farms. In 1873, for example, the highest proportion of land in estates of over 5,000 acres was in Lincolnshire and Northumberland, counties in which there were many large farms. Large estates were important in the south-west and parts of Wales, where small farms were numerous, but not in Essex, where the large farm dominated.[7]

FARMS AND THEIR FIELDS

The size of farms affected – and continues to do so – the farmer's net income and his efficiency, and has been a matter of discussion since at

[5] D. B. Grigg, 'The geography of small and large farms in England and Wales, their size and distribution', *Geography*, 48 (1963), pp. 268–79.

[6] P. G. Craigie, 'The size and distribution of agricultural holdings in England and abroad', *Journal of the Royal Statistical Society*, 50 (1887), pp. 86–142.

[7] G. E. Mingay, 'The size of farms in the eighteenth century', *Economic History Review*, 14 (1962), pp. 469–88; H. Levy, *Large and Small Holdings* (London, 1911); Grigg, *op. cit.* (1963), pp. 268–79.

least the eighteenth century. In contrast, in recent years the *layout* of farms has received little attention, but once it was thought of considerable importance.

'The chief problem of land distribution in the majority of cases probably lies within the farm itself and not in the extension or contraction of the farm boundaries.' So wrote Viscount Astor and K. A. H. Murray in 1937.[8] The layout of farms encompasses a number of features: the shape of fields, their size, their boundaries and their relationship to the central farm buildings. It includes as well the degree of fragmentation. Most farms in England consist of one block of land only, but some have two or more, separated from each other by other farmers' land. This phenomenon, more common in the past and still widespread in Africa, Asia and much of Europe, has been variously described as fragmentation, severance or scattering. There is no information at the national level on the degree of fragmentation of farms at present; however, it is certainly substantially less than it was in the eighteenth century or before.

### THE OPEN FIELDS AND THEIR SIGNIFICANCE

In late medieval England much of the arable land was farmed in open or common fields. The arable land was divided into two, three or more very large fields which surrounded the village, beyond which was woodland and grazing land used in common. The open fields were divided into narrow strips – a modal strip being 220 yards long and 22 yards wide – which in turn were in groups of strips called furlongs. The farms of the villagers varied in size, but in nearly every case their strips were not in one compact block but scattered throughout the several open fields. Villagers could turn their livestock onto the stubble after harvest and they could also use the fallow land for grazing. The number of cattle or sheep that could be kept on the commons was stinted, a function usually of the size of the farmer's arable holding. The use of the commons, fallow and stubble and the dates of sowing and harvesting were determined by a village council.

In 1500 there was little remaining open field in the south-west, Wales, the west Midlands or the north-west or in much of the south-east (see figure 10.5 and table 10.1). The open fields had either never existed in these areas or had mostly been enclosed by the early sixteenth century. On the other hand, in a broad belt from the north-east south south-west to the Dorset coast, most of the arable land was in open fields. This threefold division was paralleled by differences in the predominant form of settlement (see figure 10.6). In the west villages were few and most of the population lived in hamlets or isolated farmhouses, the latter set

---

[8] Viscount Astor and K. A. H. Murray, *The Planning of Agriculture* (Oxford, 1937), p. 5.

Table 10.1　The enclosure of open field and waste: percentage of total area of England enclosed, 1500–1914

| | |
|---|---|
| Already enclosed in 1500 | 45.0 |
| Enclosed 1500–99 | 2.0 |
| Enclosed 1600–99 | 24.0 |
| Enclosed 1700–99 | 13.0 |
| Enclosed 1800–1914 | 11.4 |
| Commons remaining in 1914 | 4.6 |
| | 100.0 |

*Source*: J. R. Wordie, 'The chronology of English enclosure, 1500–1914', *Economic History Review*, 36 (1983), pp. 483–505.

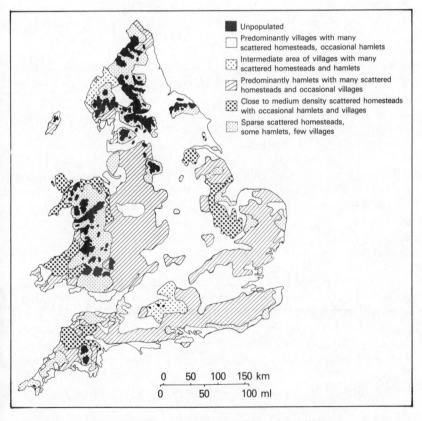

Figure 10.6　Rural settlements in England and Wales.
*Source*: Modification of map by H. Thorpe, 'Rural Settlement', in *The British Isles: a systematic geography*, ed. J. Wreford Watson and J. B. Sissons (London, 1964), pp. 360–1.

in their fields. Farms were small; so were fields, which were hedged or fenced and often irregular in shape. In the south-east hamlets and farms also predominated, although neither region entirely lacked villages or market towns. But in what has been called midland England, where the open fields were still predominant in the seventeenth century, the village was the common mode of settlement; farmhouses were in the villages, farms were highly fragmented and the strips and furlongs were without fences, walls or hedges.[9]

From 1600 onwards the enclosure of the open fields and commons of midland England proceeded apace, much of it in the seventeenth century, when enclosure by agreement was the common means. By 1700 three-quarters of the total area of England had been enclosed, but much of the arable land still remained in open fields (see table 10.1). Some 4½ million acres of open field arable were enclosed by Parliamentary Act in the eighteenth and early nineteenth centuries. In the later nineteenth century most enclosure was of common land in the upland areas of the Pennines, Wales and the moors of the south-west, together with lowland fen in Somerset and Lincolnshire and poor sandy soils in other lowland areas.[10]

The date of enclosure has had some significance for the modern layout of farms, for Parliamentary enclosure affected much of the modern arable area of eastern and southern England. The commissioners who implemented the enclosure acts attempted to group the strips of each farmer into one compact block, but this was not always possible. Enclosure also required each land-owner to hedge or fence the new farm, a costly process. New, generally straight roads were constructed, and the new fields were square or rectangular. The landscape of the Parliamentary Acts, particularly on the limestone uplands, was very distinctive, and very different from the old enclosed landscapes of the west and the south-east. This period still has significance for the present.

### FRAGMENTATION

The fragmentation of farms has many drawbacks, but nowadays of most importance is the high cost of movement. In the late 1950s it was estimated that one-third of all the man-hours worked on British farms and 40 per cent of all the energy used was spent moving commodities around the farm. Thus fragmentation can increase costs. Sadly the only survey of fragmentation in England and Wales dates from the National Farm Survey of 1941–3 when the farm boundaries of the day were marked on 6″ Ordnance Survey Maps; the survey analysed the layout of

---

[9] H. Thorpe, 'Rural settlement', in J. Wreford Watson (ed.), *The British Isles: a systematic geography* (London, 1964), pp. 358–79.

[10] M. Turner, *English Parliamentary Enclosure: its historical geography and economic history* (Folkstone, 1980), pp. 59–61.

Table 10.2   Enclosure and fragmentation in England and Wales

| Region | Percentage of holdings severed | Openfield arable enclosed by Act as a percentage of total area |
|---|---|---|
| Cornwall | 0 – 5 | 0.0 |
| Devon | 0 – 5 | 0.0 |
| Durham | 0 – 5 | 0.4 |
| Cheshire | 5 – 15 | 0.02 |
| Cumberland | 5 – 15 | 1.2 |
| Montgomeryshire | 5 – 15 | n.d. |
| Northumberland | 5 – 15 | 2.0 |
| Westmorland | 5 – 15 | 0.06 |
| Carmarthenshire | 15 – 30 | n.d. |
| Denbighshire | 15 – 30 | n.d. |
| Bedfordshire | 30 – 50 | 47.6 |
| Derbyshire | 30 – 50 | 15.8 |
| Essex | 30 – 50 | 2.2 |
| Hertfordshire | 30 – 50 | 12.3 |
| Leicestershire | 30 – 50 | 42.7 |
| Kesteven | 30 – 50 | 39.2 |
| Pembrokeshire | 30 – 50 | n.d. |
| West Suffolk | 30 – 50 | 7.6 |
| Cambridgeshire | 30 – 50 | 45.4 |
| Lindsey | 30 – 50 | 29.8 |
| Nottinghamshire | 30 – 50 | 32.1 |
| Rutland | 30 – 50 | 44.6 |
| 24 counties | 25.0 | 13.8 |

n.d. No data.
*Sources*: M. E. Turner, *English Parliamentary Enclosure* (Folkstone, 1980), pp. 182–3; Ministry of Agriculture, *National Farm Survey of England and Wales (1941–3): a summary report* (London, 1946), p. 37.

40 per cent of all the farms over 5 acres in 24 counties and found that 75 per cent of them were in one single block of land, 25 per cent were fragmented. It also found that fragmentation increased with farm size; only one-fifth of farms under 25 acres were severed, but a half of those over 700 acres. Although the survey did not deal with all counties, the degree of fragmentation seemed to be least in counties in the west, north, Wales and the south-east, and greatest in midland England, although there were some exceptions, such as Pembrokeshire. In Essex and Suffolk, counties with much old enclosure, there was also much fragmentation (see table 10.2). On the whole, however, fragmentation was greatest in the counties where the consolidation of strips was only lately and imperfectly accomplished, and least in the area of old enclosure.[11]

[11] M. Chisholm, *Rural Settlement and Land Use: an essay in location* (London, 1979), p. 38; Ministry of Agriculture, *National Farm Survey of England and Wales (1941–1943): a summary report*, (London, 1946), pp. 36–9.

The National Farm Survey noted only whether a farm was in two or more parts or not fragmented, but unfortunately not the number of parcels, the distance of each parcel from the farmstead, or the proportion of the farm fragmented, all of which would influence the time spent in moving around the farm. The only indication of the degree of fragmentation comes from a survey of part of Oxfordshire in the Second World War. Then 73 per cent of the farms surveyed consisted of only one parcel, 17 per cent of two, 7 per cent of three, and only 3 per cent of four or more. The great majority of farms consisted of one or two blocks only.[12]

There is no reliable information on the changes in the degree of fragmentation since the 1940s; the results of the few later studies are contradictory when compared with those of the 1941–3 survey. Thus on an estate in Nottinghamshire the landowner steadily reduced fragmentation in the post-war period; in contrast, in a sample of parishes in the same county the degree of fragmentation increased between 1943 and 1963, as it did in a number of Somerset parishes. Although in the long term farmers and land-owners may aim to reduce fragmentation, in the short run the need to acquire extra land to increase the size of farm often means acquiring land some distance from the home farm and is likely to increase the degree of fragmentation. There are a few farmers, such as vegetable producers in the Vale of Evesham, who believe fragmentation has an advantage, as the scattering of parcels may help avoid frost or other climatic hazards.[13]

FIELDS AND THEIR BOUNDARIES

The fields of England vary enormously in size and shape and in the type of boundary, which include hedges, walls, ditches, wooden fences and barbed wire. The size and shape often give some indication of the time they were formed and their function. The open fields of the period before the nineteenth century had no hedges or fences except around the outer perimeter, to keep out stock which were grazing the common grazing lands. There was little need to fence the strips, nor indeed is there much need for the modern farmer to fence or hedge his arable

---

[12] Agricultural Economic Research Institute, *Country Planning: a study of rural problems* (Oxford, 1944), p. 33; M. Butterwick and E. N. Rolfe, 'Yetminster Revisited', *Farm Economist*, 10 (1962–5), pp. 446–51.

[13] C. J. W. Edwards, 'The effects of changing farm size upon levels of farm fragmentation: a Somerset case study', *Journal of Agricultural Economics*, 29 (1978), pp. 143–53; G. E. Jones and A. J. Simmons, 'Towards an interpretation of change in farm structure: a Nottinghamshire case study', *Farm Economist*, 10 (1962–5), pp. 331–44; B. W. Ilbery, 'Farm fragmentation in the Vale of Evesham', *Area*, 16 (1984), pp. 159–65; B. A. Wood and P. T. Wheeler, 'Changing farm structure on a Nottinghamshire landed estate 1952–1977', *East Midland Geographer*, 8 (1985), pp. 198–205.

fields; hedges may provide some protection against wind erosion, but otherwise they have little practical function. Where livestock are kept, however, field boundaries are far more important, for they are needed to keep animals from straying onto other people's land or the farmer's own crops, and to allow the farmer to control the grazing of his grass. Hedges also provide some shelter for livestock, which in turn reduces heat-loss and thus the need for extra feed.[14]

The early hedges of the west and the south-east enclosed small and often irregularly shaped fields, and their prime function was to control the movement of cattle and sheep. The Parliamentary Acts of enclosure were later, and much of the area so enclosed was in crops. Hence fields tended to be larger and more regular in shape. Many rectangular fields of 10 acres or more were laid out by the enclosure commissioners. As long as oxen or horses were used to pull the plough, and horses pulled the reaper, such sizes were appropriate; but when the tractor and the combine replaced the horse, the optimum size became much larger; bigger fields meant that less time was spent in turning and less time was wasted moving from field to field. From the 1930s the optimum size of field began to rise. For the comparatively small combine harvesters of the 1930s, 25 acres was the optimum, but this had risen to 45 acres by 1970. Since then combines, sprayers and tractors have all further increased in size, as has the optimum size of field. Although the prime reason for enlarging fields is to save time on unproductive turning and journeying from field to field, removing hedges and other boundaries has also increased the area that can be ploughed.[15]

The great age of the hedge and fence was the eighteenth and early nineteenth centuries. Parliamentary Acts of enclosure required farmers to hedge or wall their fields, and some 100,000 miles of hedges were laid from about 1700 to 1850. The total length of field boundaries reached its maximum in the mid-nineteenth century, but many contemporaries believed there were too many hedges – particularly in Devon, where fields were ridiculously small. Between 1850 and 1940 about 50 to 70,000 miles of hedges were lost as the urban area expanded, but the remaining fields were not much larger than they had been a century before. In the early 1940s half of all the fields in a survey of part of Oxfordshire were of fewer than 10 acres, 40 per cent between 10 and 20 acres. In the eastern counties a decade earlier the average size of

---

[14] F. Sturrock and J. Cathie, *Farm Modernisation and the Countryside: the impact of increasing field size and hedge removal on arable farms*, Department of Land Economy, Occasional Papers no. 12 (Cambridge, 1980); W. W. Baird and J. R. Tarrant, 'Vanishing hedgerows', *Geographical Magazine*, 44 (1972), pp. 545–51.

[15] Baird and Tarrant, *op. cit.* (1972), pp. 545–51; E. T. Davies and W. J. Dumford, *Some Physical and Economic Considerations of Field Enlargement*, Department of Agricultural Economics, 133 (Exeter, 1962); R. McG. Carslaw, 'Size of fields in the Eastern counties of England', *Farm Economist*, 1 (1933), pp. 36–7; J. M. Caborn, 'The agronomic and biologic significance of hedgerows', *Outlook on Agriculture*, 6 (1971), pp. 279–84.

*Not all field boundaries are hedges. Stone walls predominate in one Derbyshire limestone region. (Author)*

arable fields had been 10 acres, that of pasture fields 7 acres. Clearly most fields at that time were less than the optimum size for tractor and combine harvester.[16]

Not surprisingly the post-war period has seen a substantial reduction in field boundaries and an increase in the average size of field. The total length of field boundaries has fallen by about one-fifth, that of hedges alone by approximately one-quarter. The rate of hedge removal rose in the 1950s and reached a peak in the early 1960s; it has since declined, at least partly because of protests by conservationists. The reduction in the number of hedges, although primarily to enlarge fields to utilize machines more efficiently, has also been a response to the rising cost of maintaining them. Their removal diminishes the attractiveness of many areas and also reduces sites for birds, animals and insects. Most of the hedgerow removal has taken place in the arable areas of the country and has exaggerated the long-standing difference between the large fields

[16] J. T. Coppock, 'Land use changes and the hedgerow', in M. D. Hooper and M. W. Holdgate (eds), *Hedges and Hedgerow Trees*, Monkswood Symposium no. 4 (1968), J. M. Way and B. N. K. Davis, 'Hedges as a feature of our countryside', *Agriculture*, 70 (1963), pp. 565–8; W. H. Long, 'Size of fields in Devon', *Farm Economist*, 1 (1935), pp. 224–5; W. R. Mead, 'The study of field boundaries', *Geografie Zeitschrifte*, 54 (1966), pp. 101–17; R. McG. Carslaw *op. cit.* (1933); Agricultural Economics Research Institute, *Country Planning: a study of rural problems* (Oxford, 1944), p. 44.

of the east, the small fields of the west and the intermediate sizes of those in the Midlands.[17]

SUMMARY

Although most parts of England and Wales still contain a combination of large and small farms, fields of different shape and size and farms with varying degrees of fragmentation, there is a broad regular pattern in which farms and fields increase in size when passing from west to east, while the most fragmented farms, in the 1940s, were found in a great swathe from the North Yorkshire Moors to the Dorset coast. These differences seem related to differences in morphology and land use and the history of enclosure. The last 40 years have seen marked changes, particularly in the east of England.

[17] M. D. Hooper, 'Hedgerows and small woodlands', in J. Davidson and R. Lloyd (eds), *Conservation and Agriculture* (London, 1977), pp. 45–57; 'The rate of hedgerow removal', in Hooper and Holdgate, *op. cit.*; *Countryside Commission News*, 23 (September 1986), pp. 4–5.

# 11
# The Rise and Fall of the Farm Population

For many observers of the agricultural scene the most striking feature of the post-war period has been the great fall in the numbers of people working on the land; their implements and tools have been replaced by machines, while human muscle and horse power has given way to electricity and the internal combustion engine. But the decline did not begin in 1945; although the farm labour-force in 1981 was only half of that in 1951, the numbers then were only just over half those in 1851. The decline has been going on for over 120 years (see table 11.1). Equally long term has been the decline in the labour-force as *a percentage* of the total work-force. Currently only one in 50 is employed in farming in England and Wales; no other country has a proportion so low, although the United States, Sweden and Switzerland have ratios nearly as small. But no country has had a minority of its population engaged in agriculture for so long; not since the early sixteenth century has as much as three-quarters of the total work-force been engaged in agriculture (see table 11.2), although such a figure is exceeded today in parts of Africa and Asia. By the middle of the eighteenth century only 46 per cent of the work-force was directly employed in farming, the same as the figure for the world as a whole in 1979. By the time of the battle of Waterloo only a third of England's population, but over 60 per cent of the population of France, worked on the land. Thereafter the decline continued to one-fifth in 1851, one-twelfth in 1901 and one-twentieth in 1951. No country has been so urbanized and so industrialized for so long.[1]

1 D. Grigg, *The Dynamics of Agricultural Change: the historical experience* (London, 1982), p. 110; Food and Agriculture Organisation, *Production Yearbook, 1980*, 34 (Rome, 1981).

Table 11.1  Numbers in agriculture in England and Wales, 1851–1983 (both sexes, thousands)

| Date | Farmers | Relatives | Contract workers on farms | Others | Total | % rate of change |
|------|---------|-----------|---------------------------|--------|-------|------------------|
| 1851 | 249 | 111 | 1,267 | 79 | 1,706 | – |
| 1861 | 249 | 92 | 1,204 | 95 | 1,640 | – 3.9 |
| 1871 | 249 | 76 | 997 | 116 | 1,438 | – 12.2 |
| 1881 | 223 | 75 | 891 | 84 | 1,273 | – 11.5 |
| 1891 | 223 | 67 | 800 | 108 | 1,198 | – 5.8 |
| 1901 | 224 | 107 | 649 | 137 | 1,117 | – 0.7 |
| 1911 | 228 | 114 | 687 | 154 | 1,183 | + 5.0 |
| 1921 | 264 | 95 | 627 | 151 | 1,137 | – 4.0 |
| 1931 | 248 | 80 | 538 | 130 | 996 | – 12.3 |
| 1951 | 263 | 88 | 483 | 132 | 966 | – 3.2 |
| 1981 | 202 | n.d. | 257 | n.d. | 459 | – 52.5 |

n.d. no data.
*Sources*: 1851–1931: F. D. W. Taylor, 'United Kingdom: numbers in agriculture', *Farm Economist*, 8 (1958), pp. 36–40 (based on census occupational tables; NB, Female relatives excluded in later censuses); 1951: J. R. Bellerby, 'The distribution of manpower in agriculture and industry 1851–1951', *Farm Economist*, 9 (1958), pp. 1–11; 1981: *Census of Great Britain, Economic Activity in Great Britain* (London, 1984). Change in definition in 1951 census makes comparison difficult. 1951 data are census occupations plus Agricultural Census data.

CHANGES IN THE SIZE OF THE AGRICULTURAL LABOUR-FORCE
BEFORE 1851

1851 saw the zenith of the English agricultural population. Before then it had been increasing for several centuries, although very slowly; since then it has been declining. 1851 also saw major changes in the composition of the work-force. Before that time, and since the early sixteenth century, farm-workers without land had been an increasing proportion of the labour-force, farmers a declining proportion. After 1851 this trend was reversed; the number of farm-workers has declined dramatically, so that now farmers and their relatives form a majority of the labour-force. But all such statements need to be treated with caution. It is not simply that there are no accurate statistics of occupations before the Population Census of 1851. Even since then there have been problems in distinguishing who works in farming and for how long. Seasonal variations in the amount of work on the farm, which are particularly notable in arable farming, mean that a lot of labour is hired only for short periods, especially at harvest time. Exactly how much work is done on the land by the farmer's relatives, and particularly by his wife and daughters, is never very clear. Equally unclear in the statistics has been the difference between farmer and non-farmer, and between labourer and farmer. Although much of English land was and is held in large farms, there have always been many small holdings in the occupation, and sometimes ownership, of men and women who had some other job – as craftsmen, shopkeepers, innkeepers, or in a job closely allied to farming such as brewing or butchery. They may, however, not be recorded in the census as farmers. Farm labourers often held some land, however small, and in the sixteenth and seventeenth centuries the boundary between small farmer and labourer was blurred. As late as 1662 an Act required that four acres of land be attached to every cottage built; although soon in abeyance it was indicative of the wide spectrum from the prosperous tenant farmer to the landless labourer; statistics have tended to record only these two extremes.[2]

In the sixteen century the population of England and Wales grew rapidly, but the number of labourers grew more rapidly than the number of farmers, not simply because of natural increase, but because some small farmers lost their land at enclosure and became labourers. It was not a good time for the labourers, for their numbers grew more rapidly than did demand for their work, and real wages halved between 1500 and 1640. They did, however, still have some common rights and often a small patch of land, while bye-employment, particularly in textiles, was common. But in the sixteenth and seventeenth centuries there was a steady increase in the ratio of labourers to farmers. In the early sixteenth century there were probably no more than 1.4 labourers to each farmer, but by the end of the seventeenth century the figure was 1.74.[3]

The agricultural population increased steadily until the late seventeenth century (see table 11.2). It may then have declined; but from the middle of the eighteenth century the agricultural population, like the total population, began to grow quite rapidly. The later eighteenth and first half of the nineteenth century was a period of considerable change in agriculture, and of course in other parts of the English economy. The urban population grew rapidly, and factory industry expanded. Rural fertility was high and mortality lower than in the town, so that, although there was a substantial migration from the country into the towns, the rural population nonetheless increased substantially. Much of this increased population was absorbed in farming. Parliamentary enclosure provided a great deal of short-term employment in hedging and building

2 E. A. Wrigley, 'Men on the land and men in the countryside: employment in agriculture in early nineteenth century England', in L. Bonfield, R. Smith and K. Wrightson (eds), *The World We Have Gained*, (Oxford, 1986), pp. 295–336.

3 A. Everitt, 'Farm labourers', in J. Thirsk (ed.), *The Agrarian History of England and Wales*, vol. IV: *1500–1640* (Cambridge, 1967), pp. 400, 403, 414, 425, 435; E. A. Wrigley, 'Urban growth and agricultural change: England and the continent in the early modern period', *Journal of Interdisciplinary History*, 15 (1985), pp. 683–728; J. H. Clapham, 'The growth of an agrarian proletariat 1688–1832', *Cambridge Historical Journal*, 1 (1923), pp. 92–5.

Table 11.2  The agricultural population of England, 1520–1801 (millions)

| Date | Total population | Agricultural[a] population | Agricultural population as a percentage of total |
|------|-----------------|--------------------------|-------------------------------------------------|
| 1520 | 2.40 | 1.82 | 75.8 |
| 1600 | 4.11 | 2.87 | 69.8 |
| 1670 | 4.98 | 3.01 | 60.4 |
| 1700 | 5.06 | 2.78 | 54.5 |
| 1750 | 5.77 | 2.64 | 45.8 |
| 1801 | 8.66 | 3.14 | 36.2 |

[a] Those working in agriculture and their dependents.
*Sources*: E. A. Wrigley, 'Urban growth and agricultural change: England and the continent in the early modern period', *Journal of Interdisciplinary History*, 15 (1985), pp. 683–728.

new roads and, in some places, new farms and farm buildings. Land was constantly being reclaimed in the uplands and lowlands, while in the east and south, corn production, which was more labour-intensive than livestock farming, was replacing grass. There was also a steady growth in the area in potatoes and fodder roots, which required a great deal of extra labour; their acreage probably rose fivefold from 1750 to 1850.[4]

Although the agricultural labour-force may have declined in the first half of the eighteenth century, it increased thereafter, probably by one-third between 1750 and 1850, most rapidly before 1800. Until the beginnings of the Napoleonic Wars the demand for labour and the supply were roughly in balance, but during the wars the army and the navy as well as increasing industrial production took labour from the land, and there were frequent labour-shortages. This ended when the wars ended and over 400,000 men returned to civilian life; although the adult male labour-force in agriculture increased very slowly from 1811 to 1851 – from 910,000 to 1,010,000 – there were too many people seeking too few jobs until the 1840s, particularly in the south-east, and there was unemployment, underemployment and very low real wages for the farm labourer in this period. Migration from the south-east to London was not sufficient to reduce the labour surplus; in the Midlands and the north migration was greater because of the wider opportunities of industrial employment, and as a result a gap opened

4 W. A. Armstrong, 'The influence of demographic factors on the position of the agricultural labourer in England and Wales, *c.* 1750–1914', *Agricultural History Review*, 29 (1981), pp. 71–82; E. J. T. Collins, 'Migrant labour in British agriculture in the nineteenth century', *Economic History Review*, 29 (1976), pp. 38–59.

up between agricultural wages in the north and those in the south; north of Nottingham wages were some 37 per cent above those in the south.[5]

The composition of the agricultural labour-force also changed after 1750. In the eighteenth century the amalgamation of farms on estates and the sale of land by small land-owners after Parliamentary enclosure was reducing the number of farmers, while the number of farm labourers was increasing both absolutely and as a proportion of the total farm work-force. The number of labourers to each farmer rose from 1.74 in 1700 to 2.5 in 1831, and by 1851 the ratio was one farmer to 2.9 farm labourers.[6]

This period also saw another important change. Before 1750 between one-third and one-half of the labour-force had consisted of farm servants, young men and women between 14 and 25 years of age who lived in the farmer's house and worked on the farm. They received their board and some pay, often in kind. In their twenties they married, moved to cottages and became day-labourers; they were then hired by the day or week and were often laid off for much of the winter. Farm servants were found on the larger farms, for on the smaller holdings the farmer and his wife could manage without hired labour. But the number of farm servants living in declined in the late eighteenth century as the growth in population provided an abundance of day-labourers available at low wages. By the time of the Napoleonic Wars some farmers' wives resented the servants living in, while a servant, under contract for a year, gained a parish settlement under the Old Poor Law and became a potential liability to the parish. In the early nineteenth century servants dwindled to be replaced almost entirely by day-labourers, except in Wales, the west and the north. In the north high industrial wages attracted labourers from the farms, so farmers had to offer yearly contracts to ensure they kept them. In the remoter districts it was difficult to get labour without the practice of living in, while in livestock areas the constant attention that livestock needed ensured the survival of farm servants on larger farms.[7]

THE ZENITH: THE AGRICULTURAL POPULATION IN 1851

In 1851 the agricultural labour-force reached its highest point. European visitors were much struck by the differences between England and their

5 E. L. Jones, 'The agricultural labour market in England, 1793–1872', *Economic History Review*, 17 (1964), pp. 322–8; E. A. Wrigley, *op. cit.* (1986), pp. 295–336; E. H. Hunt, 'Labour productivity in English agriculture, 1850–1914', *Economic History Review*, 20 (1967), pp. 280–92.

6 *1851 Census, Great Britain, Ages, Civil Condition, Occupations and Birth Places*, 1: *Accounts and Papers*, 88, pt. 1: *1852–53*, p. lxxlx.

7 Ann Kussmaul, *Servants in Husbandry in Early Modern England* (Cambridge, 1981), pp. 4, 15, 20–4, 100, 114–15, 125, 131; B. Short, 'The decline of living-in servants in the transition to capitalist farming; a critique of the Sussex evidence', *Sussex Archaeological Collections*, 122 (1984), pp. 147–64; D. M. Snell, *Annals of the Labouring Poor: social change and agrarian England 1660–1900* (Cambridge, 1985), pp. 68–86, 96–7.

own countries. In England occupier-owners were uncommon and much of the farmland was in the possession of a few great land-owners; farms were large, run by prosperous tenant farmers who employed day-labourers to work the land. But there were in fact very marked regional variations in ownership, farm size and the labour-force. In 1851, 38.8 per cent of all those who described themselves as farmers in the census employed no labour and worked the land themselves with help from their family; in the 1831 census the figure had been 47.4 per cent. These farms, found especially in the north and Wales (see figure 11.1), where most farms were small (see figure 10.2), were in marked contrast to the east and south, where farms were larger and there were few farms without labourers. In 1851 the national average was 2.9 labourers per farm, but this was greatly exceeded in the counties of the south-east. Indeed most of the country's farm labourers were to be found there.

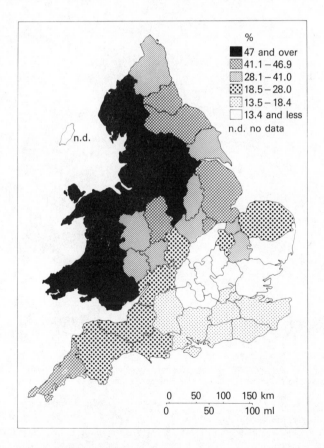

Figure 11.1   Farms of 5 acres and over without employed labour, as a percentage of all farms of 5 acres and over, 1851.
*Source: 1851 Census, Great Britain, Ages, Civil Condition, Occupations and Birth Places, 1: Accounts and Papers, 88, pt. 1 (1852–3), p. lxxix.*

Forty per cent of all labourers worked on farms of over 300 acres, which were only 8 per cent of all farms; most of these were in the east and south-east. The distribution and concentration has not greatly changed. In 1946, 46 per cent of all workers were found on only 6.1 per cent of the farms; in 1970 half of all full-time labourers were on 10 per cent of the farms, while 36.8 per cent of farms employed no labour at all. The last-named were still found in the west, south-west and Wales, while the greater number of labourers was still to be found in the east and south-east (see figure 11.2).[8]

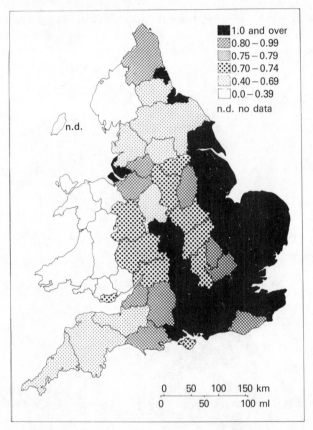

Figure 11.2   Number of farm-workers per farmer, 1981.
*Source*: Office of Population Censuses and Surveys, *Census 1981, County Reports* (London, 1982).

8 D. K. Britton, 'The distribution of agricultural workers in England and Wales by size of employment group', *Farm Economist*, 6 (1949), pp. 80–3; J. A. Mollet, 'The size of farm staffs in England and Wales in 1851 and 1941', *Farm Economist*, 6 (1950), pp. 150–3; Manpower Working Group, Economic Development Committee for the Agricultural Industry, *Agricultural Manpower in England and Wales* (London, 1972), p. 2.

In 1851 farm servants were only a small proportion of the farm labour-force; they were still numerous in the north, the west and Wales, but were very few in the east and south, where day-labourers were universal. The number of women employed full-time in agriculture had also declined since 1750; only 9 per cent of adult labourers were female. Women were most important in parts of the north, South Wales and the south-west, and their distribution is probably related to the location of the dairy industry. By the early twentieth century women were unusual as part of the permanent labour-force, found in any numbers only in Northumberland, Oxford and the Holland division of Lincolnshire. On the other hand they were still a large proportion of the casual and seasonal labour-force who undertook much of the weeding, stone-picking and gleaning.[9]

Casual and seasonal labourers were not recorded in the census but were undoubtedly common and were particularly numerous at the harvest. Local populations provided most of this labour, but from the late eighteenth century there grew up a regular flow of migrant labour from the remoter areas of the Welsh and Scottish uplands and the west coast of Ireland to the arable east and south of England. The movement from Wales and Scotland faded away in the 1830s, but that from Ireland reached a peak in the 1840s during the famine. At times one-tenth of the grain harvest was brought in by migrant Irish labour. Although the seasonal labour-force declined in the later nineteenth century, it was still thought to be about one-tenth of the total number employed in a year in 1913.[10]

THE GREAT DECLINE

Information on the agricultural labour-force is not entirely reliable. The agricultural census did not record the number of farm-workers until 1920 or the number of farmers – more exactly the number of partners, directors and farmers – until 1970. The population census is thus the only guide to long-term trends, and its figures show that the total labour-force fell by one-third between 1851 and 1901 and by only 14 per cent

---

9 Snell, *op. cit.* (1985), pp. 52, 56, 58; P. E. Dewey, 'Government provision of farm labour in England and Wales, 1914–18', *Agricultural History Review*, 27 (1979), pp. 110–21; A. Hawkins, *Poor Labouringmen: rural radicalism in Norfolk 1872–1923* (London, 1985), p. 21; D. W. Howell, 'The agricultural labourer in nineteenth century Wales', *Welsh Historical Review*, 6 (1973), pp. 262–87.

10 E. J. T. Collins, 'Labour supply and demand in European agriculture 1800–1880', in E. L. Jones and S. J. Woolf (eds), *Agrarian Change and Economic Development: the historical problems* (London, 1969), pp. 61–94; Collins, *op. cit.* (1976), pp. 38–59; W. A. Armstrong, 'The work-folk', in G. E. Mingay (ed.), *The Victorian Countryside*, 2 (London, 1981), pp. 491–505; S. Barber, 'Irish migrant agricultural labourers in nineteenth century Lincolnshire', *Saothar, Journal of Irish Labour History Society*, 8 (1982), pp. 10–22.

between 1901 and 1951, but halved between 1951 and 1981 (see table 11.1), in which year total numbers were slightly over one-quarter of those in 1851. The periods of most rapid decline were the 1860s, the 1870s, the 1920s and the 1950s and 1960s. There were only two decades of increase. The returning – if temporary – prosperity of the Edwardian era saw a slight rise and the Second World War and its immediate aftermath saw a sizable increase (see figure 11.3). Otherwise the decline has been continuous.

Not only have its numbers declined dramatically but the composition of the labour-force has altered. In 1851, 80 per cent of the full-time labour force were hired labourers, one-fifth farmers and their relatives. Between 1851 and 1951 the number of farmers showed little change and most of the decline in the work-force was due to the fall in the number of hired labourers (see table 11.3). Since 1951, however, the number of farmers has declined; but as they have not declined as dramatically as the number of farm workers, whose total halved between 1951 and 1981, farmers and their relatives have contributed an increasing proportion of the labour input on farms. Over the last 20 years seasonal and casual labour has remained fairly constant in numbers and thus has formed a growing proportion of the total labour-force (see figure 11.3), though a small proportion of the total hours worked.

Thus by the early 1980s farmers (including salaried managers) and their relatives formed a very large part of the labour-force. Of the whole-

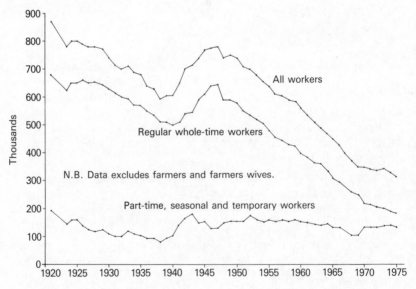

Figure 11.3  Changes in the number of agricultural workers, 1921–1975.
*Source*: Ministry of Agriculture, *Agricultural Statistics, England and Wales* (London, 1921–75).

Table 11.3  Changing composition of the labour-force in England
and Wales, 1851–1951 (as a percentage of the total)

| Date | Farmers | Relatives | Contract workers | Others | Total |
|------|---------|-----------|------------------|--------|-------|
| 1851 | 14.6 | 6.4 | 74.4 | 4.6 | 100.0 |
| 1901 | 20.0 | 9.6 | 58.2 | 12.2 | 100.0 |
| 1931 | 24.9 | 8.0 | 54.0 | 13.1 | 100.0 |
| 1951 | 27.2 | 9.1 | 50.0 | 13.7 | 100.0 |

*Sources*: F. D. W. Taylor, 'United Kingdom: numbers in agriculture', *Farm Economist*, 8 (1958), pp. 36–40; J. R. Bellerby, 'The distribution of manpower in agriculture and industry, 1851–1951', *Farm Economist*, 9 (1958), pp. 1–11.

time labour-force (see table 11.4) of just over 300,000 they were 61 per cent of the total; even if part-time labour is included, farmers, managers, spouses and relatives made up 58 per cent of the total numbers employed in agriculture in 1983 – 570,549 – but accounted for a much greater proportion of the hours actually worked. As in 1851, the farmer and his family make up a far greater proportion of the total labour-force in the west than in the east (see figure 11.4), but it is the declining relative importance of the hired farm-worker over the last 100 years which is of most significance. This is because, with the rise of modern machinery, all but the largest farms can be run with very little hired labour, while the use of contractors has also allowed farmers to dispense with whole-time hired labour. In 1983 there were fewer than 120,000 regular whole-time hired farm-workers, and 155,016 whole-time and part-time, compared with 1,267,000 in 1851.

WHY HAS THE LABOUR-FORCE DECLINED?

There has been surprisingly little discussion of why the labour-force has declined so dramatically since the 1850s. Indeed it has perhaps been seen to be self-evident that, as machines have become available, so farmers have dispensed with, or at least not replaced, farm-workers. But at least as important has been the powerful attraction of the cities not only for farm labourers, but for other people living in the countryside. Between 1850 and 1950 the average wage in agriculture was half that in manufacturing industry, and less than for most other jobs in the towns. With the spread of the railways, increased literacy and the greater mobility of the people even in the depths of the countryside, the towns presented a powerful magnet in the later nineteenth and the early twentieth centuries. Indeed even today the gap between agricultural and

Table 11.4 The composition of the agricultural labour-force in England and Wales, 1983 (thousands, and as a percentage)

| | Whole-time | | | Part-time | | | Grand Total |
|---|---|---|---|---|---|---|---|
| | Male | Female | Total | Male | Female | Total | |
| Regular family worker | 19,837 (6.8) | 3,230 (24.6) | 23,067 (7.6) | 7,993 (5.8) | 5,253 (4.2) | 13,246 (5.0) | 36,313 (6.4) |
| Regular hired worker | 107,742 (37.0) | 9,926 (75.4) | 117,668 (38.6) | 16,119 (11.7) | 21,229 (16.6) | 37,348 (14.1) | 155,016 (27.2) |
| All regular workers | 127,579 (43.8) | 13,156 (100.0) | 140,735 (46.2) | 24,112 (17.5) | 26,482 (20.8) | 50,594 (19.1) | 191,329 (33.5) |
| Seasonal or casual | – (0.0) | – (0.0) | – (0.0) | 47,906 (34.7) | 39,103 (30.6) | 87,009 (32.7) | 87,009 (15.3) |
| Salaried managers | 6,899 (2.4) | – (0.0) | 6,899 (2.3) | – (0.0) | – (0.0) | – (0.0) | 6,899 (1.2) |
| Farmers, directors and partners | 157,090 (53.8) | – (0.0) | 157,090 (51.5) | 65,930 (47.8) | – (0.0) | 65,930 (24.8) | 223,020 (39.1) |
| Spouses of farmers | – | – | – (0.0) | – (0.0) | 62,292 (48.6) | 62,292 (23.4) | 62,292 (10.9) |
| Total | 291,568 (100.0) | 13,156 (100.0) | 304,724 (100.0) | 137,948 (100.0) | 127,877 (100.0) | 265,775 (100.0) | 570,549 (100.0) |

Source: Ministry of Agriculture, Agricultural Statistics England and Wales 1983 (London, 1985).

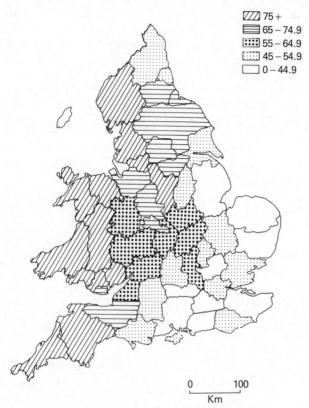

Figure 11.4 Farmers and family workers as a percentage of all workers, 1975.
*Source*: Ministry of Agriculture, *Agricultural Statistics, England and Wales 1975* (London, 1976).

industrial wages persists, although by the early 1970s the gap had diminished from one-half to four-fifths.[11]

But there have been other factors involved. Urban expansion has reduced the agricultural area by some 4 million acres since the 1870s, and even if there had been no other changes, fewer people – perhaps 15 per cent fewer – would have been needed on the land. Between 1920 and 1940 the loss of 650,000 acres to building is estimated to have led to the loss of 20,000 workers. The 1880s, 1890s, 1920s and 1930s were

11 R. Gasson, 'Industry and migration of farm workers', *Oxford Agrarian Studies*, 2 (1973), pp. 141–60; H. R. Wagstaff, 'The mobility, replacement and wage rates of farm workers', *Oxford Agrarian Studies*, 3 (1974), pp. 140–50; G. J. Tyler, 'Factors affecting the size of the labour force and the level of earnings in UK agriculture 1948–1965', *Oxford Agrarian Studies*, 1 (1972), pp. 21–45; Wagstaff, *op. cit.* (1974), pp. 140–50.

poor times for farmers, who tried to economize on labour. One way was to lay arable land down to grass and, as arable farming was more labour-intensive than most livestock production, this too would have caused a fall in labour needs; between 1870 and 1937 the arable acreage fell by 5 million, and this reduced labour needs by seven to nine men per 1,000 acres. Since 1950 the decline of mixed farming and the increasing specialization of many farms has also reduced the demand for labour. In the same period, of course, English agriculture has seen a remarkable substitution of machinery for labour, a topic that must now be discussed.[12]

12 W. A. Armstrong, 'The flight from the land' in G. E. Mingay (ed.), *The Victorian Countryside*, 1 (London, 1981), pp. 118–35; Lord Eversley, 'The decline in the number of agricultural labourers in Great Britain', *Journal of the Royal Statistical Society*, 70 (1907), pp. 217–319; F. P. Hirsch, 'Migration from the land in England and Wales', *Farm Economist*, 6 (1951), pp. 270–80; W. H. Pedley, *Labour on the Land: a study of developments between the two Great Wars* (London, 1942), p. 6.

# 12
# Power on the Land

The remarkable decline in the labour-force since 1851 has been accompanied – some would say caused – by a remarkable growth in the amount of inorganic power used on farms, while tools and implements have been replaced by machines. Although the most dramatic changes have come in the period since the end of the Second World War, the beginnings of the power and machine revolutions can be traced back to the eighteenth century.

## HUMAN AND ANIMAL MUSCLE

Until 1798 the only source of power on farms was human and animal muscle, and until the eighteenth century the principal source of draught power was the ox – horses being thought too expensive, and only used when speed was at a premium. Oxen seemed to have all the advantages: they were more powerful, their yokes were cheaper than the elaborate harness needed for the horse, they fed on grass rather than oats, and when too old for work they could be sold for meat. But the great advantage of the horse was its speed, and so between 1500 and 1800 it slowly replaced the ox. As the fallow was reduced and roots and potatoes were grown, there was more work to be done and speed became important; greater speed made more timely cultivation possible in autumn and spring, and, by allowing early sowing, both avoided the loss of a crop and increased yields. The design of lighter and less cumbersome ploughs in the early nineteenth century eased the progress of the horse. One consequence of the rise of the horse was that cattle no longer needed to be suitable for draught, and more specialized breeds for milk and meat became possible from the mid-eighteenth century. Oxen survived into the nineteenth century, notably in the Weald, the South Downs, the Cotswolds, the Wolds of Yorkshire and Lincolnshire

*Oxen ploughing on the Sussex Downs, early twentieth century.* (East Sussex County Library)

and the south-west, but they were not of national significance after the late eighteenth century.[1]

### THE AGE OF THE HORSE

In spite of the importance of steam in the nineteenth century, and the appearance of the internal combustion engine at its end, this was the age of the horse on and off the farm; the total number of horses in Britain doubled between 1811 and the 1880s, and reached a peak in the Edwardian age (see table 12.1). Thereafter the number of farm-

Table 12.1  Horses in Great Britain, 1811–1924 (thousands)

|  | 1811 | 1851 | 1871 | 1881 | 1891 | 1901 | 1911 | 1924 |
|---|---|---|---|---|---|---|---|---|
| Commercial | 251 | 264 | 444 | n.d. | 858 | 1,166 | 995 | 374 |
| Private | 236 | 277 | 414 | 585 | 500 | 600 | 537 | 549 |
| Agriculture | 800 | n.d. | 940 | 987 | 1,087 | 1,089 | 1,087 | 753 |
| Non-agriculture[a] on farms | n.d. | n.d. | 314 | 441 | 394 | 572 | 626 | 425 |
| Total | 1,287 | n.d. | 2,112 | – | 2,839 | 3,427 | 3,245 | 2,101 |

n.d. no data.
[a] Unbroken horses and non-agricultural horses kept on farms.
*Source*: F. M. L. Thompson, 'Nineteenth century horse sense', *Economic History Review*, 29 (1976), pp. 60–79.

1 G. E. Fussell, *The Farmer's Tools* (London, 1951), p. 36; J. Langdon, 'The economics of horses and oxen in medieval England', *Agricultural History Review*, 30 (1982), pp. 31–46; J. Weller, *History of the Farmstead: the development of energy sources* (London, 1982), pp. 126–7, 133; J. S. Creasey, 'The draught ox', *Heavy Horse Magazine* (March, 1977), pp. 26–9.

horses increased less dramatically, but did not begin to decline until after the First World War. Throughout the nineteenth century the horse was the principal source of power on British farms, not only for pulling implements such as the plough or the reaper, but for carrying goods in wagons to market. A considerable proportion of the country's farmland was needed to sustain the farm- and non-farm-horse population. It was estimated that 3 to 5 acres were necessary to feed a horse; if so, it would have taken over one-fifth of Britain's improved farmland to feed the total horse population. Not surprisingly, substantial fodder imports were necessary; equally important, the decline of the horse after 1920 released a considerable area – about 4 million acres – to be used for other crops.[2]

There were experiments with alternatives to the horse. Steam power was first used on a farm to drive a threshing machine in 1798, but until the 1840s horses and running water were more common. With the development of the *portable* steam threshing machine, the flail and the horse- or water-driven threshing machine were rapidly replaced, and the steam threshing machine remained the chief means of separating grain from straw until the 1940s, when it was superseded by the combine harvester. But steam was not successfully applied to any other part of farm operations, although it had revolutionary consequences in the draining of the fens (see above, pp. 28–9). However, in the 1840s there were great hopes that steam would oust the horse for ploughing, and there was much experiment. The method invested by John Fowler proved the most successful, and the number of ploughing sets in use increased steeply after 1863; but they never ploughed more than 200,000 acres in a year – less than 2 per cent of the arable area of England and Wales. They were used mainly on the bigger farms and particularly on heavy clay soils – where they were still being used by a few farmers in the 1950s – but the steam plough declined after 1914 as the tractor was introduced. Steam threshing lasted much longer.[3]

## THE TRACTOR

It was not the steam engine that replaced the horse but the internal combustion engine, initially in the tractor, which pulled not only the

2 H. Edmunds, 'The horse in modern times', *Journal of the Agricultural Society of England*, 138 (1977), pp. 52–60; J. T. Coppock, *An Agricultural Geography of Great Britain* (London, 1971), p.103; E. J. T. Collins, 'The farm horse economy of England and Wales in the early tractor age, 1900–1940', in F. M. L. Thompson (ed.), *Horses in European Economic History* (Reading, 1985), pp. 73–100; D. K. Britton, 'The disappearance of the farm horse in England and Wales', *Incorporated Statistician*, 10 (1960), pp. 79–88; R. P. Askew, 'The future changes in the number of horses in England and Wales', *Farm Economist*, 2 (1936–8), pp. 129–33.

3 Fussell, *op. cit.* (1951), p. 89; N. Harvey, *The Industrial Archaeology of Farming in England and Wales* (London, 1980), pp. 93, 101–2, 125–6; C. C. Spence, *God Speed the Plow: the coming of steam cultivation to Great Britain* (Urbana, Illinois, 1960).

plough but a variety of other implements; later many of these, such as the combine harvester, became self-propelled. The first experimental tractors were designed in the United States and Western Europe in the 1890s, and the first commercial tractor in England was produced in 1902. But very few were used in England before the First World War. Nearly all British production was exported; indeed for a short period Britain was the leading exporter of tractors. During the war tractors were imported from the United States, and later the Fordson was manufactured in the British Isles, first at Cork, then at Dagenham. The number of tractors grew slowly in the inter-war period, so slowly that their increase does not seem to have been the main cause of the decline in the number of horses on farms. The fall in the arable acreage in the 1920s and 1930s reduced the demand for horses in the east of the country, while farmers increasingly used lorries rather than horses for haulage around the farm and to market. The decline of the non-farm-horse population before the spread of the lorry, the bus and the car led to a decline in the number of breeding mares kept on farms. Indeed by the 1930s, when few experts regarded the tractor as a serious competitor to the horse, there were fears that the breeding stock available was insufficient to maintain the number of horses.[4]

The number of tractors increased very slowly between the wars. The early machines were very unreliable and few spares were available, while until 1933 they had steel wheels, not pneumatic tyres. Few implements were designed to be hitched to a tractor, rather than to a horse, and until Harry Ferguson's invention of the three-point linkage in 1934 it was difficult to connect tractor and implement. However, this advance, together with the later conversion from petroleum to diesel fuel and the introduction of power take-off points, which transformed it from being solely a means of haulage into the source of power for machines, made the tractor powerful, versatile and irresistible in the post-war period; the horse was swept away. The horsepower capacity of English tractors equalled that of horses as early as the mid-1930s, but the early tractors were rarely fully used; in 1930 horses worked 1,500 to 1,700 hours a year but tractors only 400 to 800 hours. Until the war tractor and horse were complementary rather than competitive. This ceased to be true

4 C. L. Cawood, 'The history and development of farm tractors: part 1', *Industrial Archaeology*, 7 (1970), pp. 264–91, 'Part II, 1918–51', pp. 397–423; R. Trow Smith, *Power on the Land; a centenary history of the Agricultural Engineers Association, 1875/1975* (London, 1975), p. 45; R. L. Bell and J. C. Hawkins, 'Research in agricultural engineering 1931–1981', in G. W. Cooke (ed.), *Agricultural Research 1931–1981: a history of the Agricultural Research Council* (London, 1981), pp. 203–18; Collins, *op. cit.* (1983), pp. 73–100; Askew, *op. cit.* (1936–8), pp. 129–33; T. C. Barker, 'The delayed decline of the horse in the twentieth century', in Thompson, *op. cit.* (1983), pp. 101–12; K. Blaxter, 'Power and agricultural revolution', *New Scientist* (14 February 1974), pp. 400–3; S. Plant, 'Horse displacement and land liberation resulting from the introduction of a standard tractor', *Farm Economist*, 6 (1951), pp. 301–30.

after Second World War. As engineering industires returned to peace-
time production, cheaper and more efficient tractors became available,
and until the 1970s oil was, in real terms, remarkably cheap. Farming
prosperity allowed farmers to take advantage of the new power source,
and, as the numbers of tractors increased, so the number of farm-horses
declined, until in 1959 the agricultural census ceased to record them.
By the 1970s there were only about 4,000 farm-horses in England and
Wales. Since the 1960s the number of tractors has not increased but
the horsepower of tractors has risen. In the 1930s the average capacity
of British tractors was 10 horsepower, in the 1950s, 24 horsepower, and
by the 1970s, 70 per cent of those sold exceeded 50 horsepower.[5]

POWER ON THE FARMSTEAD

Until the late nineteenth century tasks done on the farmstead were
largely undertaken by human muscle; milking cows, grinding oil-cake,
cutting feeds and feeding animals were all done by hand. At the end of
the century the steam engine, used for threshing grain and for other
tasks, began to be supplemented by petrol-driven stationary engines,
although the numbers were few: in 1908 only 7 per cent of British farms
had any form of stationary power. The revolutionary change on the
farmstead, as distinct from in the fields, came with the use of electricity.
In 1926 only 20 farms in England and Wales were supplied with
electricity. The National Grid was established in the same year, and by
1941–2, 27 per cent of farms were connected, by 1961 the National
Grid supplied 85 per cent of all farms, and now virtually all are
connected. This has been of major importance, for milking machines are
nearly all powered by electricity, while the large-scale production of
poultry and pigs is dependent upon ventilation and heating run mainly
by electricity.[6]

This century has seen a remarkable increase in the use of power, both
stationary and mobile, on farms in England and Wales. The total amount
of stationary and non-animal draught power increased tenfold between
1908 and 1939, threefold between 1939 and 1948. No equivalent
estimate has been made for the post-war period, although United

---

5 Cawood, *op. cit.* (1970), pp. 397–423; E. H. Whetham, 'The mechanization of
British farming 1910–1945', *Journal of Agricultural Economics*, 21 (1970), pp. 317–31; D.
K. Britton and I. F. Keith, 'A note on the statistics of farm power supplies in Great
Britain', *Farm Economist*, 6 (1950), pp. 163–70; Collins, *op. cit.* (1985), pp. 73–100; R.
A. Dudman, 'Of horse and tractors', *The Farm Economist*, 6 (1950), pp. 181–7; Edmunds,
*op. cit.* (1977), pp. 52-60.

6 Weller, *op. cit* (1982), p. 126; I. R. Winship, 'The gas engine in British agriculture,
1870–1925', *History of Technology*, 60 (1984), pp. 181–204; Ministry of Agriculture and
Fisheries, *National Farm Survey of England and Wales: a summary report* (London, 1946), p.
107.

LORD WILLOUGHBY D'ERESBY'S STEAM PLOUGH, AT GRIMSTHORPE.

### PLOUGHING BY STEAM.
(*To the Editor.*)

As you have already published (p. 396, vol. XVI) a notice of the Steam Plough of Lord Willoughby d'Eresby, it may be interesting to your readers to be informed of the progress which has been made in the application of such a novel and difficult application of steam power. Having had the opportunity of examining the working of the Steam Plough at Grimsthorpe, I am enabled, with his Lordship's permission, to lay the result of my observations before your readers. In the early trials a portable steam-engine was applied in the centre of the field, and the motion conveyed to a capstan fixed in the ground, on which rope was coiled. To each end of this rope ploughs were attached, which were drawn alternately towards the engine by steam power, and from the engine towards the hedge by horses. To dispense entirely with the horses, two capstans were next employed, one at each end of the field, and the ropes were endless, so that the ploughs were moved in both directions by steam power.

In the present improved arrangement two engines are employed, one at each end of the field, as represented in the Sketch, the capstans being attached to the engines. The ploughs are made double-ended, and are drawn alternately by each engine along the field, so that, whilst the rope is being wound upon the capstan of one engine, it is being unwound off the capstan of the other, and *vice versâ*. Each engine, as it is alternately idle, is moved along a temporary tramway, formed of planks laid along the side of the hedge. To prevent the rope dragging in the furrow, six small wooden frames are dropped into the furrow, and provided with rollers over which the rope runs. Two ploughs are arranged together, each turning a furrow of nine inches. With a field 180 yards long between the engines, the ploughing of each furrow 18 inches wide occupies 2½ minutes, the ploughs moving at rather less than 1½ miles per hour. Allowing for the time lost in shifting the plough, this gives 4 acres per day at the present slow speed, which I see no difficulty in increasing to 4 miles per hour, when the men, who are only agricultural labourers, shall have acquired greater dexterity in managing the engines and ploughs.

To produce this result there are required two men to drive engines, four to shift ploughs and engines, one to hold plough, and three boys at trucks, and 2½ cwt. of coke. Taking the wages of men and boys at 18s. per day, and the coke at 8s., or total 26s., the cost per acre will be 6s., which is about one-half the cost of ploughing by horse-power, with the advantage of doing it in half the time. In estimating, however, the pecuniary advantages of steam-ploughing, it must be viewed in connexion with a general system of farm machinery.

To such of your readers as desire to judge for themselves of the value of this invention, I recommend a visit to Grimsthorpe, where Mr. Scott, who has charge of the Steam Plough, informs me it may be seen at work on Monday, Tuesday, and Wednesday in each week. The farm can boast of a stud of four beautiful portable engines, constructed by Mr. Gooch, of Swindon; two of which are at work, either for Lord Willoughby's own use or that of his tenants, thrashing, grinding, sawing timber and stone, making cutters and tenons for the cottages, &c. The nearest stations to Grimsthorpe are Spalding, Peterborough, and Stamford.

In conclusion, I may express my conviction that all those preliminary difficulties, which, from the expense attending their removal, deter most persons from experiments of this class, have been overcome, and that the Steam Plough is now a "great fact," which may be taken up with advantage by our agricultural engineers, who have in this case no patent right to pay for. I am, sir, your obedient servant,

W. REID WHITEHEAD, C.E.

Cornhill, June 4, 1852.

*Steam ploughing on Lord Willoughby d'Eresby's home farm at Grimsthorpe in South Lincolnshire in 1852* (The Mansell Collection)

*Steam Ploughing. Fowler's set was the most successful and remained in use until the 1940s. Here a set is seen ploughing c. 1900.* (BBC Hulton Picture Library)

Kingdom farm-fuel consumption is estimated to have increased fourfold between 1938 and 1974. The power available *per man* has risen dramatically, from approximately 1 hp per man in 1910 – mainly horses – to 3 hp in 1939 and 50 hp in 1980, for not only has power risen but labour has fallen.[7]

MACHINES, TOOLS AND IMPLEMENTS

The distinction between a machine and a tool or an implement is not easy to make; machines, perhaps, may be defined as having moving parts. The first machine to be used on British farms was the threshing machine, followed by Patrick Bell's reaper in the late 1820s. But this was far from being the first advance in farming technology or the first adoption of a labour-saving device. Although saving labour and thus cost was probably the main motive for adopting machines or using improved implements or tools, there were other reasons for such changes. Not the least was the need to make labour less arduous, or to enable tasks to be carried out more quickly; this in turn allowed, for example, more timely sowing or harvesting, and thus higher yields.

Although cost saving is the prime motive of the adoption of machinery, replacing labour by machines is not always the cheapest way of carrying out a task. Thus Patrick Bell's reaper worked reasonably efficiently in the 1820s; but at that time labour was abundant in south-east England, and the use of the sickle or scythe cheaper, and, given its experimental nature, more reliable, than a machine. Only after the 1840s, when labour shortages became apparent, did farmers turn to a reaper for the cereal harvest, and it was the American reaper of Cyrus McCormick and not that of Patrick Bell that was adopted. A great many apparently useful innovations took some time to be taken up by farmers, for a variety of reasons. Jethro Tull's drill, for example, designed in the early eighteenth century, did not work very well in practice, and it was not until the 1780s that a workable drill was available. The early tractors were viewed with suspicion, much of it justified, for they were unreliable, poorly serviced and often dangerous to drive. There was half a century between the first commercial tractor of 1902 and the 1950s, when it replaced the horse. Although saving labour has doubtless been a major incentive for the acceptance of new machines, at many periods it has been the shortage of labour that has forced farmers to adopt them, often before they were working properly.

Changes in implements were increasing labour productivity long before 1945, and there were improvements well before the first machines. It

7 Britton and Keith, *op. cit.* (1950), pp. 163–70; Sir F. Engledow and L. Amey, *Britian's Farming Future* (London, 1980), p. 107; K. Blaxter, *op. cit.* (1974), pp. 400–3.

may be useful to note first what sort of tools and implements farmers possessed before the age of machines. The inventories of Yorkshire farmers in the late seventeenth century showed that most of them owned a plough, a harrow and carts with two wheels; forks, spades and mallets to break up clods; a flail for threshing and a fan to sort chaff from the grain; scythes and sickles for cutting grain and grass; rakes and forks for hay-making, and churns and cheese presses for the dairy.[8] The progress since then is perhaps best described by taking the major stages in the farmer's year.

PREPARING THE SEED BED

Until the 1950s farmers believed that the pulverization of the soil and the formation of a good tilth was an essential part of successful crop production; they were probably influenced, however indirectly, by Jethro Tull, who thought that pulverization increased the supply of plant nutrients. At any rate much of the farmer's year was spent ploughing in the autumn and, for spring-sown crops, again in the spring; with breaking down the clods left by the plough to give a fine seed bed; with sowing the crop; and by weeding before and after the sowing of the crop. The most common plough until the 1960s was the mouldboard; the coulter cut the sod, the share cut beneath the sod and through weeds, and the mouldboard inverted the sod. Until the eighteenth century ploughs were heavy, cumbersome and, except for the share and coulter, made from wood. From the early eighteenth century they were much better designed, and iron eventually replaced wood. The clods left by the plough were broken up by sixteenth-century farmers with mallets and harrowed with thorn-bushes nailed to a wooden frame. But the roller was introduced and the harrow improved, and by the nineteenth century they were all iron. But perhaps the crucial invention of these early centuries was that of the drill. In Jethro Tull's time seed was spread – or broadcast – into the seed bed by hand. Tull's drill planted seed in rows, but it was not very practical, and it was Cooke's improved drill of the 1780s that led to the replacement of broadcasting, slow although this was. In 1800 most seed was still broadcast; in 1815 the drill was common only in Northumberland and East Anglia, and it had not replaced broadcasting in most of England until the 1850s. Tull also designed a horse-drawn hoe, in effect a plough without a mouldboard or coulter, which could be pulled between the drilled rows of seed to cut weeds. Like the drill, it was little used in the eighteenth century and spread south from the north-east of England only after 1815; it was not

8 W. Harwood Long, 'The development of mechanization in English farming', *Agricultural History Review*, 11 (1963), pp. 15–26.

*Broadcasting seed, early twentieth century.* (Supplied by Author)

widely employed until after the 1840s. Horse-hoeing was of course supplemented by much hand-hoeing until the 1950s.[9]

9 G. Marshall, 'The Rotherham Plough', *Tools and Tillage*, 3 (1976), pp. 150–67; Fussell, *op. cit.* (1951), p. 105; R. Wilkes, 'The diffusion of drill husbandry', in *Agricultural Improvement: medieval and modern*, ed. W.E. Minchinton, Exeter Papers in Economic History (1981), pp. 65–94; T. H. Marshall, 'Jethro Tull and the new husbandry of the eighteenth century', *Economic History*, 2 (1929), pp. 41–60.

In the 1830s a great number of other farm implements began to be produced by the new agricultural machinery industry. Not only drills and horse-hoes, but rollers, clod-crushers and harrows with iron tines were continuously improved but not fundamentally changed. It is difficult to trace the adoption of these implements – there are no statistics on farmers' possession of machinery and implements until 1942 – but an indirect measure of their adoption can be obtained from the sales of second-hand implements. In Oxfordshire – which was not a particularly backward county – the widespread use of most implements did not occur until well into the nineteenth century.[10]

The preparation of the seed bed remained largely unchanged in principle until after the Second World War. Then the combined drill allowed fertilizer and seed to be drilled at the same time, and later precision drilling made possible the accurate spacing of sugar-beet seed. Much before this, in the late nineteenth century, multiple furrow ploughs had replaced the single share. But in the 1950s the whole underlying principle of seed-bed preparation was undermined. Research in the United States showed that repeated cultivation reduced soil fertility and damaged soil structure. Indeed the only value of ploughing was to destroy weeds. But by the 1950s herbicides had been produced that could do this without any cultivation at all. Some farmers, on suitable soils, then turned to new techniques of sowing. Ploughing was much reduced, the minimum of cultivation was undertaken – not with a mouldboard plough but with tines or discs – and then seed was directly drilled into the thinly disturbed soil.[11]

HARVESTING

Cereals were the main crop before the mid-nineteenth century and have recovered this dominance in the last 30 years (see above, p. 52). The harvesting of these crops was always time-consuming, and their mechanization is a good guide to the general progress of mechanization in English farming.

In the late eighteenth century harvesting wheat required a great many people and a series of different stages. Wheat was cut with a sickle, leaving straw about a foot high; the grain was gathered into a sheaf by followers, who tied it with twine. It was then stooked to dry before being loaded onto a wagon and taken to a barn. After Christmas, in the slack time of the agricultural year, the grain was separated from the straw by

10 J. R. Walton, 'Mechanization in agriculture: a study of the adoption process', in H. S. A. Fox and R. A. Butlin (eds), *Change in the Countryside: essays on rural England 1500–1900*, Institute of British Geographers, Special Publication no. 10 (1977), pp. 23–47.

11 H. C. Pereira, 'Agricultural science and the traditions of tillage', *Outlook on Agriculture*, 8 (1975), pp. 211–12.

thrashing with a flail – two lengths of wood joined by leather. The harvest in the field had to be carried out very rapidly to prevent any loss of yield and needed a large labour-force. Threshing, in contrast, was carried out in an almost leisurely fashion over quite a long period. For the first 35 years of the nineteenth century there was little advance in this method of harvesting, which was barely changed from the Middle Ages. However, between the 1830s and the 1870s crop yields increased; the heavier crop needed more labour, and in the 1830s and 1840s there began to be labour shortages during the harvest.[12]

From the 1850s the full-time labour-force began to fall as the higher wages of the towns attracted agricultural workers away from the country, and the number of casual labourers available declined as urban wages rose. Harvest wages began to rise faster than prices and there was every incentive to use machinery. At first it was not machines but improved implements that solved the problem. The scythe, long used for cutting hay, oats and barley, began to replace the sickle in the wheat harvest, reducing labour needs by a quarter. More fundamental was the adoption of the reaper-binder. McCormick's reaper had been displayed at the Great Exhibition of 1851 and was quite rapidly adopted. In 1878 the self-binding function was added to the cutting of the grain, eliminating

*A self-binder harvesting wheat in Gloucestershire in the 1930s. Sheaves are thrown out to the right and stooked by hand.* (University of Reading, Institute of Agricultural History and Museum of English Rural Life)

12 E. J. T. Collins, *Sickle to Combine: a review of harvest techniques from 1801 to the present day* (Reading, 1967).

*The elevator introduced from the United States in the late nineteenth century made the building of hay-stacks and wheat ricks much easier.* (BBC Hulton Picture Library)

the need for a follower to tie the sheaves; the reaper-binder spread rapidly in the 1890s and by the 1920s had long ousted the reaper. The sheaves were still stacked in rows to dry, but were now stored in ricks rather than barns, thatched against the weather. The use of the elevator, which like the reaper and the reaper-binder was an American invention, eased the making of these ricks. The proportion of the area cut by reaper rose, compared with that in the rest of Europe, very rapidly, from zero in 1851 to 25 per cent in 1871, 80 per cent in 1900 and, by the 1930s, when the first combines were at work in the English countryside, to 95 per cent. Rapid as was this rate of adoption, it was slow compared with that in the United States, possibly because much of the arable land of England and Wales was on poorly drained ridge and furrow, which retarded the use of machines.[13]

13 E. J. T. Collins, 'Harvest technology and labour supply in Britain', *Economic History Review*, 22 (1969), pp. 453–75; 'The Age of Machinery', in G. E. Mingay (ed.), *The Victorian Countryside*, 1 (London, 1981), pp. 200–13; P. A. David, 'The landscape and the machine: technical interrelatedness, land tenure and the mechanization of the corn harvest in Victorian Britain', in D. N. McCloskey (ed.), *Essays on a Mature Economy: Britain after 1840* (London, 1971), pp. 145–214.

### THE THRESHING MACHINE

The threshing of grain, unlike its harvesting, was not performed under pressure; nor was it an expensive process, for in early nineteenth-century England there was an abundance of labour seeking work in the winter. Yet the first threshing machine was constructed in Scotland in 1786 and steam power was first applied in Denbigh in 1798, long before the first reaper. Initially, however, it was powered by horses or water and made little progress outside the north-east; in the south-east labourers were abundant, and if farmers did not employ them to thresh with the flail they had to support them on poor relief through the rates. As the machine was slowly adopted in the south-east, so opposition from labourers grew, culminating in the Captain Swing riots of 1830–2, when 200 machines were destroyed. This delayed their adoption for some time, and it was not until the decline of the agricultural labour-force began to be felt in the 1840s and 1850s that the threshing machine was widely taken up. In 1850 only half the harvest in the south-east was threshed by machine, the rest by flail, and most of the machines were driven by horsepower. However the development of the portable steam threshing machine changed all this, and by the 1880s nearly all the harvest was threshed by steam machines. It was labour scarcity, and also the extreme slowness of the flail, that finally led to the triumph of

*Steam threshing in north Berkshire (Nalder and Nalder, Challow nr. Wantage).* The engine is a Davey Paxman Colchester. (University of Reading, Institute of Agricultural History and Museum of English Rural Life)

the thresher. It might take up to 40 days to thresh the produce of ten acres of corn with a flail.[14]

The replacement of the sickle and scythe by the reaper-binder, and the flail by the threshing machine, led to a considerable increase in labour productivity. In the 1840s most of the harvest was still brought in with hand tools, and the cultivation and harvest of one acre of corn took 11 days. By 1900 the use of the horse, the seed drill, the reaper and the steam thresher reduced this time to only $7\frac{1}{2}$ days per acre, an increase in productivity of 70 per cent.[15]

### THE COMBINE HARVESTER

From the 1880s to the 1940s the majority of the English grain acreage was harvested with a reaper-binder, stacked by hand, built into ricks with the aid of an elevator and then steam threshed. But the machine that was to perform all these tasks, the combine harvester, was first tried in the Mid-west of the United States in the 1850s; an improved version drawn by numerous horses was in use in California in the 1880s, but not employed in the wheat belt of the Great Plains until the 1920s; the first combines in England were tried in Gloucestershire in 1927, almost a century after the first use of Patrick Bell's reaper. The combine was initially drawn by tractors, but by the 1950s most of them were not only much larger but self-propelled. The diffusion of the combine was very slow before the war. The early machines were not very reliable and were very expensive, and it was estimated that they were not economical if a farmer had fewer than 300 acres of corn; by the 1960s, however, rising farm wages had lowered this threshold to 100 acres, and the post-war period saw a remarkable increase in their numbers and a comparable decline of the reaper-binder. Reaper-binders remained surprisingly common, however; there were still 65,000 of them in use in Great Britain in 1965, mainly in areas where fields were small, only small totals of grain were grown, or on sloping land where the bigger combines were impracticable. They remained especially important in the west, where the combine had made little progress in the early stages of its diffusion. Since the 1960s the number of combines has not increased, but their power and capacity has.[16]

14 E. J. T. Collins, 'The diffusion of the threshing machine in Britain, 1790–1880', *Tools and Tillage*, 2 (1972), pp. 16–33; N. E. Fox, 'The spread of the threshing machine in central southern England', *Agricultural History Review*, 26 (1978),pp. 26–8; S. MacDonald, 'The progress of the early threshing machine', *Agricultural History Review*, 23 (1975), pp. 63–77.

15 Collins, *op. cit.* (1981), pp. 200–13.

16 Collins, *op. cit.* (1969), pp. 453–75; G. E. Jones, 'The diffusion of agricultural innovations', in I. Burton and R. W. Kates (eds), *Readings in Resource Management and Conservation* (Chicago, 1970), pp. 475–92.

*A modern combine harvester in Nottinghamshire, 1980s.* (Author)

### LONG-TERM PRODUCTIVITY GAINS IN HARVESTING

The mechanization of grain led to major changes in productivity in farming long before the age of the combine harvester, although the precise extent of this increase is in doubt. F. W. Bateson has estimated that between 1830, when grain production was still entirely with the aid of hand tools, and the 1930s, when tractors, drills and combine harvesters were in use, the hours required to produce one acre of grain fell from 55.7 to 3.3. E. J. T. Collins has calculated that between 1800 and 1965 labour productivity in the grain harvest rose twentyfold, while J. S. Nix's data show that labour requirements to produce an acre of wheat or barley in 1960 were only one-quarter of those in 1930, and by 1983 only one-eleventh (see table 12.2)[17]

### RAISING THE ROOTS

The potato was not a major field crop until well into the nineteenth century, sugar-beet not until the 1920s; it is not surprising therefore

17 F. W. Bateson, 'Farm sizes and layouts', in F. W. Bateson (ed.), *Towards a Socialist Agriculture: studies by a group of Fabians* (London, 1946), pp. 106-23; E. J. T. Collins, *op. cit.* (1969), pp. 453–75.

Table 12.2   Labour requirements for cash crops, 1930–1983 (man-hours per acre)

| Crop | 1930 | 1950 | 1960 | 1983 Average | 1983 Premium |
|---|---|---|---|---|---|
| Potatoes | 215 | 195 | 140 | 50 | 37 |
| Sugar-beet | 235 | 180 | 120 | 27 | 12 |
| Wheat | 53 | 33 | $17\frac{1}{2}$ | $5\frac{1}{2}$ | $3\frac{1}{2}$ |
| Barley | 54 | 23 | $12\frac{1}{2}$ | 5 | 3 |

*Sources*: 1930, 1950 and 1960 are from J. S. Nix, 'Labour for cash crops, 1930–1970', *Agriculture*, 68 (1961), pp. 119–25. The figures for 1983 are from J. S. Nix, *Farm Management Textbook* (Ashford, 15/1985). Average requirements refer to the whole range of farming conditions and farm size; premium are the requirements on larger farms with good husbandry.

that efforts to mechanize both their sowing and harvesting were later than those for the cereal crops. In addition, they were far more difficult to harvest, as the mature root is underground, while planting potato tubers mechanically is more difficult than drilling grain seed.

Until the mid-nineteenth century the potato was grown mainly by smallholders and planted and harvested by hand. However, from then on it was increasingly cultivated on large arable farms and in large acreages, and there was a growing incentive to mechanize. There were experiments with mechanical diggers for harvesting in the 1870s, and these were adopted in parts of Lancashire in the 1890s, followed later by potato planters. Potato spinners, which spun the potato to the surface where it was picked by hand, began to be replaced by harvesters, which dug and picked up the potato, in the 1960s; although there has been a substantial decline in labour needs in potato production since the 1930s, like sugar-beet, the crop still requires far more labour per acre than do the cereals (see table 12.2). Although sugar-beet harvesters were known as early as 1931, the mechanization of the harvest has been completed only since the 1950s. But there has also been dramatic labour-saving elsewhere in the production process. Until the 1950s sugar-beet seed gave a cluster of seedlings, which had to be greatly reduced to allow one to grow – a form of weeding known as singling. The introduction of monogerm seed has thus greatly reduced labour need.[18]

### LIVESTOCK AND MECHANIZATION

The mechanization of livestock production has for the most part come later than that of most of the crops grown in England. The fodder crops

18 A. Mutch, 'The mechanization of the harvest in south west Lancashire', *Agricultural History Review*, 29 (1981), pp. 125–32; Bell and Hawkins, *op. cit.* (1981), pp. 203–18; Harvey, *op. cit.* (1980),p. 105.

proved particularly difficult to mechanize. Indeed it was the high labour cost of the turnip, swede and mangold crops, which required large labour inputs, that led to their decline from the 1880s (see above, pp. 53–5). It is only in the 1970s that it has been possible to mechanize the harvest of the fodder roots and make their production economically viable again. Grass remains, as it always has been, the major source of feed for livestock in Great Britain, and part of the summer grass growth has always been cut and kept as hay for winter feed. In the mid-nineteenth century hay-making required a great deal of labour in a very short period. Three or four consecutive, dry, sunny days are necessary to make good hay. The grass was first cut with a scythe, then gathered into windrows with a fork and rake to dry, and then forked into haycocks, which were scattered to dry before recocking. Finally, the grass was made into haystacks. This process was partially mechanized at the same time as the cereal harvest. A horse-drawn mower, working on much the same principle as the reaper, began to replace the scythe in the 1860s. In Lancashire, for example, 17 per cent of farms had a mower in 1867, 64 per cent in 1877, and 75 per cent in 1881, while in Oxfordshire over half all farms had a horse-rake in the 1880s. In contrast, in many parts of Wales the scythe was not replaced until well into the twentieth century. Once the tedder had been added to these implements the means of hay-making remained largely unchanged until the middle of the twentieth century. Since then the principal change has been not so much any technical advance in machinery, but the steady change from hay-making to silage-making, a process that requires only cutting and rapid transfer to the silo.[19]

Perhaps the principal change in livestock production has been the mechanization of milking, and this has become effective only since the end of the Second World War. Until this century a pail and a stool was all that was needed to milk by hand. In 1895 a milking machine called the Thistle was invented in Scotland. It had to be considerably modified before it became effective and was very slowly adopted in England and Wales. By 1939 only one-fifth of the herds were milked by machine, but after the war mechanization spread rapidly. By 1975 all but 3 per cent of all cows were mechanically milked. Dairying – and other branches of livestock production – have also benefited from further technical changes. In milking the design of milking parlours and the management of cows has been radically changed, while the milk-churn has been replaced by the bulk tanker. Dairy and other cattle have also benefited by improved systems of feeding; semi-automated feeding has greatly increased the number of animals that one man can manage. Nearly 40 million tons of forage, concentrates and bedding for livestock have to be

19 Mutch, *op. cit.* (1981), pp. 125–32; Walton, *op. cit.* (1977), pp. 23–47; Harvey, *op. cit.* (1980), pp. 103–4; Fussell, *op. cit.* (1951), pp. 139–41, 147–8.

moved each year in England and Wales and the partial mechanization of this has led to marked, if not obvious, savings in labour.[20]

SUMMARY

Until the middle of the nineteenth century there was only a slow increase in the power per man on English farms as the horse replaced oxen and then the steam engine began to be used for threshing. After 1850, however, the labour-force declined and steampower was more widely used and supplemented by petrol-driven engines at the end of the century. In the twentieth century the increase in the power per man was slow until the Second World War, in spite of the adoption of the tractor and the spread of electricity. It is only since the end of the Second World War that there has been such a major increase in power per man.

In contrast, while mechanization has been dramatic since the Second World War – only a few vegetables and soft fruit remain dependent upon hand harvesting – there had been very considerable advances long before 1945. The mechanization of threshing began in 1798, of harvesting grain in 1851, and of grass only a little later, while the early use of milking machines dates from the end of the nineteenth century. Thus considerable gains in labour productivity were possible long before the massive application of power in the post-war period.

20 Whetham, *op. cit.* (1970), pp. 317–31; D. J. B. Calverley, 'Mechanization in livestock husbandry', *Journal of the Royal Agricultural Society of England*, 128 (1967), pp. 69–76; P. A. Clough, 'Systems of machine milking', *Journal of the Royal Agricultural Society of England*, 132 (1971), pp. 205–14; Harvey, *op. cit.* (1980), p.107; Bell and Hawkins, *op. cit.* (1981), pp. 73–100.

# 13
# Types of Farming and Agricultural Regions

THE REGIONS AND TYPES OF FARMING

So far the changes in farming have been traced by considering different aspects of the systematic agricultural geography of England and Wales – land use, crop patterns, livestock distributions, land tenure and farm size. But this is not the only or indeed the most common approach. Since the late eighteenth century many contemporary writers have used the regional approach to describe the farming of the country, and historians and geographers have used this method in explaining both the past and present.

Although there is much description of agriculture in the topographies of writers from the sixteenth century onwards, the first comprehensive account of the farming of Britain came during the Napoleonic Wars. Fears of food shortages led to the formation of the Board of Agriculture, which collected some agricultural statistics and commissioned accounts of the agriculture of every county in England and Wales. The reports are of very variable quality, but many of them adopted a regional approach to a description and analysis of farming. For the most part the regions were topographic divisions or very simple soil regions – this was at a time when the first geological maps were being prepared but were probably not widely known; most writers assumed that the primary cause of regional differences in the type of farming were differences in the environment.[1]

This tradition of environmentally based regional description was maintained in the mid-nineteenth century; the Royal Agricultural Society

1 F. V. Emery, 'English regional studies from Aubrey to Defoe', *Geographical Journal*, 124 (1976), pp. 315–25; H. C. Darby, 'Some early ideas on the agricultural regions of England', *Agricultural History Review*, 2 (1954), pp. 30–47; D. B. Grigg, 'The changing agricultural geography of England: a commentary on the sources available for the reconstruction of the agricultural geography of England, 1770–1850', *Transactions of the Institute of British Geographers*, 41 (1967), pp. 73–96.

offered prizes for the best essays on the agriculture of the counties of England and Wales and 38 winning essays were published in the society's journal between 1845 and 1869. By then soil and geological maps were becoming available, and most of the essays organized their description of farming on the basis of these regions, although the terms district or division were used rather than region.[2]

After the 1860s there were few attempts at the regional description of English farming: although the reports of Select Committees on Agricultural Depression do contain much local information, they were not organized in a regional manner. An attempt just before the First World War by P. M. Roxby to provide a comprehensive regional account of the agricultural geography of England and Wales was never completed.[3] However, in the 1930s the regional approach became common again, most notably in the Land Utilization Survey country reports. L. D. Stamp organized the mapping of the land use of the whole of the United Kingdom,and maps at the 1″ scale were published. There was also a memoir on the agricultural geography of each county; most of these contain a map and description of land-use regions. Stamp's summary of this work, *The Land of Britain: its use and misuse*, also contains the first map of the type of farming areas of England and Wales. This was undertaken by the Economics Branch of the Ministry of Agriculture and completed in the summer of 1939, although the map was not generally available until published at the 1 :625,000 scale in the National Planning Series. Two principles were used to classify areas. First, areas were designated arable if over two-thirds of the land was in crops, pastoral if less than one-third; the remaining areas were described as intermediate. Second, the dominant enterprise or enterprises were identified. A combination of these two criteria gave 17 different types of farming – five pastoral, six intermediate and six arable – and some 200 separate areas were shown on the map; figure 13.1 is a simplified version.[4] This map was widely used until in the 1960s the Ministry of Agriculture began to classify farms on a new basis, which led to several attempts to produce new maps of type of farming areas. The two processes –

2 Darby *op. cit.* (1954), pp. 30–47; Grigg, *op. cit.* (1967), pp. 73–96.

3 P. M. Roxby, 'The agricultural geography of England on a regional basis', *Geographical Teacher*, 7 (1914), pp. 316–21; A. Angelbeck, 'The agricultural geography of England on a regional basis, pt. III: Staffordshire', *Geographical Teacher*, 8 (1915), pp. 154–63; E. M. Ward, 'The agricultural geography of England on a regional basis, pt. II: Yorkshire', *Geographical Teacher*, 7 (1914), pp. 382–94; 8 (1915), pp. 27–38.

4 J. P. Maxton, ed., *Regional Types of British Agriculture* (London, 1936); E. C. Sykes, 'The agricultural geography of Northumberland', *Geography*, 18 (1933), pp. 269–81; W. Smith, 'The agricultural geography of the Fylde', *Geography*, 22 (1937), pp. 29–43; L. D. Stamp, *The Land of Britain: its use and misuse* (London, 1950), pp. 299–314: the titles of the county memoirs and their authors are listed on pp. 455–9.

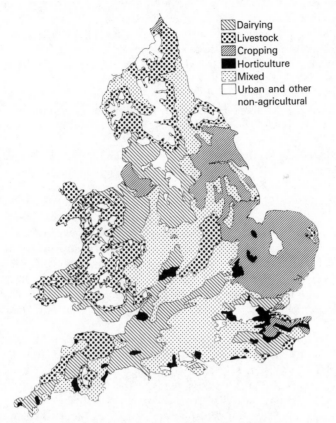

Figure 13.1   Type of farming areas, 1939.
*Source*: Simplification of map in L. D. Stamp, *The Land of Britain: its use and misuse* (London, 1950), p. 301.

classifying farms and demarcating type of farming areas – should be distinguished.[5]

From 1963 to 1976 the Ministry of Agriculture published each year a great deal of information on types of farms. Farms – or a sample of farms – which returned forms to the annual census were allocated to one of 13 different types upon the basis of the predominant enterprise. An enterprise is a product, for example pigs or cereals, and the predominant enterprise was ascertained by calculating the number of

5 L. Napolitan and C. J. Brown, 'A type of farming classification of agricultural holdings in England and Wales according to enterprise patterns', *Journal of Agricultural Economics*, 15 (1962), pp. 595–617; Ministry of Agriculture, *Farm Classification in England and Wales* (London, 1963–76).

man-hours spent in a year on that product. If more than 50 per cent of all man-hours were spent on an enterprise then the holding was allocated to that class; if no one enterprise accounted for 50 per cent or more of the man-hours then the holding was described as mixed. The results of this classification were published annually in *Farm Classification*, where the average characteristics of each type – land use, farm size, number of livestock and so forth – were printed for the country as a whole and for each of the Ministry of Agriculture's divisions. In addition, in the parish summaries of the annual census, the number of holdings in each class in the parish was recorded.[6]

In 1980 the Ministry of Agriculture changed the basis of farm classification in order to be consistent with the European Community classification. The importance of an enterprise is now defined by the Standard Gross Margin, a measure of the value of output; farms are allocated to a class if an enterprise accounts for more than two-thirds of the value of total output, or if it is less than two-thirds but more than one-third and also the leading enterprise. The Ministry now publishes each year the number of holdings and the area they occupy in each of six types – Pigs and Poultry, Cropping, Dairying, Horticulture and Upland and Lowland Cattle and Sheep; there is no Mixed Farming category. Further details on each type are published in *Farm Incomes in England*.[7]

The data collected by the Ministry of Agriculture on farm classification have been used to produce a number of maps of types of farming areas in England and Wales. The first of these, by B. M. Church and associates, uses the 10 km grid squares of the Ordnance Survey as the basic mapping unit; a sample of holdings in the 1968 census for each square was analysed and the square allocated to one of 13 enterprise types. In figure 13.2 the number of types has been reduced to five to make the map comparable with that of K. Anderson. Anderson used the 1970 census data for the 374 ADAS (Agricultural Development and Advisory Service) districts as his base. He then allocated each of these districts to one of ten types of farming on the basis of the similarity of the agricultural characteristics of each district. In figure 13.3 the ten types are also reduced to five to make them more easily comparable with Church's map and also with the 1939 map by the Ministry of Agriculture.[8]

6 Ministry of Agriculture, *Farm Classification in England and Wales* (London, 1963).

7 D. Grigg, 'Types of farming in England and Wales', *Geography Review*, 1 (1988), pp. 20–4; Ministry of Agriculture, *United Kingdom Agricultural Statistics 1983* (London, 1984); Welsh Office, *Welsh Agricultural Statistics 1984*, 6 (Cardiff, 1984); Ministry of Agriculture, *Farm Incomes in England 1984*, Farm Income Series no. 37 (London, 1985), Appendix C, pp. 55–7; *Official Journal of the European Communities* (5 June 1978).

8 B. M. Church, D. A. Boyd, J. A. Evans and J. I. Sadler, 'A type of farming map based on agricultural census data', *Outlook on Agriculture*, 5 (1968), pp. 191–6; K. E. Anderson, 'An agricultural classification of England and Wales', *Tijdschrift voor economische en sociale geographie*, 66 (1975), pp. 148–58.

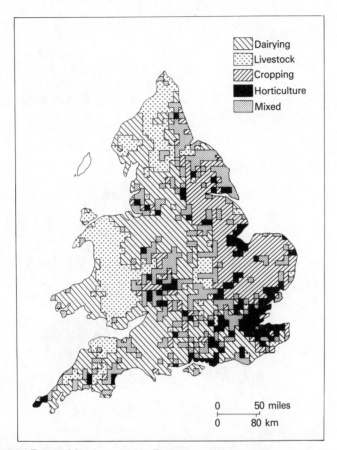

Figure 13.2 Types of farming areas in England and Wales, 1968.
*Source*: B. M. Church, D. A. Boyd, J. A. Evans and J. I. Sadler, 'A type of farming map based on agricultural census data', *Outlook on Agriculture*, 5 (1968), pp. 191–6.

The Ministry of Agriculture has published a very detailed series of maps of type of farming using the parish summaries for 1968. Every holding in the parish is allocated to a type on the basis of the number of standard man-days (see above, p. 170). Two series of maps were published at 1 : 250,000; in one series each holding in each parish was shown by a circle, its type identified by colour and the size of the holding in acres indicated by the size of the circle. The second series of maps showed type of farming by colour, the size of farm again proportional to the size of the circle, but in this case size is measured by the number of standard man-days worked in a year.[9]

All these maps are now out of date. The basis of classifying farms has been greatly changed, but the data currently published by the Ministry

9 Ministry of Agriculture, Fisheries and Food, *Types of Farm Maps: explanatory note*, Agricultural Development and Advisory Service, Land and Farm Research Group (1974).

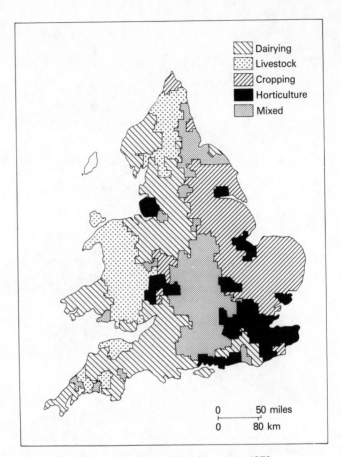

Figure 13.3   Types of farming areas, 1970.
*Source*: Simplification of map by K. Anderson, 'Agricultural classification of England and Wales',
*Tijdschrift voor economische en sociale geographie*, 66 (1975), pp. 148–58.

does not allow a map showing type of farming to be produced. However, it does allow a map, using county data, of the relative importance of each of six types to be constructed (see figure 13.4).[10]

### MODERN DISTRIBUTIONS

Although there have been striking changes in the agriculture of England and Wales since 1939, the type of farming pattern has remained

10 Grigg, *op. cit.* (1988), pp. 20–4; B. G. Jackson, C. S. Barnard and F. G. Sturrock, *The Pattern of Farming in the Eastern Counties*, Occasional Papers no. 8, Farm Economics Branch, School of Agriculture, University of Cambridge (Cambridge, 1963).

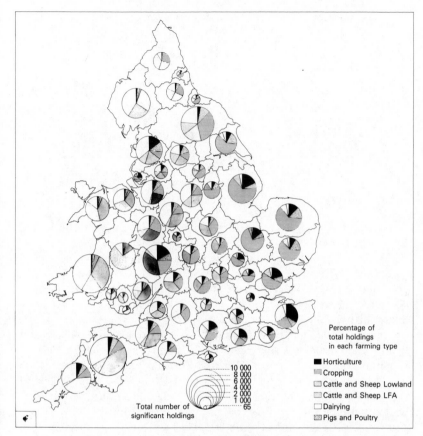

Figure 13.4   Types of farming in England and Wales, 1983.
*Source*: D. Grigg, 'Types of farming in England and Wales', *Geography Review*, 1 (1988), pp. 20–4.

remarkably unchanged. In all four maps the broad distribution of the major types of farming remain much the same. Arable farming predominates in the east from the North Yorkshire Moors, south through the East Riding into Lincolnshire and then south-east into East Anglia. This region is bordered to the west by the Pennines, and the northern part of these hills is occupied by sheep and cattle-rearing, a type which also occupies the uplands of Wales and is found in the hills of the south-west peninsular, notably on Exmoor and Dartmoor. In the western lowlands dairying is the leading type of farming – on the plains of the Solway Firth, in Lancashire south into Shropshire, and, *par excellence*, in Cheshire, but it is also found at higher altitudes, in the uplands of East Lancashire and, most notably, on the limestone plateau of Derbyshire. This great zone narrows southwards until a second zone of dairying appears, from the Vale of Gloucester southwards into Wiltshire and

Table 13.1   Classification of agricultural holdings, England and
Wales (as a percentage of the total)

|  | Numbers | Area |
|---|---|---|
| Dairying | 22.3 | 20.8 |
| Upland cattle and sheep | 10.2 | 9.1 |
| Lowland cattle and sheep | 27.0 | 13.3 |
| Cropping | 24.0 | 50.9 |
| Pigs and Poultry | 7.5 | 3.4 |
| Horticulture | 8.5 | 2.5 |

*Sources*: Ministry of Agriculture, *United Kingdom Agricultural Statistics 1983*
(London, 1985); Welsh Office, *Welsh Agricultural Statistics 1984* (Cardiff,
1984).

Dorset, and south-westwards into Somerset and parts of Devon and
Cornwall.

Horticulture and pigs and poultry occupy a small fraction of England's
agricultural land (see table 13.1). The extent of the former varies
according to how it is defined, but certain areas emerge, however
specified: the environs of London, particularly in Kent; the Fens; the
Sandy district; the Vale of Evesham and the Lancashire mosses.

This leaves one major type of farming – mixed farming – where both
livestock and crops are sold off the farm, and both grass and arable are
prominent in the land use. Although allegedly in decline since 1945,
mixed farming has a distinctive location south of Birmingham between
the arable farming of the east and the dairy farming of the west,
while north of the arable zone, in the North Riding, Durham and
Northumberland, mixed farming replaces more specialized arable cropping (see figures 13.1, 13.2 and 13.3).

PAST REGIONAL PATTERNS

It would be illuminating to compare the modern pattern of types of
farming with that of the past, and show how the distribution has
changed. But this is not possible, for there are no comprehensive statistics
before 1866, nor are there any attempts by past writers to produce a
map of the agricultural regions of England and Wales before that of the
Ministry of Agriculture in 1939, although in 1851 James Caird did
distinguish between the corn and the grazing counties (see figure 13.5).
However, Joan Thirsk has recently produced a map of the agricultural
regions of England and Wales for the period between 1640 and 1750.
She divided the types of farming of England and Wales into three major
classes, Pastoral, Intermediate and Arable, and each of these into six
sub-classes. This classification is simplified in figure 13.6 to make it

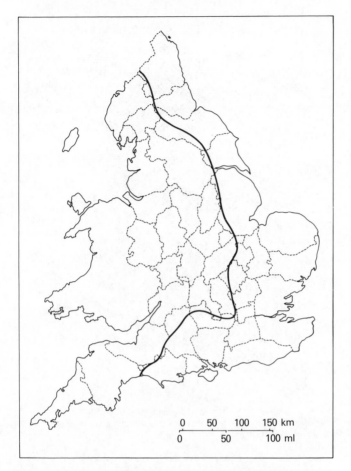

Figure 13.5   Arable and grazing districts in England and Wales, 1851.
*Source*: James Caird, *English Agriculture in 1850–51* (London, 1852).

more easily comparable with the modern maps. The broad distinction between arable and intermediate types in the east and south and pastoral types in the west is apparent, although areas where dairying was predominant were far fewer than today, while market gardening was also less extensive. The difference between intermediate and arable types was less marked than at present; there were fewer lowland farms where only crops or livestock were produced, while in many of the pastoral areas grain was produced for consumption on the farm.[11]

11 James Caird, *English Agriculture in 1850–51* (London, 1852); Joan Thirsk, 'The farming regions of England', in J. Thirsk (ed.), *The Agrarian History of England and Wales*, vol. IV; *1500–1640* (Cambridge, 1967), pp. 1–113; *England's Agricultural Regions and Agrarian History 1500–1750* (London, 1987).

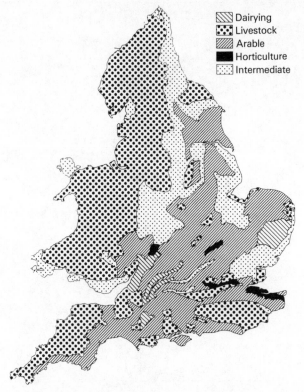

Figure 13.6   Types of farming areas, 1640–1750.
*Source*: Simplification of map in Joan Thirsk, ed., *The Agrarian History of England and Wales*, vol. IV: *1500–1640* (Cambridge, 1967).

SUMMARY

There are many problems in defining types of farm and producing maps of type of farming areas;[12] these problems have not been dealt with here – suffice to say that modern maps, based upon data in 1939, 1968, 1970 and 1983, show a consistency in the distribution of the major

12 Of the very large literature on the methodology of farm classification and regional delimitation, see G. Clark, 'The meaning of agricultural regions', *Scottish Geographical Magazine*, 10 (1984), pp. 34–44; M. Chisholm, 'Problems in the classification and use of farming type regions', *Transactions of the Institute of British Geographers*, 35 (1964), pp. 91–103; B. W. Ilberry, 'Dorset agriculture: a classification of regional types', *Transactions of the Institute of British Geographers* (second series), 6 (1981), pp. 214–27; T. N. Jenkins, *The Classification of Agricultural Holdings in Wales* (Aberystwyth, Department of Agricultural Economics, 1982); R. B. Jones, *The Pattern of Farming in the East Midlands* (School of Agriculture, University of Nottingham, 1954).

types. It is impossible to say whether this is a persistent feature of English agricultural history, although the difference between east and west and upland and lowland is obviously an enduring characteristic. What is clear is that the major types of farming, if not their distribution, have shown dramatic changes in the past, and particularly since the middle of the nineteenth century. In the following chapters the evolution of some – but not all – of the major types of farming is traced.

# 14
# Farming in the Lowlands: Mixed Farming and its Decline

## INTRODUCTION

In the east of England arable land predominates, crops are the main source of income and livestock are of importance only locally. Many farms obtain a high proportion of their income from cereals and grow few other crops; more common are farmers who grow a variety of cash crops – cereals, oilseed rape, sugar-beet and potatoes – but have few animals. Westwards and northwards from this core of arable farming, the predominant type of farm changes. More grass is grown, the cash crops, other than the cereals, are less important, and livestock densities are much higher. In the 1960s these were the areas of mixed farming (see figures 13.2 and 13.3) as they had been in the 1930s (see figure 13.1). In the 1870s, it has been said, all English lowland farming was mixed farming. Yet when in 1980 the Ministry of Agriculture began to publish the number of holdings in each county belonging to each major type of farming, no mixed farming class was included. Thus one useful way to interpret the present pattern of farming in lowland England is in terms of the decline of mixed farming.[1]

## THE NATURE OF MIXED FARMING

Mixed farming reached its apogee in the period of Victorian prosperity, and indeed was more or less synonymous with what the Victorians called High Farming. It had taken, however, some two centuries for this type of farming to develop (see above, pp. 47–53). On the medieval farm livestock and crops were kept, but their production was not integrated;

---

1 Ministry of Agriculture, *Farm Incomes in England 1984*, Farm Income Series no. 37 (London, 1985); *Agricultural Statistics United Kingdom 1983* (London, 1984); Viscount Astor and B. Seebohm Rowntree, *Mixed Farming and Muddled Thinking* (London, no date [c. 1946]), p. 67.

in the Victorian period most farms raised both crops and livestock for sale, but their production was so organized as to be mutually beneficial. There are, however, other characteristics of mixed farming.[2]

First, more than one product is for sale; strictly speaking, specialized farming implies only one product, mixed or diversified farming two or more. In practice the production on most English farms has always been far higher; in East Anglia in the 1930s a majority of farms produced ten or more commodities and sold at least five off the farm. This diversification had several advantages. Where only one product is sold off, the farmer is at great risk both from price fluctuations and the hazards of climate and disease. If livestock commodities, such as eggs, milk and meat are produced, income comes not once a year as it does with crop monoculture, but at regular intervals. Keeping livestock and growing crops also evens out the use of labour. Crops have seasonal peaks in spring and late summer and early autumn; keeping livestock utilizes labour in the slacker periods of the year.[3]

But there is more to mixed farming than the diversification of production. Central to most definitions of mixed farming is that such farms produce both crops and livestock, and that the two enterprises are integrated. This is reflected in the land-use pattern. Most mixed farms have some permanent grass – about one-third – and arable, which occupies between one-third and two-thirds of the total area. However, because in the past temporary grass was an important part of the arable acreage, there was generally an approximate balance between grass and crops.[4]

Keeping crops and livestock was mutually beneficial. Part of the arable was used to grow crops to be fed to animals; temporary grass provided hay and grazing, and the clover in the sward added nitrogen to the soil. Fodder root crops could be fed *in situ* to sheep or lifted and fed to cattle kept in stalls. The animals provided a liberal supply of dung and farmyard manure, which maintained the yield of cereal crops. Cereals, roots and clover were grown in rotation, and this allowed thorough weeding during the year in roots and limited the spread of plant disease. Byproducts were utilized. Thus straw could be used as litter in stalls as the basis of farmyard manure and as a feed, while poor grain could be fed to livestock, as could sugar-beet tops and poor-quality potatoes.[5]

---

2 E. L. Jones, 'The changing basis of English agricultural prosperity 1853–73', in E. L. Jones (ed.), *Agriculture and the Industrial Revolution* (London, 1974), pp. 191–210.

3 R. McG. Carslaw, 'In defence of mixed husbandry', *Journal of the Royal Agricultural Society of England*, 96 (1935), pp. 5–22; H. T. Williams, *Principles of British Agricultural Policy* (London, 1960), p. 145

4 Astor and Rowntree, *op. cit.* ([*c*. 1946]), pp. 32–3, 43–4.

5 McG. Carslaw, *op. cit.* (1935); J. H. Kirk, 'The agricultural industry: an introduction', in A. Edwards and A. Rogers (eds), *Agricultural Resources: an introduction to the farming industry of the United Kingdom* (London, 1974), pp. 1–20.

The slow diffusion of turnips and clover after 1650 has been traced earlier (see above, pp. 49–51); it was not until the nineteenth century that the farming of much of eastern and southern England, with the combination of the Norfolk rotation and its modifications, the keeping of both sheep and cattle, partly fed on crops, partly on grass, and the application of large amounts of manure either by the folding of sheep or the carting of farmyard manure, developed into mixed farming. In 1852 James Caird distinguished between the corn-growing counties and the livestock-raising counties with a line running east of the Pennines, south to Rutland and then London, and from there south-west to the Dorset coast (see figure 13.5). But even these arable counties had a significant area in grass in 1875 (see table 14.1). Although three-quarters of the agricultural land was in crops, temporary and permanent grass made up one-third of the total area.[6]

Farms in the east produced wheat and barley as cash crops; oats was grown, but was largely consumed on the farm by horses. Potatoes were not of much importance, being cultivated, as were most vegetables and fruit, upon small market-gardening holdings, so that most of the area in

Table 14.1  Land use in the arable[a] and mixed[b] farming counties, 1875–1983 (percentage)

|  | 1875 | | 1938 | | 1983 | |
|---|---|---|---|---|---|---|
|  | Mixed | Arable | Mixed | Arable | Mixed | Arable |
| Cereals | 33.2 | 47.5 | 14.7 | 33.7 | 39.3 | 62.6 |
| Fodder crops | 11.2 | 15.7 | 3.4 | 8.3 | 1.7 | 2.5 |
| Horticulture | – | – | 0.5 | 1.0 | 0.9 | 5.6 |
| Potatoes | – | – | 0.9 | 4.5 | 0.9 | 3.1 |
| Sugar-beet | – | – | 0.2 | 5.1 | 0.2 | 7.6 |
| Oilseed rape | – | – | – | – | 4.1 | 5.2 |
| Temporary grass | 9.6 | 11.1 | 5.3 | 8.4 | 14.4 | 3.4 |
| Other crops | 2.6 | 2.0 | 3.2 | 5.2 | – | – |
| Arable | 56.6 | 76.3 | 28.2 | 66.2 | 61.5 | 90.0 |
| Permanent grass | 43.4 | 23.7 | 71.8 | 33.8 | 38.5 | 10.0 |
| Cattle per 100 acres | 16.8 | 11.4 | 27.9 | 13.3 | 40.4 | 12.4 |
| Sheep per 100 acres | 81.8 | 71.5 | 53.8 | 29.2 | 82.2 | 15.0 |
| Pigs per 100 acres | 7.3 | 9.4 | 10.9 | 15.7 | 31.2 | 54.1 |

[a] Berkshire, Buckinghamshire, Durham, Hampshire, Leicestershire, Northamptonshire, Oxfordshire, Warwickshire.
[b] Bedfordshire, Cambridgeshire, Essex, Huntingdonshire, Lincolnshire, Norfolk, Suffolk, East Riding, Humberside.
Source: Ministry of Agriculture, *Agricultural Statistics of England and Wales.*

6 James Caird, *English Agriculture in 1850–51* (London, 1852).

crops other than cereals was devoted to fodder crops. Sheep and cattle were kept, yielding beef – the single most important product – mutton, wool and sometimes milk. Most farms maintained pigs and poultry, although they were apt to be incidental to the main tasks of producing wheat and beef. Within Caird's arable counties there were, of course, considerable variations in the type of mixed farming practised. Perhaps the areas of mixed farming *par excellence* were the limestone uplands –the Yorkshire and Lincolnshire Wolds, Lincoln Heath, Salisbury Plain and the Cotswolds (see figure 4.1). On these thin, poor, but easily cultivated soils a mixed husbandry based upon sheep, barley and turnips had developed in the eighteenth century. In the north of England most of the land was enclosed and in crops by the nineteenth century, but in the south sheep grazing on grass downland lasted longer. In the clay vales of the arable counties wheat, fallow and beans replaced barley and turnips, while cattle were more important than sheep. Grass occupied more of the farmland than on the limestone soils.[7]

Caird put the midland counties in his grazing zone. But in the 1870s, as in the 1970s, these counties were areas of mixed farming. Although there were parts of Northamptonshire and Leicestershire where grasssland predominated, in most of the Midlands grass and crops were in balance (see table 14.1). Livestock densities – of sheep and of cattle – were above those in the arable counties; both the regions, however, derived many of their sheep and some of their young cattle for fattening from the uplands. In parts of the Midlands ley farming was practised rather than the crop rotations of the east. In this system (see above, p. 49) crops – mainly cereals and fodder crops – alternated not with one year in temporary grass, but with several years in clover and grass.[8]

Between 1850 and 1880, the High Farming period, mixed farming reached its apogee. Indeed the practices of farmers in this period became established as the principles of good husbandry, since held up to students of agriculture and advocated as the basis of agricultural policy by numerous committees and in many books. Indeed many of the modern proponents of 'organic' farming appear to be advocating a return to the principles of the mid-nineteenth century, although they are often unaware of this. However, from the 1850s to the 1930s mixed farming was undermined by the decline in agricultural prices, and since the 1950s the advance of chemical and mechanical technology has rendered many of the principles of mixed farming obsolete.[9]

7 C. S. Orwin and E. H. Whetham, *History of British Agriculture 1846–1914* (London, 1964), pp. 3, 10, 124; E. L. Jones, *The Development of English Agriculture 1815–1873* (London, 1968), p. 22.

8 Hilary Chew, 'The post-war land use pattern of the former grasslands of east Leicestershire', *Geography*, 38 (1953), pp. 286–95.

9 Astor and Rowntree, *op. cit.* ([*c.* 1946]), is an early critique of mixed farming; Williams, *op. cit.* (1960), defends it, as does more recently Sir F. Engledow and L. Amey, *Britain's Farming Future* (London, 1980).

THE DECLINE OF MIXED FARMING

From the 1870s the import of cheap wheat, meat and wool led to a continuous decline in prices, with a brief interruption in the First World War, until the late 1930s. This undermined mixed farming. The fall in wool prices made sheep less and less profitable, and the high labour-cost of folding and employing shepherds accelerated their decline. Between the 1880s and the 1930s there was a dramatic fall in the number of sheep in the lowland counties, although those in the uplands of Wales and the north of England decreased less, or indeed in some places increased. The old breeds of the lowlands such as the Southdown, the Cotswold, and the Lincolnshire Longwood diminished.[10]

As the sheep population fell, so too did the area in root crops; turnips were expensive to hoe, lift and cart to farmyards, as was folding; in contrast, imported feeds such as grains and oil-cakes fell in price and made home-grown feeds of all kinds expensive by comparison. Consequently the fodder acreage, and particularly that of the root crops, declined from the 1870s. The fodder root in its role as a cleaning crop was replaced by the potato, and after 1925, by the sugar-beet. The latter crop required much intensive cultivation and provided an invaluable source of income when sold to sugar factories, while the tops, cut before sale, and the pulp, bought back from the factories, provided nearly as much feed as a turnip. The sugar-beet consequently replaced the turnip in the rotation in many parts of eastern England after 1925; before then the potato had played a similar role.[11]

Turnips were also fed to cattle, bought in autumn from the uplands and fattened during the winter. The import of beef from Argentina and elsewhere undercut the prices of all but prime English beef, and so beef production declined. Cattle and sheep had been kept, in mixed farming, not only for cash sales off the farm, but to provide manure for the cereal crops; indeed before the 1840s, for many farmers in eastern England, this was the prime reason for keeping cattle, which were fed on purchased oil-cake to improve their dung as much as their flesh. The fall in wheat prices from the 1870s combined with the fall in wool and mutton prices made not only the folding of sheep uneconomic: because wheat was uncompetitive with imports, the cost of producing manure – whether

10 J. Fraser Hart, 'The changing distribution of sheep in Britain', *Economic Geography*, 32 (1956), pp. 260–74; Sir E. J. Russell, 'Agriculture', in A. F. Martin and R. W. Steel (eds), *The Oxford Region: a scientific and historical survey* (Oxford, 1954), pp. 132–41; R. P. Askew, 'Recent changes in sheep breeding in the arable areas', *Journal of the Ministry of Agriculture*, 44 (1937), pp. 450–7.

11 *Report of the United Kingdom Sugar Industry Inquiry Committee*, HMSO, Cmd. 4871 (1935), pp. 39–40; F. Raynes, 'The beet crop in Norfolk farming', *Journal of the Ministry of Agriculture*, 43 (1936), pp. 38–47.

from sheep or cattle – for a cereal with an ever-falling price was becoming prohibitively expensive.[12]

MIXED FARMING IN THE 1930s

The response of the lowland farmers was very varied. Some turned to the production of commodities not hitherto part of the mixed-farming system. Thus in Essex in the 1890s and on the Wiltshire chalk in the 1920s dairy herds were added to the existing enterprises, while in eastern England many farmers began to grow one or two of the hardier vegetables on a large scale, encouraged in the 1920s and 1930s by the establishment of canning factories (see below, pp. 206–7). Sugar-beet and potatoes were also adopted by many farmers in the eastern counties. But it is the negative consequences that were most noteworthy. Cereal acreage declined before the import of wheat and barley (see table 14.1 and figure 5.2), as did the area occupied by fodder crops, which included not only roots, but peas and beans. The area under grass increased,modestly in the arable east, but dramatically in the midland counties, where by 1938 three-quarters of the agricultural area was in grass; most of the rest was in cereals, and potatoes, sugar-beet and horticultural crops had made little advance.[13]

Yet in 1939 most of this midland region was described by local farm economists as an area of mixed farming (see figure 13.1). True, much of Northamptonshire and Leicestershire were overwhelmingly in grass, but to the west cereals, fodder crops and dairying were combined, while in the south on the Hampshire chalk dairying had been added to the sheep and cereals combination. A substantial proportion – 28 per cent – of the farmland of England and Wales was occupied by farms classified as mixed, mainly in the midland counties. But in addition the farms of the arable eastern counties, described as arable types in contemporary classifications, were essentially mixed farms, even though two-thirds of their area, on average, was in arable. The farms of the east differed from those of the Midlands in having less land in grass and more in cereals and much lower livestock densities, but most notably in that horticulture, sugar-beet and potatoes occupied one-tenth of the farm area, compared with less than 2 per cent in the mixed counties (see table 14.1).[14]

12 Jones, *op. cit.* (1968), pp. 21–2; Askew, *op. cit.* (1937), pp. 450–7; A. Bridges, 'General features of farming in Great Britain', in J. P. Maxton, *Regional Types of British Agriculture* (London, 1936), pp. 13–36.

13 L. D. Stamp, 'Wartime changes in British agriculture', *Geographical Journal*, 109 (1947), pp. 39–57.

14 Ministry of Agriculture and Fisheries, *National Farm Survey of England and Wales (1941–1943): a summary report* (London, 1946), pp. 14–18, 78–87.

THE END OF MIXED FARMING?

The Second World War saw a remarkable plough-up of land in lowland England, so that by 1941 farms in the arable districts were three-quarters in arable and the mixed farms of the Midland counties over half in arable. Indeed during the war much of the long-established fattening pastures in the Midlands, notably in Leicestershire and Northamptonshire, were ploughed, and were not returned to grass after the war. Perhaps the most important initial change in land use after 1945 was the spread of alternate or convertible husbandry in eastern and midland England, and thus the increase in the area in temporary grass (see figure 4.3). However, this increase came to an end in 1961 and since then mixed farming has rapidly declined.[15]

In the 1950s mixed farming was still to be found widely in eastern and southern England, although it had many critics who argued than an increase in productivity was possible only if mechanization and specialization were pursued, while others believed that the maintenance of crops and livestock production on the same farm was unnecessary since the cost of chemical fertilizers had fallen. In the 1930s chemical fertilizer was not greatly used except upon potatoes and sugar-beet (see table 7.4), pesticides were confined to fruit, and herbicides were experimental. However, further technical advances and the falling real cost of these methods has had dramatic consequences.[16]

First, it has been possible to maintain – and indeed substantially to increase – crop yields by using only chemical fertilizers. Although there remains some debate about the value of the organic matter that is obtained from farmyard manure, for the rest there is no doubt that chemical fertilizers alone are perfectly capable of maintaining long-term soil fertility. Consequently, there is no longer any need to keep livestock to provide manure. Similarly, the use of herbicides to control weed growth has made wide-row cleaning crops unnecessary, so that the fodder roots continued their decline in acreage until the late 1970s. Sugar-beet and potatoes continued to be cultivated, although their acreage is limited by quotas imposed by the European Community and the Potato Marketing Board respectively; they are grown of course as cash crops, but also serve as cleaning crops. The use of insecticides and fungicides has given the farmer some protection against plant disease that was formerly controlled – and only partly at that – by crop rotations. Hence from the 1960s many farmers in the eastern counties began to experiment with the continuous cropping of cereals, particularly of barley; the principal obstacle to this was not soil exhaustion, as was at first thought, but plant disease, and it was found necessary to grow

15 Ministry of Agriculture, *op. cit.* (1946), p. 16; Chew, *op. cit.* (1953), pp. 286–95.
16 Astor and Rowntree, *op. cit.* ([*c.* 1946]).

break crops that prevented the build-up of diseases specific to wheat or barley. The most successful of these break crops has been oilseed rape.[17]

The chemical revolution undermined the biological fundamentals of mixed farming – the use of manure and rotations to control weeds and disease and to preserve soil fertility. Other factors reduced the number of enterprises that farmers pursued upon their farms. One powerful deterrent to producing a wide variety of commodities was the high cost of mechanizing every crop. Hence the popularity of growing crops that could be harvested with a combine harvester – such as cereals, oilseed rape, and beans. Because of the favourable prices established for cereals since 1947, and the great progress both in the mechanization of these crops and the breeding of new high-yielding varieties, a large number of farmers in the eastern counties have simplified their farm systems by concentrating upon cereals. This has given rise to much criticism of 'prairie' farming, particularly when it is found associated with the removal of hedgerows, the pollution of rivers by nitrates and the burning of straw. The production of large quantities of cereals has also undermined the livestock side of mixed farming. Now that large quantities of relatively cheap grain are available to livestock producers, there is less need to grow the traditional fodder crops such as roots, peas and beans, kohl rabi and cabbage, and purchased concentrates and grass have provided most of the diet of the modern ruminant.[18]

The simplification of farming has led to fewer enterprises being found on English farms, although admittedly there is only limited information on this. However, between 1968 and 1974 the average number of enterprises on full-time holdings in England and Wales fell from 3.18 to 2.85; one reason for this decline has been because farmers have withdrawn from pig and poultry farming and left it to quasi-industrial specialists (see below, pp. 189–95). Although keeping these animals was once all but ubiquitous, by 1974 breeding sows were kept on only one-fifth of holdings and hens one-third.[19]

One result of these changes has been the decline in the number of mixed farms. This cannot be traced with any accuracy over more than a short period, not least because of the difficulty of defining and measuring a mixed farm. However, the data presented in table 14.2 are suggestive, if not definitive. In 1924, 22 per cent of all agricultural holdings had between 70 per cent and 30 per cent of their total area in arable and were defined as mixed farms, occupying 37 per cent of the

17 Ministry of Agriculture, *Modern Farming and the Soil: report of the Agricultural Advisory Council on soil structure and soil fertility* (London, 1970).

18 J. A. L. Dench, A. K. Giles, H. Casey, D. J. Ansell, J. A. Burns, J. Wright, E. G. Hunt, W. Brooker and R. G. Hughes, *Break Crops: an economic study in Southern England*, Agricultural Enterprise Studies in England and Wales, Economic Report no. 13 (Reading, 1972).

19 D. K. Britton, 'Some explorations in the analysis of long-term changes in the structure of agriculture', *Journal of Agricultural Economics*, 28 (1977), pp. 197–208.

Table 14.2    Types of farming, 1925–1983 (as a percentage of all holdings)

|                    | *1925* | *1941* | *1963* | *1975* | *1983* |
|--------------------|-------|-------|-------|-------|-------|
| Dairying           | –     | 32.4  | 40.3  | 35.8  | 22.3  |
| Livestock          | –     | 21.3  | 14.6  | 21.9  | 37.2  |
| All livestock      | 56.1  | 53.7  | 54.9  | 57.7  | 59.5  |
| Pigs and Poultry   | 1.4   | –     | 5.4   | 7.3   | 7.4   |
| Cropping           | 12.0  | 17.8  | 15.4  | 17.4  | 24.6  |
| Horticulture       | 8.5   | 3.2   | 9.7   | 10.9  | 8.5   |
| Mixed              | 22.0  | 25.3  | 14.6  | 6.7   | n.d.  |
| Total              | 100.0 | 100.0 | 100.0 | 100.0 | 100.0 |

n.d. no data.
*Sources*: Ministry of Agriculture, *National Farm Survey of England and Wales (1941–1943): a summary report* (London, 1946), p. 16; *The Agricultural Output of England and Wales 1925*, HMSO, Cmd. 2815 (1927), *Farm Classification in England and Wales* (London, 1984).

area in crops and grass. In 1941 one-quarter of all holdings were defined as intermediate, between the arable types which had two-thirds or more of their total area in arable and pasture types which had two-thirds in grass; these farms occupied just under one-third of the area. Between 1963 and 1975 the Ministry of Agriculture recorded the number of holdings in each of several classes; mixed farming was a residual category, where no one enterprise accounted for more than half of the standard man-days worked in a year. Thus, although not comparable with the earlier estimates, the data for 1963 and 1975 suggest a continuing decline. The classification of farms adopted since 1980 has no category of mixed farming. This does not of course mean that mixed farming has totally disappeared. Outside the horticultural types, there are probably few farms in England and Wales which do not grow crops and keep some livestock. However, the trend towards specialization and simplification is reflected in the land-use data (see table 14.1). In 1983 farms in the eastern arable counties were overwhelmingly in crops, with grass accounting for only 13 per cent of the area, cereals nearly two-thirds, and potatoes, sugar-beet, rape and horticulture over one-fifth. Not surprisingly livestock densities were much lower than in the counties of mixed farming, and indeed lower than those in the arable counties in 1938. The greatest decline has been in sheep, now only one-fifth the density of 1875; not surprisingly fodder crops are now of little importance.

The midland counties are the only region where mixed farming can be said to have any persistence. Here there are farms with on average more grass than in the east and much higher livestock densities than in 1938 or 1875, but with still 60 per cent of their area in crops (see table 14.1). What is conspicuously absent are the cash crops so important in the east and fodder crops. The Midlands are now largely in cereals and grass.

TOWARDS SPECIALIZATION

Since the 1950s the production of pigs and poultry has been concentrated into specialist holdings using industrial techniques. Many of the dairy herds kept on mixed farms in the 1920s and 1930s have disappeared, and milk production has focused in the west of the country (see below, pp. 213–29). Sheep, which were once an indispensable part of lowland mixed farming, are kept at a fraction of the densities found in the 1870s, and the fodder roots once used to feed sheep and cattle have gone. The great revival of sheep numbers since 1947 has come in the hills and uplands and only to a lesser extent in the lowlands, where flocks are kept, among other things, to feed off leys used to break up continuous cereal cropping. Cattle fed on winter roots are no longer the key to the production of farmyard manure on mixed farms; chemical fertilizer does the job. Thus livestock densities are now lower in eastern England than in 1938 and 1875. Excluding horticulture, the two predominant types of farm – on neither of which are livestock very important, although rarely absent – are *general cropping*, where cereals, potatoes, sugar-beet, oilseed rape and vegetables are grown and livestock are kept, and the *specialist cereal producers*, with four-fifths of their area in cereals; few other cash crops are grown, and few animals are kept (see table 14.3).

Table 14.3   Arable types of farming, 1983 (acres)

|  | General cropping | Specialist cereals |
|---|---|---|
| Average size | 311.0 | 291.0 |
| Arable as % of total | 87.5 | 92.0 |
| **As a % of arable:** | | |
| Cereals | 64.0 | 82.0 |
| Potatoes | 4.5 | 0.0 |
| Sugar-beet | 6.4 | 0.9 |
| Oilseed rape | 4.5 | 3.7 |
| Other cash crops | 2.7 | 2.7 |
| Horticulture | 2.7 | 0.0 |
| Fodder crops | 1.8 | 0.0 |
| Temporary grass | 10.9 | 6.5 |
| **Per 100 acres of crops and grass:** | | |
| Cattle | 20.0 | 8.0 |
| Sheep | 37.0 | 21.0 |
| Pigs | 20.0 | 3.0 |
| Fowls | 69.0 | 20.0 |
| All livestock units | 20.0 | 8.0 |
| Labour units | 1.0 | 0.7 |

*Source*: Ministry of Agriculture, *Farm Incomes in England 1984*, Farm Income Series no. 37 (London, 1985).

SUMMARY

The mixed farming of the nineteenth century was undermined first by economic forces, which made its major products, wheat and meat, unrewarding, and second by technological advances, which made it unnecessary to keep livestock to produce manure or to follow rotations to control disease and allow thorough weeding. Since the 1960s farms in the east of England have become overwhelmingly arable with comparatively few livestock, differing from each other mainly as to whether or not they specialize in cereals.

# 15
# Pigs and Poultry

The growing specialization of agriculture is best demonstrated by considering the production of pigs and poultry; they are classed together as a type of farming by the Ministry of Agriculture not so much because the two enterprises always occur side by side on the same holding, but because of their differences from other types of farming. First, neither pigs nor poultry are ruminants and grass plays a small part in their diet. In the past they were scavengers – medieval pigs being excellent foragers – and they have always been able to live on kitchen leftovers, spent grain and other wastes. Modern poultry, however, are fed largely on grain; the pig also relies on grain, although is fed a wider variety of foods including soya beans and fishmeal.[1]

Second, poultry and pigs are biologically far more productive than sheep or cattle. Sheep, at best, produce two lambs a year; the modern pig, in contrast, has two litters and more than 20 piglets a year, hens on average have 270 eggs. Broiler chickens are raised from chicks to slaughter weight in about seven weeks. Consequently the food output per acre of pigs and poultry measured in calories is two to four times that of sheep and beef cattle, although less than that of milk output. The pig, though not the broiler, is also a very efficient converter of feed into meat.[2]

Third, poultry, almost entirely, and pigs, mainly, live in controlled environments that are independent of climate, soil and land use. Modern poultry are kept for eggs or for meat (broilers), in cages at a very high density, with controlled ventilation, heating, lighting and automated feeding. In most cases the holdings on which they are managed grow none of their feed, which is purchased from compounders. Not surprisingly

1 J. Wiseman, *A History of the British Pig* (London, 1986, pp. 1, 2, 7–8.
2 V. R. Fowler, 'The future of the pig as a meat animal', *Proceedings of the Nutrition Society*, 39 (1980), pp. 151–9; W. Bolton, 'The role of poultry', *Proceedings of the Nutrition Society*, 29 (1970), pp. 253–62; T. C. Carter, 'The poultry industry: progress and prospects', *Span*, 21 (1978), pp. 71–2.

it could be written 20 years ago that 'Poultry has moved out of the category of farming into that of industry . . .'. Modern piggeries exhibit many similar characteristics, but are more commonly found upon conventional farms which may grow some of their feed, although most pig feed is purchased. Finally, it should be noted that poultry and pig holdings occupy very little land, for their feeds are grown by other farmers.[3]

POULTRY AND PIGS BEFORE 1900

Before the nineteenth century poultry and pigs were found on most farms in England and Wales, except those in upland areas. Little attention was paid to their feeding; the medieval pig foraged in forests for beech nuts and acorns, but in the modern period has relied more upon waste, particularly the whey and skimmed milk of farm butter- and cheese-makers, spent grain and inferior potatoes. In the eighteenth century Chinese pig breeds were imported into Europe and in England cross-bred to produce an animal that was smaller than the native breeds, and which reached slaughter-weight earlier. By the 1870s there were just over 2 million pigs and the highest densities were in three regions: in Lancashire and Cheshire and in the south-west pigs were kept on dairy farms and fed with whey and skimmed milk; in East Anglia they were found on mixed farms and fed with cereals, skimmed milk, potatoes, peas and beans.[4]

Pig-meat could be relatively easily preserved, compared with beef or mutton, by salting or smoking. In the middle of the century the Harris family of Calne in Wiltshire introduced American methods of curing and began to organize the collection of pigs from farmers for their factory. In 1933 the Pig and Bacon Marketing schemes extended this system to the rest of the country. But the growing demand for bacon and ham in Britain was not met by the emergence of a successful British pig-meat industry. Indeed from the 1880s the Danes assumed control of the market. Native pigs increased in numbers but had only reached 2.6 million in 1914; they were still an incidental feature of farm output. Much of the increase came in Lancashire, where pigs were widely kept, being fed on the by-products of dairying, damaged potatoes and, because of the nearness of Liverpool, imported grain. The dominant breed in

3 P. Bolam, 'Norfolk Farming', *Journal of the Royal Agricultural Society of England*, 130 (1969), pp. 29–42.

4 Wiseman, *op. cit.* (1986), pp. 1, 2, 21; D. B. Bellis, 'Pig farming in the United Kingdom – its development and future trends', *Journal of the Royal Agricultural Society of England*, 129 (1968), pp. 24–42; C. S. Orwin and E. H. Whetham, *History of British Agriculture 1846–1914* (London, 1964), p. 362.

Britain – half the pigs – was the Large White; the Berkshire and Middle White each accounted for one-quarter of all pigs.[5]

Poultry were ubiquitous in England, but only a few were kept on each farm; indeed they were more part of the domestic than the farm economy and remained so into this century. However, some local specialities did develop. Poultry and pigs in Hertfordshire were being fed barley to fatten them for the London market at least as early as the seventeenth century. In the eighteenth century geese and turkeys were driven from Norfolk to London, while in the mid-nineteenth century small holders and farmers around Aylesbury fattened ducks for the capital. To the south of London in the High Weald artificial fattening of chickens began in the 1830s and persisted for a century. But poultry – whether kept for eggs or table-meat – were not very important in England, and in the late nineteenth century much of British egg consumption was imported from Denmark and the Netherlands.[6]

THE BEGINNINGS OF SPECIALIZATION

By the First World War both pigs and poultry were dependent upon imported feeds, and consequently their numbers fell during the latter part of the war. The inter-war period saw, however, some important changes. First, the number of fowls kept doubled between 1924 and 1934, particularly in the eastern counties (see figure 15.1). Second, intensive methods began to be adopted, so that by the 1930s there were half a million fowls maintained in battery cages, mainly by specialist poultry keepers, though most birds were still to be found upon ordinary farms.[7]

There were fewer changes in pig production, although the decline of farm butter- and cheese-making meant there was less whey and skimmed milk and, consequently, continued import of feeding stuffs. Hence by the outbreak of the Second World War the south-west had lost ground to East Anglia and Lancashire, where dairy byproducts were more easily replaced by home-grown and imported grain respectively. The dependence

5 Orwin and Whetham, *op. cit.* (1964), p. 361; T. W. Fletcher, 'Lancashire livestock farming during the Great Depression', *Agricultural History Review*, 9 (1961), pp. 17–42; Bellis, *op. cit.* (1968), pp. 24–42; Wiseman, *op. cit.* (1986), p. 61.

6 P. Brassley, 'Northumberland and Durham', in J. Thirsk (ed.), *The Agrarian History of England and Wales*, vol. V: *1640–1750*, pt. 1: *Regional Farming Systems* (Cambridge, 1985), p. 36; Joan Thirsk, 'The farming regions of England', in J. Thirsk (ed.), *The Agrarian History of England and Wales*, vol. IV: *1500–1640* (Cambridge, 1967), p. 51; J. D. Chambers and G. E. Mingay, *The Agricultural Revolution 1750–1880* (London, 1966), p. 24; J. T. Coppock, *An Agricultural Geography of Great Britain* (London, 1971), p. 238; D. W. Fryer, *The Land of Britain*, pt. 54: *Buckinghamshire* (London, 1942), pp. 81–2; Brian Short, 'The Art and Craft of Chicken Cramming: poultry in the Weald of Sussex 1850–1950', *Agricultural History Review*, 30 (1982), pp. 17–30.

7 J. T. Coppock, *op. cit.* (1971), pp. 238–9.

*Pigs and Poultry*

*Turkeys have been produced in Norfolk since at least the eighteenth century. A flock in 1906 is pictured here.* (BBC Hulton Picture Library)

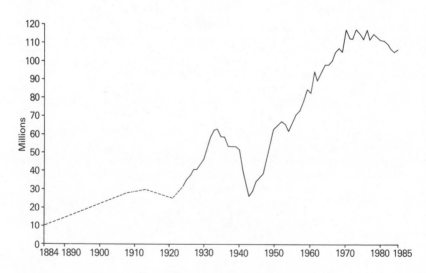

Figure 15.1   Growth of poultry numbers in England and Wales, 1884–1985.
*Source*: Ministry of Agriculture, *Agricultural Statistics, England and Wales.*

of pig and poultry production on overseas feeds had a disastrous effect on their numbers in the Second World War, as imports diminished and home-grown fodder went primarily to dairy cattle. But the post-war recovery was rapid and the transformation of production, particularly that of chickens for meat, was radical.[8]

BROILERS

Most chickens were kept on farms in the 1930s – and those mainly for eggs. Table-meat came from hens past laying, and the meat was expensive. In the 1940s chickens were kept upon 90 per cent of all agricultural holdings, and very few holdings had more than 200 adult fowls; only 1 per cent had more than 500. By the 1960s the production of eggs and especially of meat had been totally transformed. In the United States the idea of keeping large numbers of chickens in enclosed areas, either on deep litter or in cages, had emerged in the 1920s, as had the breeding of birds specialized for either egg or meat production. The management of broilers began there in 1942, and later ventilation, heating, the control of lighting and automated feeding were added. These techniques were promulgated in England by a Ministry of Agriculture team which visited the United States just after the war, and the adoption of intensive production for both layers and meat spread from 1950.[9]

However, the rapid expansion of broilers did not come until the rationing of feeding stuffs was abandoned in 1953. Since 1947 there had been guaranteed prices for eggs, but not for meat. It was, however, in the production of broilers that the new techniques were most rapidly adopted. Between 1953 and 1959 the total number of table fowls kept in England and Wales rose fivefold, the number of broilers twentyfold, and between 1955 and 1972 poultry-meat consumption rose from one-twentieth to one-fifth of all meat consumption. The number of fowls continued to increase until the 1970s, since when the high cost of grain in the EEC has hampered expansion (see figure 15.1).[10]

The most striking feature of the growth of broilers and indeed of all fowls has been the concentration of an increasing proportion of all birds on very few holdings, the decline in the number of agricultural holdings that keep poultry, and the virtual end of free-range fowls. In the 1940s very few birds were kept indoors, but by 1968 this figure was 95 per

8 Margaret F. Davies, *The Land of Britain*, pt. 32: *Pembrokeshire* (London, 1939), pp. 124, 145, 161; H. W. B. Luxton, 'Agriculture', in F. Barlow (ed.), *Exeter and its Region* (Exeter, 1969), pp. 217–39.

9 R. Coles, *Development of the Poultry Industry in England a:d Wales, 1945–1959* (London, 1960), pp. 24, 64, 60; G. Sykes, *Poultry: a modern agribusiness* (London, 1963), pp. 93, 139.

10 Coles, *op. cit.* (1960), p. 66; Economist Intelligence Unit, 'Broiler chickens in the UK', *Retail Business*, no. 189 (1973), pp. 21–2.

cent, four-fifths of which were in battery cages, 13.6 per cent on deep litter. Although poultry were still widely maintained in the 1960s, output of both meat and eggs was being concentrated increasingly in the hands of a few companies on a few holdings. Thus in 1960 90 per cent of the United Kingdom's broiler output came from 1,000 holdings, and three companies controlled half the output. This concentration has continued uninterruptedly. Most of the output comes from holdings with over 10,000 birds, and by the early 1970s 5 per cent of the holdings accounted for half the output.[11]

By the 1970s the production of both eggs and table-meat had been concentrated onto a few holdings with little land, and could perhaps be described as hardly part of farming at all. However, the growth of this industry had been possible only because of biological advances. In the 1920s and 1930s attempts to develop large-scale intensive poultry units foundered on outbreaks of disease; only with advances in vaccines and antibiotics was it possible to have such large flocks. The development of separate breeds for eggs and for meat – mainly American hybrids – combined with improved management has led to substantial improvements in productivity. Thus in 1940 poultry needed 3 kg of feed to produce each 1 kg of meat, but by the 1970s only 2 kg of feed, while broilers were brought to market-weight much quicker. Hens, on average, produce 270 eggs a year compared with 176 before the Second World War.[12]

The consequences of the broiler and egg explosion of the post-war period – the number of broilers produced rose from 5 million in 1953 to 200 million in 1970 – has been to make Britain self-sufficient in egg production – one-third were imported in 1938 – and greatly to increase the consumption of poultry-meat as the real price fell compared with beef and mutton. Consumption per capita doubled between the 1930s and the early 1960s.[13]

The changing location of egg and meat production is hard to trace. Lancashire and Cheshire were early specialists in poultry and indeed remain so. But since the rise of the broiler industry an increasing proportion are located in the east. However, the major locational change is away from the farm so that broiler and egg production are in the hands not of farmers, but of specialist producers.[14]

11 Bolton, *op. cit.* (1970), pp. 253–62; Sykes, *op. cit.* (1963), pp. 7, 17; Economist Intelligence Unit, *op. cit.* (1973), pp. 21–2.

12 Coles, *op. cit.* (1960), p. 31; A. C. L. Brown, 'Animal health: present and future', *Philosophical Transactions of the Royal Society*, 281B (1977), pp. 181–91; Carter, *op. cit.* (1978), pp. 71–2.

13 Coppock, *op. cit.* (1971), p. 242; Coles, *op. cit.* (1960), pp. 56–61.

14 Coppock, *op. cit.* (1971), pp. 234, 241; Bolton, *op. cit.* (1970), pp. 253–62.

Since 1945 pig production has experienced many changes similar to those that poultry production has undergone but has not become divorced from farms, although pig units have become increasingly independent enterprises on farms. Like poultry, pigs have become concentrated on a few holdings, and the number of pig producers has steadily – indeed even dramatically – declined. In the 1960s the number of pig producers halved and in the 1970s two-thirds of the pig holdings in the United Kingdom went out of production. By 1979 pigs were kept on only 13 per cent of the agricultural holdings in England and Wales. In contrast, as the total number of pigs increased in the post-war period, so the average size of herd rose from 6.9 in 1960 to 18.5 in 1971. By the end of the 1970s four-fifths of all sows were in herds of 50 or more. Sows have become predominantly Large White, with some imported Finnish Landrace, and their litters have grown with the number of piglets produced in a year rising from 11 in 1946 to 17 in 1976. The health of these animals is better – swine fever was eradicated in 1966 – and like poultry they convert feed into meat more efficiently than in the past.[15]

But production has been less industrialized than for poultry. Still raised for the most part on conventional farms, there is continued debate as to whether they should be run in the open air or kept continually indoors. Their location also reflects past location. Pigs are now less important in the south-west than they were in the nineteenth century, but it is here that the declining number of specialist breeders are to be found. Also in decline are those producers who fatten only; the units that both breed and fatten are now well over half of all units. To the traditional areas of pig production in Lancashire and East Anglia has been added the edge of towns in the West Riding, and Humberside, where there is easy access to imported grain.[16]

There has been a considerable increase in the consumption of pig-meat since the end of the Second World War, particularly in the 1970s, when it doubled; hence pig- and poultry-meat now constitute a much larger proportion of the meat consumed in Britain than in the 1930s; pigs and poultry also form a far greater proportion of livestock output than they did in the 1870s, having risen from one-fifth then to nearly one-third today.[17]

15 W. J. K. Thomas, *The Structure of Pig Production in England and Wales* (University of Exter, Agricultural Economics Unit, 1981); Brown, *op. cit.* (1977), pp. 181–91; Wiseman, *op. cit.* (1986), p. 99; Anon, 'Pigmeat in the United Kingdom', *Retail Business*, 180 (1973), pp. 19–31.

16 Thomas, *op. cit.* (1981).

17 C. W. R. Spedding, ed., *Fream's Agriculture* (London, 1983), p. 692.

SUMMARY

Until the 1920s pigs and poultry were found in small numbers on most English farms. Since then they have been concentrated onto a small number of holdings, where they are kept in a controlled environment and fed on purchased feeds. Although pigs are still kept on conventional farms, poultry production, like glasshouse production, has moved out of agriculture into industry.

# 16

# From Market Gardening to Horticulture

DEFINITION AND CHARACTERISTICS

One authority on horticulture has described it as an un-English activity;[1] it is certainly true that many horticultural crops were not widely grown in England until comparatively late, and that English farmers, unlike those in western and particularly southern Europe, were reluctant to integrate these crops into their farming systems. It has also, because of the great changes of the last century, been increasingly difficult to define horticulture as a type of farming. This was not always so; market gardening has been widely accepted as a distinctive type.

Horticultural crops occupy a very small part of the agricultural area of England and Wales (see table 16.1), but this greatly understates their importance, for their production accounts for one-tenth of the value of British farm output and employs one-eighth of the agricultural labour-force. But horticulture, unlike, for example, livestock production, uses few inputs from the rest of the agricultural economy; if the value added by horticulture is calculated, then this type of farming accounts for 17 per cent of the total farm output.[2]

It is difficult to define horticultural crops, save that they were all once produced by highly intensive hand-methods, and were, until this century, rarely grown by conventional farmers. Since the 1920s this distinctiveness has broken down, although most horticultural crops remain labour-intensive whether grown upon conventional farms or in market gardens.

The range of modern horticultural crops includes first and, in terms of area, by far the most important, vegetables (see table 16.1); second, orchards (or top fruit), now mainly apples and pears and in the past also considerable areas of plums, cherries and damsons; third, small or

1 R. R. W. Folley, *Intensive Crop Economics* (London, 1973), p. 13.
2 Folley, *op. cit.* (1973), p. 40; W. L. Hinton, *Outlook for Horticulture*, Farm Economics Branch, Occasional Papers no. 12 (Cambridge, 1968), p. 8.

Table 16.1  Horticultural crops in England and Wales, 1983

| | Acres | As a % of horticulture | As % of England and Wales | | As a % of value of horticulture output, 1970 |
|---|---|---|---|---|---|
| | | | Crops and grass | Arable | |
| Vegetables | 349,722 | 68.7 | 1.5 | 2.6 | 41.9 |
| Orchards | 88,137 | 17.3 | 0.37 | 0.6 | 23.0 |
| Small fruit | 33,611 | 6.6 | 0.14 | 0.2 | 10.4 |
| Flowers, Bulbs | 27,915 | 5.5 | 0.1 | 0.2 | 24.2 |
| Glasshouses | 5,253 | 1.0 | 0.02 | 0.04 | 0.5 |
| Others | 4,651 | 0.9 | 0.02 | 0.03 | |
| All horticulture | 509,291 | 100.0 | 2.2 | 3.7 | 100.0 |
| Crops and grass | 23,592,321 | | | | |
| Arable England and Wales | 13,681,342 | | | | |

Sources: Ministry of Agriculture, Agricultural Statistics United Kingdom 1983 (London, 1985); R. W. Folley and J. A. Wicks, Determinants of Location of Horticultural Crops in England and Wales: an experimental enquiry (Wye College, 1975), p. 90.

soft fruit, of which strawberries are the most important, but also currants and raspberries; fourth, flowers and bulbs; and fifth, the production of young plants for gardens in nurseries, an economic activity which flourished first in the eighteenth century when the market was primarily the gardens and parks of the rich but which has revived with the popular demand of the last 30 years. Glasshouse production occupies only 1 per cent of the area devoted to horticultural crops but produces one-quarter of the value of their output (see table 16.1).[3]

Such a remarkable range of crops – at least 50 are grown – makes generalization difficult. However, they are all without exception cultivated more intensively than the conventional field crops of the farmer, whether grown in allotments in cities, in commercial market gardens or on large mechanized arable farms. Thus the number of standard man-days needed to complete the production of a hectare of horticultural crops in 1975 ranged from 20 for winter cauliflower to 350 for watercress, while glasshouse production required 1,300 (see figure 16.1). In contrast, field crops, with the exception of potatoes, have labour requirements of fewer than 20 standard man-days; the latter were grown mainly in market gardens until the middle of the nineteenth century and thereafter became almost exclusively a field crop, except for earlies. Horticultural crops are grown intensively not only in terms of their labour requirements but also in fertilizer usage; they also give a far higher gross output and net return per hectare than do field crops (see figure 16.1).[4]

Some horticultural crops are highly perishable and have to be consumed soon after harvest. It is for this reason, in addition to the cost of moving vegetables and fruit long distances, that market gardens were traditionally near – or indeed often within – towns. But by no means all crops are perishable; the root crops, such as turnips, parsnips, carrots and potatoes, can be stored for quite long periods. Most of the vegetables are harvested in the summer and early autumn; only a few such as brussels, cabbage and celery can be cut in winter. Hence the production of vegetables and fruit that do mature in early summer gains a high premium, although 'early' crops are only about one-tenth of the value of total output. Horticultural production suffers from very considerable fluctuations in price, reflecting the frequent swings in output. This is because, first, the British market is unprotected from imports from the rest of the EEC, and second, because horticultural crops are peculiarly sensitive to climatic hazards. Thus, for example, in 1985 four-fifths of Kent's winter cauliflower acreage was destroyed by frost in January and February.[5]

3 M. Thick, 'Market Gardening in England and Wales', in *The Agrarian History of England and Wales*, vol. VII: *1640–1750*, pt. 2: *Agrarian Change* ed. J. Thirsk (Cambridge, 1985), pp. 503–32.

4 Ministry of Agriculture, *Farm Classification in England and Wales 1975* (London, 1976); C. Whitehead, 'The cultivation of hops, fruit and vegetables', *Journal of the Royal Agricultural Society of England*, 39 (1978), pp. 723–60.

5 R. R. W. Folley and J. A. Wicks, *Determinants of the Location of Horticultural Crops in England and Wales: an experimental enquiry* (Wye College, 1975), p. 28.

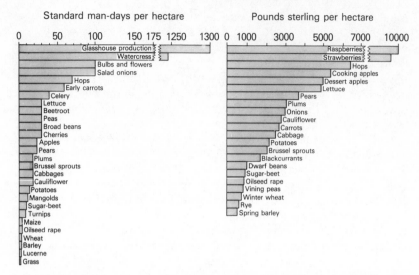

Figure 16.1   Intensity of horticultural products: labour inputs per hectare and value of output per hectare.
Sources: J. Nix, *Farm Management Pocketbook* (Ashford, 1975); Ministry of Agriculture, *Farm Classification in England and Wales* (London, 1975).

Unlike that of most agricultural products, horticultural output receives, and has received in the past, little protection or government support. Until 1932 fruit and vegetables were freely imported into Britain, but in that year an *ad valorem* duty was imposed on all but Commonwealth produce. Horticulture was excluded from the guarantees and subsidies of the 1947 Agricultural Act, although later tariffs were imposed on some imports, and in 1960 the Horticultural Improvement Scheme offered support for the building of new glasshouses and the grubbing-up of old orchards. Entry into the Common Market resulted in tariffs being imposed upon some traditional suppliers, such as North American apple growers, but also the abolition of tariffs on Italian, Spanish and Dutch products. Intervention prices for horticultural products do exist but are very low, and so prices are established by the market rather than by the Commissioners.[6]

6 Tony Gardener, 'Government and the horticultural industries', in E. D. Sargent and S. J. Rogers (eds), *The Economic Prospects for Horticulture* (London, 1970), pp. 21–36; R. Giles, 'The changing face of United Kingdom horticulture: statistical background to the horticultural industry', in Sargent and Rogers, *op. cit.* (1970), pp. 1–20; W. L. Hinton, 'Horticulture and the Common Market', *National Westminster Bank Quarterly Review* (November 1972), pp. 51–8; 'Outlook for horticulture in Europe', *Outlook on Agriculture*, 9 (1977), pp. 108–14.

THE BEGINNINGS OF HORTICULTURE

A wide range of vegetables and fruit was grown in medieval England – although not of course American crops – but they were probably confined to the gardens of monasteries, castles and great houses in the twelfth, thirteenth and fourteenth centuries. Vegetables at this time were eaten mainly as part of a pottage, rather than as an accompaniment to meat. Their cultivation is thought to have declined in the fourteenth and fifteenth centuries, but production revived in the sixteenth century. Henry VIII's gardener imported French apple trees in 1533 and grew them at Teynsham in Kent. More important, Walloon and Dutch immigrants who fled from religious persecution in the 1560s brought their skills as market gardeners to Sandwich and later to London.[7]

By 1600 the rudiments of the future pattern of horticulture were apparent. In the west – Herefordshire, Somerset and Worcestershire – applies were grown mainly for cider; in Kent apples and other fruit were cultivated, and in London, on the terrace gravels of the Thames flood plain, market gardening, mainly for vegetables but with some fruit, was well established. In 1605 the Gardeners' and Fruiterers' companies were formed. Their members were the market gardeners, generally with fewer than 10 acres, who grew a number of vegetables and fruits for sale rather than for private consumption.[8]

Market gardening expanded in the seventeenth century; there is early evidence of the production of vegetables for the market near Norwich and Colchester in the late sixteenth century, and by the mid-seventeenth century near other provincial towns such as Oxford, Nottingham, Ipswich and, significantly for the future, Evesham, Pershore and Sandy. In the late seventeenth century Evesham was supplying Bristol and Birmingham. It has been suggested that most of this vegetable production was for the poor who could not afford meat; the diet of the rich was primarily of meat, although they developed a taste for the more exotic vegetables in the eighteenth century, when the French custom of serving vegetables with meat became more common.[9]

By the middle of the eighteenth century market gardening was well established. In places its origins had been associated with Dutch immigrants; water transport was important for the London market, and parts of Essex and Kent could supplement the considerable industry in London itself. But Evesham and Sandy had to rely upon pack-horses to market their produce, much of it the more robust roots. In places such

---

7 Lord Ernle, *English Farming: past and present* (London, 1978), p. 101; J. H. Harvey, 'Vegetables in the Middle Ages', *Garden History*, 12 (1984), pp. 89–99; R. Webber, 'London's market gardens', *History Today*, 23 (1973), pp. 871–8.

8 Thick, *op. cit.* (1985), pp. 503–30; J. Thirsk, 'Farming techniques', in J. Thirsk (ed.), *The Agrarian History of England and Wales*, vol. IV: *1500–1640* (Cambridge, 1967), pp. 195–6; 'The farming regions of England', in Thirsk, *op. cit.* (1967), pp. 62–75, 105, 176.

9 Thick, *op. cit.* (1985), pp. 503–30.

as the Thames gravels or around Sandy the early market gardens were on very light soils that warmed up early in spring and were easily tilled by hand, but production soon moved onto other soils. Similarly, much of the early market gardening was first established in areas where the open fields had been enclosed; but by the mid-eighteenth century vegetables were being grown on open fields at Sandy.[10]

Probably closeness to market was the single most important location factor; not only did it reduce the costs of transport and make the marketing of perishable produce possible, but it allowed the purchase of horse-dung from urban stables. This remained an important factor until well into the twentieth century. The location near towns ensured that market gardening was on a small scale and highly intensive. Both rents and wages were very high, and so returns per acre had to be high. Cultivation was entirely with hand tools, and the soil was frequently dug over with spades and repeatedly weeded; an abundance of manure was used, and near the Thames irrigation was practised. Seed was sown in rows in beds, and both intercropping and multiple cropping were observed. By the eighteenth century most of the vegetables grown at present were cultivated: beans, peas, carrots, parsnips, cabbage, potatoes, turnips, cucumbers, radishes, lettuces, asparagus and celery. Vegetables were also grown by some farmers away from the city edges, but as part of a rotation – a small part of their total area, and a sign of things to come.[11]

By the early nineteenth century the leading area of market gardening was in and around London, especially to the west of the built-up area. In addition the Vale of Evesham and Sandy were well established and the west of Cornwall was sending potatoes and cauliflowers by sea to west-country towns and also to London. There was vegetable production elsewhere – notably at Cottingham near Hull – but as late as the 1850s London still accounted for most of the country's market gardening. But from the mid-nineteenth century a series of changes began to transform horticultural production.[12]

10 Thick, *op. cit.* (1985), pp. 503–30; F. Beavington, 'Early market gardening in Bedfordshire', *Transactions of the Institute of British Geographers*, 37 (1965), pp. 91–100; J. M. Martin, 'The social and economic origins of the Vale of Evesham market gardening industry', *Agricultural History Review*, 33 (1985), pp. 41–50.

11 Thick, *op. cit.* (1985), pp. 503–30.

12 G. B. G. Bull, 'T. Milne's Land Utilization map of the London area in 1800', *Geographical Journal*, 122 (1956), pp. 25–30; N. J. Hurford, 'Early potatoes in West Cornwall', *Agriculture*, 79 (1972), pp. 510–14; K. H. Johnstone, 'Early potatoes in Cornwall', *Agriculture*, 63 (1957), pp. 124–6; K. H. Johnstone, 'Cornish cauliflowers', *Agriculture*, 70 (1963), pp. 216–19; J. Sheppard, 'Horticultural developments in East Yorkshire', *Transactions of the Institute of British Geographers*, 19 (1953), pp. 73–80; H. Evershed, 'Market gardening', *Journal of the Royal Agricultural Society of England*, 32 (1871), pp. 420–36.

THE SPREAD OF MARKET GARDENING, 1850–1914

From the 1850s the real incomes of most of the population began to increase. This had effects upon English agriculture, particularly in the case of dairying, but higher incomes also led to an increased demand for fresh vegetables and fruit. This in turn was partly due to changes in middle-class eating habits. The adoption of French cuisine with its greater emphasis upon fruit and vegetables influenced all but the poorest, while the American custom of eating fruit as a first course slowly spread. Much of this increased demand was met initially by imports – notably of canned American fruits in the 1880s – and English market gardeners responded only slowly.[13]

However, it was possible for this increased demand to be met from a larger cultivated area, for the railways could move the most perishable vegetables and fruits to market before their freshness was lost; consequently areas remote from markets increased their acreage. London was linked to Sandy in 1851, and to Cornwall by 1859. The most important result of this was that market gardening was no longer confined to the edge of towns. Nor was the production of vegetables and fruit the concern only of market gardeners. In the 1880s the fall of wheat, wool and other prices forced farmers to look for alternative enterprises; some took to fruit and vegetables. The development of soft-fruit production in eastern England is one such response and can be seen perhaps as an early instance of agri-business. One way of preserving fruit was to convert it into jam, which needed cheap sugar. The repeal of sugar duties in 1874 prompted the expansion of jam-making in England. A. C. Wilkins grew fruit at Tiptree Heath in Essex in 1862 and subsequently a jam factory was built, while later Smedley's at Wisbech, Chivers at Histon, near Cambridge, and Beach and Son at Pershore all encouraged the spread of gooseberries, blackcurrants and plums. There was a good market for jam, which the poor used instead of butter.[14]

The prosperity of the late nineteenth century and the problems of traditional farming led to the expansion of fruit and vegetable production. The long-established market-gardening regions of Evesham, Sandy and London expanded their area; the acreage in market gardening in the Vale of Evesham doubled between 1875 and 1895. But they were joined by the silt fens of Lincolnshire and Norfolk and the mosslands of

---

13 P. Atkins, 'The production and marketing of fruit and vegetables 1850–1950', in D. Oddy and D. Miller (eds), *Diet and Health in Modern England* (London, 1985), pp. 102–33; A. Torode, 'Trends in fruit consumption', in T. C. Barker, J. C. McKenzie and J. Yudkin (eds), *Our Changing Fare: two hundred years of British food habits* (London, 1966), pp. 115–34.

14 P. E. Cross, 'Extension of market gardening into agriculture', in E. J. Russell (ed.), *Agriculture: today and tomorrow* (London, 1945), pp. 129–48; Ministry of Agriculture, *Horticulture in Britain*, pt. 1: *Vegetables* (London, 1967), p. 348.

Lancashire, which had been reclaimed only in the later nineteenth century. Both these were areas of very fertile soils and the existing farms were predominantly small. In the Fens the bulb industry dated from the 1850s, and potatoes became a major farm crop there at much the same time. Flowers were also taken up in the 1880s in the Scilly Isles, while the market gardeners of west Cornwall added to their range of crops by growing the Roscoff variety of cauliflower.[15]

By 1914 most of the modern regions of vegetable and fruit production were well established. Statistics of horticultural production are unreliable until the 1930s, but there seems to have been a substantial increase in the area between 1866 and 1914 (see figure 16.2). Production remained labour-intensive, and even in the farming regions was carried out mainly on small holdings. Thus at Sandy in the early twentieth century most market gardeners had 10 to 15 acres, while around Wisbech half the area was in holdings of fewer than 20 acres. Although some market gardening became established in regions where small farms already existed, as in the Fens, in other regions small farms were created. Thus in the Vale of Evesham large farms were broken up in the late nineteenth century, while the Smallholdings Act of 1908 encouraged the creation of farms appropriate for market gardening. In the Vale of Evesham, Bedfordshire and other market-gardening regions, farms were – and remain – highly fragmented. Some of these farmer-gardeners used the plough rather than the spade, but weeding, picking and lifting still depended upon hand labour. Holdings producing vegetables rarely kept livestock, and so buying in manure – particularly horse-dung – was essential. Except for the soft-fruit growers, most output was for immediate consumption.[16]

THE INTER-WAR PERIOD

The changes that were set underway in the 1880s continued in the inter-war period, but there were new trends. In the 1920s the lorry began to supplement the railway in moving the produce to market, in 1952 diesel lorries were introduced, and road transport has since largely replaced the railway. The lorry, of course, allowed production to move into areas away from the railway line. The lorry also replaced the horse, and its decline led to some problems for the small market gardeners who relied

15 G. M. Robinson, *West Midland Farming 1840s to 1970s*, Department of Land Economy, Occasional Paper 15 (Cambridge, 1983), p. 38; Johnstone, *op. cit.* (1963), pp. 216–19; D. Grigg, *The Agricultural Revolution in South Lincolnshire* (Cambridge, 1966), p. 164.

16 F. Beavington, 'The development of market gardening in Bedfordshire 1799–1939', *Agricultural History Review*, 23 (1975), pp. 23–47; E. A. Pratt, *The Transition in Agriculture* (London, 1906), p. 43; P. Allington, 'Combe Martin: a study of horticultural isolation', *Agriculture*, 69 (1962), pp. 279–82; G. M. Robinson, *Late Victorian Agriculture in the Vale of Evesham*, School of Geography, Research Paper no. 16 (Oxford, 1976), p. 18.

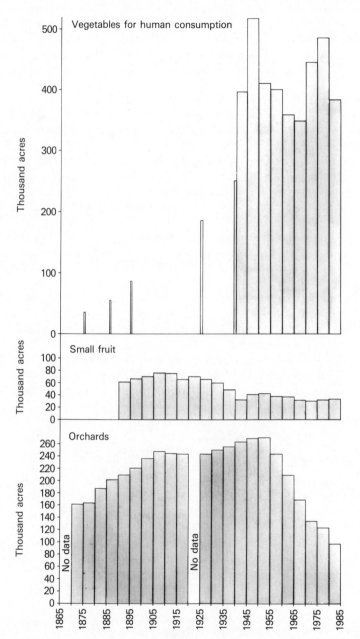

Figure 16.2   Changes in the area in vegetables, small fruit and orchards, 1870s–1985.
*Source*: Ministry of Agriculture, *Agricultural Statistics, England and Wales.*

upon horse-dung to maintain soil fertility; in the 1930s there was some evidence of declining crop yields in the Sandy and Evesham areas, but the falling real price of fertilizer arrested this in the post-war period, since when the yield of most horticultural products has risen, if less spectacularly than that of cereals.[17]

The 1920s saw a further extension of the processing of horticultural products that had begun with the jam factories of the 1870s and 1880s. The canning of fruit and vegetables began in the United States in the 1880s but was uncommon in the United Kingdom until after 1925. There was then a rapid expansion of canning output, using at first imported fruit, but this encouraged the home expansion of peas and small fruit, mainly in Eastern England. The output of canned fruit and vegetables in Britain rose from 7 million tons in 1926 to 100 million in 1932, when 60 factories were engaged in the business, mainly in the Fens and East Anglia.[18]

The inter-war period also saw the beginnings of the most important of changes in market gardening. Some of the more robust vegetables were grown on the large arable farms of eastern England before the First World War, but the continued decline of wheat prices encouraged farmers there to expand. A number of other factors encouraged the rise of vegetable production in the arable east. First the rapid spread of suburban London was reducing the area under market gardens. The expansion of housing east of West Ham, in north-west Kent and especially in Middlesex greatly reduced the area in crops. Half the market-gardening area of Middlesex was built upon between 1919 and 1936, leaving by 1943 only one substantial tract in crops, at Heathrow, which eventually became the airport. In contrast, the slow mechanization of farming began to give the large-scale production of vegetables a cost advantage over the small-scale intensive market gardeners, although the harvesting of most vegetables was not fully mechanized until after the Second World War. The use of tractors made the cultivation of heavy clays possible, for market gardeners with spades alone could not easily have utilized these soils: the expansion of vegetable production onto clays was particularly noticeable in Bedfordshire. The rise of canning factories also encouraged relocation in the 1920s and 1930s. Canning factories contracted with farms to deliver fresh vegetables; they needed large amounts, of good quality, delivered on time. It was far more satisfactory for such factories to contract with big farmers, who were to

17 F. Beavington, 'The change to more extensive methods in market gardening in Bedfordshire', *Transactions of the Institute of British Geographers*, 33 (1963), pp. 89–100; Beavington, *op. cit.* (1975), pp. 23–47; Ministry of Agriculture, *op. cit.* (1967), p. 43.

18 Cross, *op. cit.* (1945), pp. 129–48; L. D. Stamp and S. H. Beaver, *The British Isles: a geographic and economic survey* (London, 1933), pp. 180–204; Ministry of Agriculture, *op. cit.* (1967), p. 348; Ministry of Agriculture, *Horticulture in Britain*, pt. 2: *Fruit and Flowers*, (London, 1970), p. 148–50.

be found, of course, in the east and not in the traditional market-gardening areas.[19]

The potato was the first crop lost by market gardeners. It began to become a field crop in the 1840s and 1850s and then rapidly expanded in the Fen silts and the Lancashire mossland, leaving by the 1930s only some early varieties for the market gardeners. Carrots and cabbages had become part of farm rotations before 1914, and peas had become the prerogative of the farmer by the 1930s. Since 1945, with canning and freezing the main market, they have become almost exclusively a product of the east. Competition from the eastern arable farmers has forced market gardeners either to specialize in the more delicate crops that required a great deal of care, such as lettuce, cucumbers, radishes and salad onions, or to become even more intensive by using cloches and Dutch lights or producing fruits and vegetables in glasshouses.[20]

The modern glasshouse industry dates from the 1830s, when the tax on glass was reduced and manufacturers began to produce plate glass. In 1837 Joseph Paxton designed the conservatory at Chatsworth and this, together with the erection of the Crystal Palace in 1851, showed that buildings made of glass were feasible. The area under glass steadily expanded from the 1850s, when there were 200 acres, to 1900, when there were 1,500 acres, with some in nearly every county in England. The tomato was the principal crop. Hitherto it had been grown in the open but was very unreliable. By the 1880s glasshouses were particularly notable in Worthing, where demand from sanatoriums was the original cause, in the Lea Valley in north-east London, and on a very small scale in the Blackpool district; by the end of the century glass was used for forcing bulbs in the Fens. In the 1920s and 1930s there was rapid expansion in the Blackpool district, but the Lea Valley, with half the national acreage, remained the leader.[21]

LOCATION AND TYPE BEFORE THE SECOND WORLD WAR

Thus there had been major changes in market gardening before the outbreak of the Second World War. The more robust vegetables were

19 Cross, *op. cit.* (1945), pp. 129–48; L. D. Stamp, *The Land of Britain: its use and misuse* (London, 1950), p. 134; Atkins, *op. cit.* (1985), pp. 102–33; Beavington, *op. cit.* (1963), pp. 89–100; Ministry of Agriculture, *op. cit.* (1967), p. 42.

20 Cross, op. cit. (1945), pp. 129–48; Ministry of Agriculture, *op. cit.* (1967), p. 36; E. M. Whetham, *The Agrarian History of England and Wales*, vol. VIII: *1914–1939* (Cambridge, 1978), p. 307.

21 R. Webber, *Market Gardening: the history of commercial flower, fruit and vegetable growing* (London, 1972), pp. 74, 78, 82–3, 85; A. D. Grady, 'Changes in the Lea Valley glasshouse industry', *Geography*, 44 (1959), pp. 120–2; C. E. Pearson, 'Joseph Paxton: father of the British glasshouse industry', *Agriculture*, 52 (1951), pp. 132–5; E. A. Pratt, *op. cit.* (1906), p. 90.

being grown increasingly in eastern England on large arable farms; the less robust were cultivated either in the traditional market-garden regions, where crops such as asparagus received the attention the large farmer could not give them, or in glasshouses. As a result the relative importance of the old established market-gardening regions around London, in Bedfordshire and in the Vale of Evesham declined, while the eastern counties rose to become the principal vegetable producers. The east also assumed a predominance in fruit production. With the decline of cider consumption in the nineteenth and early twentieth centuries, the apple acreage of the west fell. In 1905 the fruit-growing counties of the west had 60 per cent of the area, but by 1950 this had fallen to 34 per cent. The new markets for fruit were the canners and jam-makers and they were concentrated in the east, so that new planting of fruit – small and top – was mainly in the east from the 1880s. Kent, which had only 10,000 acres in fruit in 1873, by 1952 had 82,000 acres, 29 per cent of the total of England and Wales.[22]

HORTICULTURAL CROPS SINCE 1939

The Second World War saw a remarkable expansion of potatoes (see figure 5.1) and vegetable crops which reached its zenith in the late 1940s (see figure 16.2 and table 16.2). The post-war period saw a continuation of trends established in the 1920s.

Table 16.2  Horticultural crops in England and Wales, 1910–1985 (thousand acres)

| Crop | 1910 | 1920 | 1930 | 1950 | 1960 | 1970 | 1985 |
|------|------|------|------|------|------|------|------|
| Vegetables | – | 184 | – | 490 | 385 | 487 | 362 |
| Orchards | 251 | 220 | 247 | 272 | 249 | 153 | 84 |
| Small fruit | 84 | 58 | 66 | 51 | 38 | 31 | 31 |
| Hardy nursery stock | – | 10 | – | 10 | 13 | 15[b] | 16 |
| Bulbs | – | – | – | 5 | 13 | 12[b] | 10 |
| Flowers in open | – | 5[a] | – | 7 | 6 | 2[b] | 2 |
| Glasshouse crops | – | 2[a] | – | 5 | 5 | 4 | 5 |
| Total | | 479 | | 840 | 709 | 704 | 510 |

[a] 1925.
[b] 1975.
*Sources*: Ministry of Agriculture, *Agricultural Statistics of England and Wales; The Agricultural Output of England and Wales 1925*, HMSO Cmd. 2815 (1927), p. 130; R. R. W. Folley, *Intensive Crop Economics* (London, 1973), p. 47.

22 Cross, *op. cit.* (1945), pp. 129–48; Ministry of Agriculture, *op. cit.* (1970), p. 10; Stamp, *op. cit.* (1950), pp. 108, 118–21; R. Gasson, 'The changing location of intensive crops in England and Wales', *Geography*, 51 (1966), pp. 16–28; R. G. Halton, 'Landmarks in the development of scientific fruit growing', in *Agriculture in the Twentieth Century: essays to be presented to Sir Daniel Hall* (Oxford, 1939), pp. 310–60; D. W. Harvey, 'Fruit growing in Kent in the nineteenth century',*Archaeologia Cantania*, 79 (1964), pp. 95–108; Stamp, *op. cit.* (1950), p. 144.

First, real incomes continued to increase and indeed rose much faster than in any previous period. This led to a growing demand for vegetables and fruits – but not for the staple vegetables. Consumers now wanted a wider range of crops, and especially the salad crops; this prompted an expansion of the area in glasshouses for the cultivation of cucumbers and tomatoes.

Second, vegetables and fruit were produced increasingly for processors. Before 1939 the only markets – other than for fresh produce – had been jam-makers and canners. However, in the 1920s Clarence Birdseye had pioneered a quick-freezing technique in the United States and this had been introduced into England for the freezing of fish; Great Yarmouth, Lowestoft, Grimsby and Hull were the major sites. After 1947 this capacity was adapted to the freezing first of peas, later of beans and then of other vegetables. The process required vegetables to be frozen within 90 minutes of picking, and so the crop could not be grown more than 20 miles or so from the freezers. Freezers, like canners, dealt only with farmers who would grow large acreages of peas and beans, would follow prescribed methods of cultivation to ensure high quality, and would grow for specific harvesting dates to ensure that the freezers received an even flow of the crop. Hence much of this vegetable production was concentrated near the coastal freezing plants in Norfolk and Lindsey and later in the East Riding.[23]

Third, since 1945 the production of all but the most sensitive vegetables has passed to the large arable farms of the east. This has been because technical advances have reduced the former high labour needs. The use of herbicides had reduced that needed in weeding, while the harvesting of vegetable crops has been slowly mechanized; the mobile pea viner has ended the hand-picking of peas and beans that prevailed until the 1940s; the harvesting of bulbs has been mechanized by adapting potato-pickers; and the harvesting of orchard fruit has been quickened by the use of vibrators and the breeding of dwarf varieties. It is only the harvest of soft fruit that has not been successfully mechanized. Some farmers have resolved the problems of harvesting by inviting customers to pick their own fruit and vegetables.[24]

Fourth, there have been major changes not only in the location of fruit and vegetable production, but in the national acreage. From the 1870s to the late 1940s the area in all horticultural products increased; but since 1950 that in vegetables, small fruit and orchards has declined, the acreage in orchards dramatically (see table 16.2 and figure 16.2).

23 J. T. Coppock, *An Agricultural Geography of Great Britain* (London, 1971), p. 278; R. T. Dalton, 'Peas for freezing: a recent development in Lincolnshire agriculture', *East Midland Geographer*, 33 (1971), pp. 133–41; Ministry of Agriculture, *op. cit.* (1967), pp. 355–6.

24 J. K. A. Bleasdale, 'Two decades of change in horticulture', *Span*, 21 (1978), pp. 59–61; Ministry of Agriculture, *op. cit.* (1967), p. 18; R. F. Clements, 'The influence of herbicides on horticultural production', *Agriculture*, 74 (1967), pp. 405–9.

Only the production of hardy nursery stock has steadily increased, while glasshouse acreage has held its own. There are a number of reasons for this decline. First, it should be recalled that the British horticultural industry has not received guaranteed prices either under the Common Agricultural Policy or under the previous British system of agricultural support. Hence, inefficient producers have been more likely to go to the wall. Second, although some protection against imports has existed, over much of the post-war period the British consumer has had a wide choice of home and foreign fruit and vegetables. Third, growing incomes have led to the falling consumption of some vegetables – such as the cabbage and the potato – but increases in those of products previously little eaten. Changes in taste rather than income have also been significant; the decline of the plum and the gooseberry may be attributed to this.

But the decline in acreage does not mean that output has necessarily fallen. Although yields have not risen as greatly as those of the cereals, there have been significant increases. Market gardening has always been an innovative industry; thus it was fruit to which insecticides were first applied in the inter-war period, and among market gardeners that the first herbicides were tried in the 1930s. Since the end of the war fertilizers, herbicides and pesticides have been widely used, and there have been some major advances in plant breeding. The continued expansion of glasshouse production has exemplified the rapidly changing technology of the horticulturalist. Crops are now grown in heated glasshouses in artificial soils with photosynthesis encouraged by the addition of $CO_2$ to the air. Increased efficiency has been necessitated by the competition with Dutch producers and the rapid increase in heating costs in the early 1970s.[25]

THE PRESENT LOCATION OF HORTICULTURAL PRODUCTION

The typical market gardener harvested a variety of vegetables and some fruit. Modern production of horticultural crops is quite difference. Of all the growers of horticultural commodities 70 per cent produced only one crop in the early 1970s. Nor is production any longer carried out only on small farms; 70 per cent of all horticultural output in the early 1970s was on holdings which had labour inputs of 1,200 standard man-days a year or more, a greater concentration of output on large farms than any other type of farming. Consequently, three-quarters of all output was centred on only 10 per cent of the holdings.[26]

25 H. Phillips, 'Change in the UK glasshouse industry and its impact on the rural environment', in M. J. Healey and B.W. Ilberry (eds), *The Industrialisation of the Countryside* (Norwich, 1985), pp. 121–43.

26 Folley, *op. cit.* (1973), p. 72; Hinton, *op. cit.* (1972), pp. 51–8.

Although vegetable production is thus concentrated upon large farms, it provides a small part of the output of these farms. In contrast, there are still many small farms where horticultural output is the leading enterprise. These farms are typically about 50 acres in size and still highly labour-intensive – on average five people are employed upon them – and about half the farm is devoted to horticultural crops. Nowhere do these farms occupy much of the agricultural area, but they are relatively most important in the Fens, Bedfordshire, Essex, the counties south of London, the West Midlands and Lancashire. They are the old market-garden areas (see figures 13.2, 13.3 and 13.4)[27]

It is impossible to deal with the current distribution of every horticultural crop; and even when they are grouped into categories of orchards, small fruit and vegetables they occupy but a small proportion of the agricultural area. Orchards – now mainly apples and pears – are found only in southern England in Kent and East Anglia, in the West Midlands and in the south-west. This shows the impact of climate; most of Britain lacks the long, warm, sunny ripening periods and the accumulated hours of solar radiation that give high yields. Italian apple yields are double those in Britain. Small fruit – of which strawberries, currants, gooseberries and raspberries account for most of the area – have a slightly more northerly location than do orchards; indeed most of British raspberry output is in Scotland. Climate has a role in the location of glasshouse production, for a southerly location reduces heating costs. In theory tomatoes in the open can give a good yield south of the Wash–Bristol line, but the high probability of a cold summer means that most are now grown under glass, as are cucumbers. A line drawn from the Humber to the Bristol Channel divides the country into two: to the south there are on average above four hours mean daily sunshine a day, to the north and west there is less. Most of the fruit producers lie to the south and east of this line; so too does most of the vegetable production. Nowadays the latter takes place mainly in eastern England, where most of the output is for processing. Lancashire and the Vale of Evesham produce more labour-intensive crops which are mainly for fresh consumption.[28]

One of the most distinctive features of horticultural production is the very marked localization of some crops. In the 1960s three-quarters of the country's celery was produced within 15 miles of Littleport in the Isle of Ely, half the brussel sprouts near Biggleswade, and nearly half

27 Ministry of Agriculture, *Farm Incomes in England 1984*, Farm Income Series no. 37 (London, 1985).

28 J. T. Coppock, *op. cit.* (1971), p. 287; *An Agricultural Atlas of England and Wales* (London, 1976), p. 151; Folley and Wicks, *op. cit.* (1975), pp. 28–90; R. R. W. Folley and R. A. Giles, *Locational Advantages in Tomato Production* (Wye College, 1960); I. A. Barne and D. Gray, 'Mapping areas of England and Wales suitable for outdoor tomato production', *ADAS Quarterly Review*, 38 (1980), pp. 138–44.

the rhubarb in the West Riding. In 1960, 67 farms in Norfolk grew one-quarter of the carrots in England and Wales, while 70 per cent of the tulips are to be found in Holland, Lincolnshire. All can be transported some distance before their quality deteriorates. Lettuces, which have to be consumed quickly, are grown mainly on the edge of towns.[29]

## SUMMARY

The intensive production of fruit and vegetables began in the sixteenth century and was found mainly on the edge of towns, particularly London, until the mid-nineteenth century. The spread of the railway then allowed fresh fruit and vegetables to be grown in areas some distance from their markets. But from the 1880s fruit and notably vegetable production began to be concentrated on large arable farms in eastern England; furthermore an increasing proportion of output has gone to canners and freezers. Traditional market gardeners now produce only the more delicate crops, while those most susceptible to frost – tomatoes and cucumbers – are grown mainly under glass.

29 M. Chisholm, *Rural Settlement and Land Use* (London, 1962), p. 92; J. B. Briggs, 'Flower bulb production', *Agriculture*, 77 (1970), pp. 358–63; Ministry of Agriculture, *op. cit.* (1976), pp. 43–7; K. M. Round, 'Celery growing in the Fens', *Agriculture*, 67 (1960–1), pp. 189–91.

# 17
# Dairying

Dairying is perhaps the most important type of farming in England and Wales: it accounts for over one-fifth of all farm income; 37,000 farmers produce milk; and at least half of all the beef produced in the country comes from dairy herds. Forty years ago milk production was even more important, accounting for 31 per cent of national farm income (see table 2.7), while 162,000 farmers were then producing milk. Since 1950 the number of milk producers has declined (see figure 17.1), as has the relative importance of dairying in the farm economy, but the output of milk has greatly increased (see figure 17.2). Indeed milk production under the Common Agricultural Policy has greatly outrun demand, and in 1984 the EEC introduced a quota system which has reduced output. But the importance of dairying is relatively modern. Before 1850 milk, butter and cheese accounted for less than one-tenth of national farm income. Modern dairying is very much a product of recent technological change.[1]

## DAIRYING BEFORE THE NINETEENTH CENTURY

Comparatively little is known of dairying before the nineteenth century. Cows were kept for milking in nearly all parts of the country; they were found, for example, grazing in the undrained Lincolnshire fens and in transhumance on Snowdonia. Herds were invariably small – two or three cows were common – and most of the milk was produced in summer when grass was abundant. Milk goes sour quickly and so most of it was converted on the farm into butter and cheese. By the seventeenth

---

1 M. E. Castle and P. Watkins, *Modern Milk Production: its principles, and applications for students and farmers* (London, 1979), p. 22; M. H. R. Soper, *Dairy Farming and Milk Production* (London, 1983); S. Baker, *Milk to Market: forty years of milk marketing* (London, 1973), p. 118; Centre for Agricultural Strategy, *Strategy for the UK dairy industry*, CAS Report (Reading, 1975).

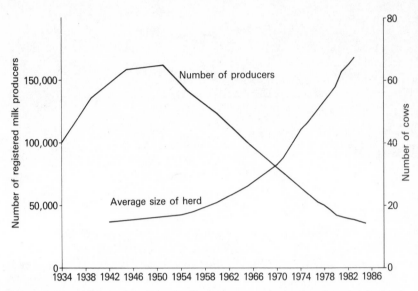

Figure 17.1   Number of registered milk producers and average size of dairy herd, England and Wales, 1934–1985.
*Source*: Federation of UK Milk Marketing Boards, *UK Dairy Facts and Figures* (Thames Ditton, various dates).

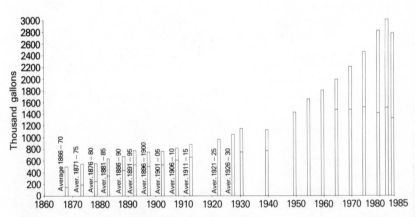

Figure 17.2   Milk output and the percentage sold to the liquid market, 1866–1984.
*Sources*: F. A. Barnes, 'The evolution of the salient patterns of milk production and distribution in England and Wales', *Transactions of the Institute of British Geographers*, 25 (1958), pp. 167–95; D.Taylor, 'The English dairy industry, *Economic History Review*, 29 (1976), pp. 585–601; Federation of UK Milk Marketing Boards, *UK Dairy Facts and Figures* (Thames Ditton, various dates).

and eighteenth centuries a considerable trade in cheese had developed, and most of the better-known varieties such as Stilton and Cheddar emerged then.[2]

Although dairying was widespread, it seems to have been most common in the west. It was the predominant type of farming in only a few regions such as the Vale of Gloucester and parts of Wiltshire and Dorset, but was an important subsidiary activity in Wales, Cheshire, Lancashire the Solway plains and parts of the West Midlands (see figure 13.6). It was less important in the arable east and south, although locally it was significant in the Weald, the clay areas of East Anglia, and the dales of the eastern Pennines from Derbyshire north to the Scottish border.[3]

### DAIRYING IN EARLY VICTORIAN TIMES

By the 1860s milk was still comparatively unimportant – 12 per cent of farm income – and was used mainly to make butter and cheese. Fresh milk was not an important part of the diet. Little more than a pint a week per capita was consumed, and butter and cheese were expensive. Milk still came from small herds, and yields were very low, about 300 to 350 gallons per year. As in earlier times cows were fed mainly on grass, by grazing in summer and hay in winter; supplementary feeds were uncommon. In the 1850s and 1860s there were few specialist dairy breeds. The Shorthorn was replacing the Longhorn as the leading breed, but although dual-purpose it became increasingly a beef animal. Milk came mainly from Shorthorns, Welsh Blacks and South Devons; only in the south of the country were a few Channel Island cows kept.[4]

Grass was the principal feed for cattle in the mid-nineteenth century, as it still is, and, as there was little import of foreign grains or oilseeds, cow densities were highest in the areas where grass growth was good. The best areas were the western lowlands, where temperatures allowed early spring, and late autumn, growth and cooler and moister summers were also favourable – in contrast to the lower rainfall and higher evaporation rates of the east and south. The uplands – of either west or

2 J. Thirsk, 'The farming regions of England', in J. Thirsk (ed.), *The Agrarian History of England and Wales*, vol. IV: *1500–1640* (Cambridge, 1967), pp. 2, 5, 7, 30, 33, 40, 47, 56, 58, 67, 72, 79–80, 81, 83, 89, 94–5, 103; F. V. Emery, 'The farming regions of Wales', in J. Thirsk,*op. cit. (1967), pp. 117, 125, 133–8.*

3 Joan Thirsk, *England's Agricultural Regions and Agrarian History 1500–1750* (London, 1987).

4 A. Harris, *The Milk Supply of East Yorkshire 1850–1950* (East Yorkshire Local History Society, 1977), pp. 25–6; A. Henstock, 'Cheese manufacture and marketing in Derbyshire and North Staffordshire 1670–1870', *Derbyshire Archaeological Journal*, 89 (1967), pp. 32–46; C. S. Orwin and E. H. Whetham, *History of British Agriculture 1846–1914* (London, 1964), pp. 131, 134, 359, 360.

north – with much cooler and wetter conditions, did not give good grass. Thus in 1875 the highest cow densities were in the lowlands of south-west Wales and in a great zone from Shropshire, Cheshire and Staffordshire north-west to the Solway plains. In the south-west the highest densities were in Somerset and Dorset; Devon and Cornwall were not of any note at this time (see figure 17.3).[5]

Although grass dairying regions were of most importance, producing nearly all the butter and cheese, there was a further location, within and on the immediate edges of towns, where cows were kept to provide fresh milk for daily consumption. London and most other major towns had dairies, where cows were kept in sheds and fed on hay brought from the pastures on the urban fringe and on spent grain from maltsters. These sheds were remarkably unhygienic, and the milk that was hawked in London's streets was often infected and invariably thinned with water. Cows were kept not only within the bigger cities but on the edges, where they were fed mainly on grass. In Lancashire much of the land within five miles of the many industrial towns was in grass; around Liverpool milk was brought into the city from as far away as 15 miles, but given the slow transport of the time and the high perishability of milk this was about the limit of movement.[6]

DEMAND AND TRANSPORT

From the 1850s to the 1950s there was a slow but steady rise in the consumption of milk in England, from about 1 pint per head per week in the 1850s, 2 pints in the 1890s, to 3.2 pints in 1939 and a peak of 5.2 pints in 1951, since when consumption has declined to just over 4 pints. The main reason for this increase has been rising incomes. Fresh milk, butter and cheese were expensive, but as incomes rose in the late nineteenth century, so also did consumption. However, there have been other factors. First, in the late nineteenth century milk had a poor reputation; not only did many retailers mix milk with water, but the fear of infection was considerable and justifiable. Consumer resistance was slowly overcome by legislation, notably in 1875 and 1901, which specified the composition of milk. The great outbreak of cattle plague in 1865 had reduced the number of cows kept in towns and led to a

---

5 W. Smith, *An Economic Geography of Great Britain* (London, 1953), p. 65.

6 P. J. Atkins, 'London's intra-urban milk supply, circa 1790–1914', *Transactions of the Institute of British Geographers* (new series), 2 (1977), pp. 383–99; 'The growth of London's railway milk trade, c.1845–1914', *Journal of Transport History*, 4 (1978), pp. 208–26; 'The retail milk trade in London, c. 1790–1914', *Economic History Review*, 33 (1980), pp. 522–37; E. H. Whetham, *The London Milk Trade 1900–1930*, Institute of Agricultural History, Research Paper no. 3 (Reading, 1970); 'The London milk trade 1860–1900', *Economic History Review*, 17 (1964), pp. 369–80; D. Taylor, 'London's milk supply 1850–1900, a reinterpretation', *Agricultural History*, 45 (1971), pp. 33–8.

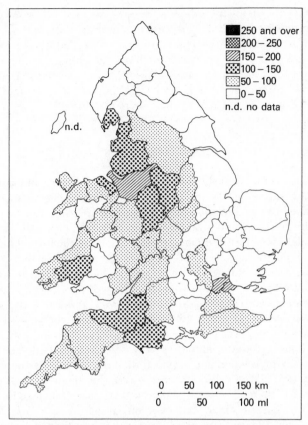

**Figure 17.3** Cows and heifers per 1,000 acres of total agricultural land, 1875.
*Source*: Board of Agriculture, *Agricultural Statistics, England and Wales 1875* (London, 1876).

series of Acts which aimed at improving hygiene both in dairies and on farms; these improvements were reluctantly adopted by farmers in the 1920s and 1930s. Pasteurisation of milk reduced the risk of infection but as late as 1925 only half of London's milk supply was so treated. The principal improvement was the slow reduction of tuberculosis; in 1930 40 per cent of the cattle in England and Wales were still infected with TB, but the spread of attested herds had virtually eliminated the disease by 1960.[7]

7 E. L. Crossley, *The UK Dairy Industry* (London, 1959), p. 4; Federation of UK Milk Marketing Boards, *UK Dairy Facts and Figures, 1985* (Thames Ditton, 1985), p. 169; R. H. Rew, 'An inquiry into the statistics of the production and consumption of milk and milk products in Great Britain', *Statistical Journal*, 55 (1892),pp. 244–78; Soper, *op. cit.* (1983); Orwin and Whetham, *op. cit.* (1964), pp. 367–8; J. A. F. Rook, 'Milk and milk products', in G. W. Cooke (ed.), *Agricultural Research 1931–1981* (London, 1981), pp. 325–36; Whetham, *op. cit.* (1970); A. S. Foot, 'Changes in milk production, 1930–1970', *Journal of the Royal Agricultural Society of England*, 131 (1971), pp. 30–42.

Second, in the 1930s the sale of milk was promoted by its subsidy for welfare purposes, notably for school children from 1934 but also in the depressed areas after 1936. Third, during the Second World War the production of milk was given a very high priority on nutritional grounds, at the expense of meat production. Fourth, since 1947 milk production has received guaranteed prices under the policies both of the British government and, since 1973, of the Common Market.[8]

### THE DEPRESSION AND ITS SIGNIFICANCE

In the 1850s comparatively little butter or cheese was imported into Britain; but in this decade the factory production of cheese and butter in the United States and the application of refrigeration to ships led to imports from the United States, New Zealand, Denmark and the Netherlands. These factory-made products undercut the home farmhouse cheese and butter because they were cheaper, of consistent standard and, in the case of butter, of better quality. In England factories were opened in Derbyshire in the 1870s but were not very efficient. Neither the farmhouse nor the factory product could withstand the foreign imports. Between 1860 and 1910 the home output of cheese fell by two-thirds, and that of butter from 0.5 million to 0.2 million hundredweight. The farmhouse producer of butter very soon lost to both home and foreign factory production and survived the First World War only in the remoter parts of Wales and the south-west. Farmhouse cheese lasted longer; in 1933 there were still 1,300 farmhouse cheese-makers, including over 300 in Cheshire alone, but by 1980, in spite of a recent revival, there were only 49 farmhouse producers of cheese in the whole country.[9]

Foreign competition was disastrous for cheese- and butter-makers on the farm or in factories. By the beginning of the twentieth century 87 per cent of the butter and 75 per cent of the cheese consumed in Britain was imported. But it was not disastrous for English and Welsh milk producers; far from output declining, it steadily increased from the 1860s to the 1930s (see figure 17.1) because of the growing urban market for fresh milk. Not only did the existing dairy farmers divert their milk from butter, but in the poor years for cereals in the 1880s and 1890s many East Anglian and Home Counties farmers added a dairy herd to their farm. The proportion of milk output sold liquid, rather than converted to butter, cheese, cream or skimmed milk, rose from 25 per cent in 1860 to 76.1 per cent in 1924 (see table 17.1). This change was possible only

8 Baker, *op. cit.* (1973), pp. 84–6.

9 M. A. Dockery, 'Developments in the farmhouse cheese making industry in England and Wales', *Geography*, 68 (1983), pp. 263–5; E. S. Simpson, 'The Cheshire grass dairying region', *Transactions of the Institute of British Geographers*, 23 (1957), pp. 141–62; D. Taylor, 'The English dairy industry', *Economic History Review*, 29 (1976), pp. 585–601.

Table 17.1  Proportion of total milk output manufactured and sold liquid, England and Wales (percentage)

| Date | Liquid | Total manufactured | Butter | Cheese | Cream | Other |
|------|--------|--------------------|--------|--------|-------|-------|
| 1860 | 25.0 | 75.0 | 30.0 | 40.0 | – | – |
| 1870 | 40.0 | 60.0 | 20.0 | 40.0 | – | – |
| 1890 | 40.0 | 60.0 | 23.0 | 16.0 | – | – |
| 1914 | 70.0 | 30.0 | 15.0 | 10.0 | – | – |
| 1924 | 76.1 | 23.9 | 15.8 | 7.0 | – | – |
| 1933 | 75.5 | 24.5 | 16.0 | 7.0 | – | 1.5 |
| 1939 | 69.0 | 31.0 | 9.4 | 8.1 | – | 13.5 |
| 1964 | 73.5 | 26.5 | 3.3 | 10.9 | 4.6 | 7.7 |
| 1969–70 | 66.4 | 33.6 | 10.1 | 9.8 | 6.5 | 7.2 |
| 1975–6 | 61.8 | 38.2 | 9.8 | 15.3 | 7.5 | 5.6 |
| 1980–1 | 49.1 | 50.9 | 25.6 | 14.4 | 6.7 | 4.2 |
| 1984–5 | 48.3 | 51.7 | 26.5 | 15.0 | 4.4 | 5.8 |

*Sources*: D. Taylor, 'The English Dairy Industry', *Economic History Review*, 29 (1976), pp. 585–601; C. S. Orwin and E. H. Whetham, *History of British Agriculture 1846–1914* (London, 1964), p. 149; R. H. Rew, 'An inquiry into the statistics of the production and consumption of milk and milk products in Great Britain', *Statistical Journal*, 55 (1892), pp. 244–78; F. A. Barnes, 'The evolution of the salient patterns of milk production and distribution in England and Wales, *Transactions of the Institute of British Geographers*, 25 (1958), pp. 167–95; Federation of Milk Marketing Boards, *UK Dairy Facts and Figures, 1985* (Thames Ditton, 1985).

because of a number of important changes both on the farm and in retailing.

CHANGES IN TRANSPORT AND LOCATION

As long as the horse and cart was the only means of transport fresh milk production had to take place a few miles from the point of consumption. But with the spread of the rail network, the area that London and the other major urban areas could draw upon steadily widened. The first milk sent by rail was from Romford to central London in 1845, when the rail network was very limited. The railway companies were slow to respond to this considerable new market; it was not until 1860 that the first train solely for milk was run, by the Great Western Railway, and the milk churn was adopted only slowly after 1860. On the farm the use of Lawrences' cooler from 1872 ensured milk was in a fresh condition before it left the farm, and chemical preservatives were used on the journey to market. By 1910 some milk for daily consumption in London was brought 130 miles, and by the 1920s was regularly transported from Derbyshire and Cornwall.[10]

10 Atkins, *op. cit.* (1978), pp. 208–26; Orwin and Whetham, *op. cit.* (1964), pp. 363–4; F. A. Barnes, 'The evolution of the salient patterns of milk production and distribution in England and Wales', *Transactions of the Institute of British Geographers*, 25 (1958), pp. 167–95; E. Whetham, *op. cit.* (1964), pp. 131, 134, 359–60.

The rise of milk transported by railway led to the decline of the urban dairy. Their costs rose as regulations on hygiene were enforced after the 1865–6 plague. Thus in London, by far the largest market, urban milk accounted for 80 per cent of consumption in 1850 when most of the rest was brought in by road from the farms on the edge of the city (see table 17.2). But by 1910 not only had consumption risen nearly tenfold, but four-fifths was brought by rail and less than 5 per cent was provided by urban dairies. In other cities the urban dairies lasted longer. In York they still provided one-fifth of consumption in 1908, and in Hull one-tenth in the 1930s. In London and the other big cities the distribution of milk from the railheads, initially by small retailers, became the business of a few very large companies; by 1915 United Dairies controlled two-thirds of London's wholesale milk and one-third of the retail trade.[11]

As the urban dairy declined so there were other changes in the location of milk production. In 1913, as in 1875, the grass-growing regions of the north-west, south-west Wales, and the south-west had the highest densities of dairy cows. But between 1875 and 1915 the greatest increases in the number of cows was not in the traditional western regions but in the south and east, where arable farming had predominated in the 1870s. These regions were suffering from the fall in cereal and wool prices; however they grew fodder crops as part of the rotation, and these could be fed to cows in the winter when milk prices were higher than in summer. In addition the East Anglian arable areas had the advantage of nearness to the London market, while in the 1880s and 1890s Scots immigrants brought to parts of Essex an expertise in dairying which local farmers lacked. Milk production also developed to the west of London on the chalk uplands of Wiltshire. Hence by the 1920s the south and east was producing one-third of the milk output of England and Wales (see table 17.3).[12]

Table 17.2   Sources of London's milk, 1850–1914 (million gallons)

| Date | Town milk | Road milk | Railway milk | Other | Total |
|---|---|---|---|---|---|
| 1850 | 12.0 | 2.0 – 3.0 | 0.8 | | 14.8 – 15.8 |
| 1870 | 8.8 | 2.2 – 4.5 | 7.2 – 11.5 | 0.3 | 18.5 – 25.1 |
| 1890 | 6.8 – 8.0 | 0.0 – 0.5 | 39.3 – 41.7 | 4.6 | 50.7 – 54.8 |
| 1910 | 2.7 | 0.0 – 0.2 | 66.9 – 90.5 | 10.0 – 20.0 | 79.6 – 113.4 |

*Source*: P. J. Atkins, 'The growth of London's railway milk trade, *c*.1845–1914', *Journal of Transport History*, 4 (1978), pp. 208–26.

11  Harris, *op. cit.* (1977); Atkins, *op. cit.* (1980), pp. 522–37.
12  Orwin and Whetham, *op. cit.* (1964), pp. 274, 359; D. Taylor, 'Some aspects of the development of English dairying 1860–1930, and their relation to the south-west', in W. E. Minchinton (ed.), *Farming and Transport in the South-West*, Exeter Papers in Economic History, no. 5 (1972), pp. 31–46.

Table 17.3   Percentage of liquid milk sales off the farm, by region

| Region | 1924–5 | 1933–4 | 1938–9 | 1946–7 | 1954–5 | 1984–5 |
|---|---|---|---|---|---|---|
| Eastern | 6.1 | 4.8 | 5.6 | 5.9 | 5.8 | 3.1 |
| East Midlands | 8.4 | 7.6 | 7.4 | 6.8 | 6.2 | 4.9 |
| Southern | 7.5 | 7.7 | 7.2 | 6.5 | 6.5 | 4.9 |
| South-eastern | 11.5 | 11.2 | 10.2 | 8.5 | 8.0 | 5.2 |
| Arable England | 33.5 | 31.3 | 30.4 | 27.7 | 26.5 | 18.1 |
| Mid-west | 14.5 | 16.1 | 14.5 | 13.2 | 13.5 | 15.1 |
| West Midlands | 8.1 | 8.6 | 8.5 | 9.2 | 9.7 | 10.5 |
| North-west | 27.3 | 28.9 | 27.6 | 24.8 | 23.1 | 22.4 |
| Pastoral core | 49.9 | 53.6 | 50.6 | 47.2 | 46.3 | 48.0 |
| Far west | 3.6 | 3.5 | 4.8 | 6.4 | 7.3 | 11.5 |
| North | 6.8 | 6.1 | 7.0 | 8.8 | 9.0 | 10.4 |
| North Wales | 2.8 | 2.1 | 2.7 | 4.2 | 4.5 | 4.0 |
| South Wales | 3.4 | 3.4 | 4.5 | 5.7 | 6.4 | 8.0 |
| Pastoral periphery | 16.6 | 15.1 | 19.0 | 25.1 | 27.2 | 33.9 |
| Total pastoral | 66.5 | 68.7 | 69.6 | 72.3 | 73.5 | 81.9 |
| All England and Wales | 100.0 | 100.0 | 100.0 | 100.0 | 100.0 | 100.0 |

*Sources*: F. Barnes, 'The evolution of the salient patterns of milk production and distribution in England and Wales', *Transactions of the Institute of British Geographers*, 25 (1958), pp. 167–95; Federation of Milk Marketing Boards, *UK Dairy Facts and Figures, 1985* (Thames Ditton, 1985).

### THE GROWTH OF OUTPUT, 1850–1933

The growing demand for fresh milk after the 1860s was met by an increase in output of about 75 per cent by 1914, and output had doubled by 1930, when three-quarters was going to the fresh-milk trade (see table 17.1). This increased output was supplied partly by extra cows, whose numbers rose from 1.7 million to 2.4 million between 1860 and 1913, partly by a 20 per cent increase in milk yield, which, however, was still very low; on the eve of the First World War it was about 420 gallons per cow per year (see figure 17.4). There were comparatively few changes in dairy farming in this period. The most noticeable was the slow mechanization of the hay harvest after the 1860s (see above, pp. 163–5) and the changes in the way cattle were fed. The area in grass increased in the 1880s and 1890s (see above, p. 39) but dairy cows in the east began to be fed on turnips and mangolds and, in the 1920s, on sugar-beet tops. More important, dairy cattle began to be fed upon grain and oilseeds, mainly imported. This began in Cheshire and Lancashire, where there was easy access to imports of cottonseed and

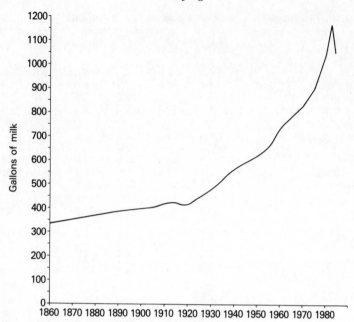

Figure 17.4   Gallons of milk per cow, 1860–1985.
*Source*: D. Taylor, 'The English dairy industry', *Economic History Review*, 29 (1976), pp. 585–601; Federation of UK Milk Marketing Boards, *UK Dairy Facts and Figures* (Thames Ditton, various dates).

maize at Liverpool, but spread elsewhere in the country. This was only possible because of the great decline in the price of grain and oilseeds after 1880, while the price of milk remained little changed.

At the beginning of the century few cows were specialist milk producers. The Shorthorn was still the dominant animal in 1908 and the Friesian had made little progress by the 1920s, while the Channel Island herds were still few and confined largely to the south of England. Milking remained overwhelmingly by hand in the 1920s, although machines had been available since the 1890s.[13]

## OVERPRODUCTION AND THE MMB

In the early 1930s English farming was suffering from falling grain, wool and meat prices; for some time milk producers, safe from foreign competition – unless they turned their milk into cheese or butter – had been relatively prosperous, but by the late 1920s overproduction and a chaotic marketing system brought financial difficulties to them as well.

13 E. S. Simpson, 'The cattle population of England and Wales: its breed structure and distribution', *Geographical Studies*, 5 (1958), pp. 45–60.

Although the government was still loath to protect home agriculture, it was prepared to help in the reorganization of milk marketing, and in 1933 the Milk Marketing Board was established. The Board, whose directors consisted – and still consist – of elected representatives of dairy farmers, and which has a large permanent staff, was at first concerned mainly with negotiating the price milk producers received from retailers and manufacturers. The former was consistently higher than the latter,. and since 1945 the price the farmer receives has been an average of the sales to retailer and manufacturer. As any surplus went to manufacturers, and hence lowered the price received, this acted as a restraint on output. From 1942 the MMB also organized the collection of milk from farmers. Farmers were charged for this, but the price within one of the board's 11 regions was standard, hence encouraging the development of milk production within the remoter parts of the region. All milk producers had to register with and sell their milk to the board; however, some producer-retailers were licensed to sell direct to the customer, and in the 1930s these farmers were half all the registered producers and accounted for one-fifth of milk output; since then they have greatly declined and are now of little significance.[14]

### THE GROWTH OF OUTPUT

Since the 1930s milk output has risen continuously and rapidly, only to falter in the 1980s as the dairy quotas were introduced, which cut back national output. From 1,000 million gallons in 1930 total output rose to 1,500 million in 1950, and by 1982–3 it had doubled to 3,000 million gallons (see figure 17.2). Until the late 1960s three-quarters of this output went to the fresh-milk market; but then demand for liquid milk began to fall, and increasingly milk was sent to manufacturers. The proportion of milk manufactured has risen from one-quarter to one-half. Under EEC financing there was, until 1984, little restraint upon output; guaranteed prices led to overproduction, which took the form of butter surpluses. As imports of butter and cheese from outside the EEC have been greatly reduced, Britain now produces two-thirds of its cheese and butter.[15]

### THE TRANSFORMATION OF DAIRY FARMING

Dairy farming has been greatly changed since the 1930s. Output has doubled, although the number of cows has increased by only 25 per

14 Baker, *op. cit.* (1973), pp. 4, 16–17; E. Straus, 'The structure of the English milk industry', *Journal of the Royal Statistical Society*, 123A (1960), pp. 140–73; E. H. Whetham, *The Agrarian History of England and Wales*, vol. VIII: *1914–1939* (Cambridge, 1978), pp. 249–51.

15 R. E. Williams, 'Perspectives on milk marketing', *Journal of Agricultural Economics*, 37 (1986), pp. 295–310.

cent. Most of the increase in milk has been achieved by a considerable rise in output per cow, yields having more than doubled (see figure 17.4). There are several reasons for these higher yields.

Of great importance has been the radical change in the breed structure. In the 1930s there were few specialist dairy herds, and Friesian cows accounted for only 7 per cent of all cattle (see table 7.8). But by the 1970s virtually all milk came from specialist breeds, of which the Friesian was dominant (see table 17.4). It was adopted so rapidly not only because it gave higher yields but also because it gives a reasonable beef; most of Britain's beef continues to be derived from the dairy herd. The comparatively rapid shift from Shorthorn and other dual-purpose cattle since the 1930s has been eased by the adoption of artificial insemination. The first centre opened in Cambridge in 1942 and now 75 per cent of all dairy cows are inseminated in this way.[16]

British livestock are afflicted by some 400 diseases, and the control of many of these since the 1930s has greatly contributed to the increased output of milk. The reduction of tuberculosis was achieved by providing financial incentives for attested herds in 1935, and TB had been eliminated by 1960. But of equal importance has been the use of antibiotics to treat disease and of vaccines to grant immunity. Brucellosis has been ended largely by the use of vaccines developed in the early 1950s, while deaths from respiratory diseases have been much reduced.[17]

Better and healthier cattle have also been better fed. In the 1920s ideas on balanced rations were introduced from Germany; feed is now

Table 17.4  Composition of the dairy herd in England and Wales, 1955–1984 (percentage of all dairy cows in each breed)

| Breed | 1955 | 1973–4 | 1983–4 |
|---|---|---|---|
| Ayrshire | 18.7 | 3.6 | 2.1 |
| Friesian | 40.5 | 81.4 | 86.8 |
| Holstein | – | – | 2.9 |
| Guernsey | 5.3 | 2.8 | 1.9 |
| Jersey | 2.6 | 2.2 | 1.6 |
| Dairy Shorthorn | 25.3 | 0.5 | 0.4 |
| Others | 7.6 | 9.5 | 4.3 |
| Total | 100.0 | 100.0 | 100.0 |

*Sources*: Federation of Milk Marketing Boards, *UK Dairy Facts and Figures, 1985* (Thames Ditton, 1985); E. S. Simpson, 'The cattle population of England and Wales: its breed structure and distribution', *Geographical Studies*, 5 (1958), pp. 45–60.

16 Simpson, *op. cit.* (1958), pp. 45–60; Soper, *op. cit.* (1983); Foot, *op. cit.* (1971), pp. 30–42.

17 K. N. Burns, 'Diseases of farm animals', in Cooke, *op. cit.* (1981), pp. 255–76.

adapted to need, and is varied with changing age and purpose. Although cows will give milk on a grass diet, the very high yields now obtained are dependent upon feeding them concentrates. Since the 1950s much of this has been home-grown (see above, pp. 90–2). But grass output has also risen as improved grass varieties have replaced traditional; whereas hardly any fertilizer was used on grass in Britain in the 1930s, half the total consumption now goes on grass (see above, p. 87). Thus stocking rates are now well above those of the pre-war period.

Dairying was – and still is – a remarkably labour-intensive activity, for animals demand a great deal of attention. Before the Second World War 90 per cent of the herds in Britain were milked by hand; but so rapid was the adoption of milking machinery under the pressure of rising labour costs that by 1963 only 3 per cent were hand milked, mainly in Wales and the south-west peninsular. In spite of the growing use of concentrates grass remains the primary source of feed. In the summer cows are grazed – there has been much experiment with various grazing strategies – but most farmers still rely on hay to provide much of their winter feed. In the 1850s this was still brought in with the scythe and a pitch-fork alone; these hand tools were slowly replaced by the horse-rake, the mechanical mower and the tedder, and since 1950 mechanization has progressed rapidly. Perhaps the most significant change has been from hay to silage, which gives a better quality feed and needs fewer harvesting processes (see above, p. 88).[18]

There have been other major changes on dairy farms. Until 1960 most cows were both kept and milked in the same cowsheds, but since then special milking parlours have been designed and widely adopted, while the feeding of cows, which is remarkably time-consuming, has been partly automated. This, together with other changes, has meant that the number of cows one man can deal with has risen. In the 1930s one man could manage 10 cows, by the early 1980s, over 100. This has had a number of implications. First, mechanization has allowed a substantial increase in average herd size (see table 17.5). Second, because the production costs of dairy farmers have risen more than milk prices in the post-war period, the smaller herds have become uneconomic; the threshold of what is economically viable has been constantly rising, and the number of small herds diminishing. In the 1950s one-third of all herds were of fewer than 10 cows, only 3 per cent of more than 50 cows. By 1984 only 4 per cent of cows were in herds of fewer than 10 cows and half in herds of more than 50 cows; yet the majority of cows were still kept in herds below the optimum size (see table 17.5). Although

---

18 E. H. Whetham, 'The mechanization of British farming 1910–1945', *Journal of Agricultural Economics*, 21 (1970), pp. 317–33; Milk Marketing Board, *The Structure of Dairy Farming in England and Wales during 1963/64* (Thames Ditton, 1965), p. 30; T. H. Davies, 'The evolution of modern dairy cow grazing systems', *ADAS Quarterly Review*, 22 (1976), pp. 275–82.

Table 17.5 Herd size in England and Wales, 1955–1984 (cows in each size group as a percentage of all cows)

| Number of cows[a] | 1955 | 1970 | 1984 |
|---|---|---|---|
| Under 10 | 31.9 | 10.8 | 4.2 |
| 10–19 | 37.3 | 25.1 | 8.0 |
| 20–9 | 18.2 | 21.0 | 11.0 |
| 30–9 | 7.2 | 14.1 | 13.1 |
| 40–9 | 3.5 | 9.3 | 10.8 |
| 50–9 | | 6.7 | 9.8 |
| 60–9 | | 4.4 | 8.4 |
| 70–99 | 3.9 | | 17.5 |
| 100–99 | | 8.6 | 14.8 |
| 200 and over | | | 2.4 |

[a] Excluding herds of 3 cows and fewer.
*Sources*: Centre for Agricultural Strategy, *Strategy for the UK Dairy Industry* (Reading, 1975); Federation of Milk Marketing Boards, *UK Dairy Facts and Figures, 1985* (Thames Ditton, 1985).

herd size rather than farm size is the best guide to the size of business in dairying, the average dairy farm is small, nearly half being fewer than 100 acres, only 15 per cent over 250 acres.[19]

SPECIALIZATION AND TYPE OF FARMING

Milk production was found on a wide range of farms in the 1930s; since then it has tended to be concentrated onto farms where it is either the only, or by far the most important enterprise. In 1975, 72 per cent of all dairy cows were to be found on specialist Dairy farms, 20 per cent on Mainly Dairy farms and very few on other farms. In the past dairying was often combined with pig production, notably in Cheshire, for the pigs would be fed partly on skimmed milk. Dairying became economical in upland areas when the Milk Marketing Board established uniform regional freight rates in 1942, and so dairying was combined with rearing and fattening, but this has become less viable since the introduction of quotas. In eastern England many mixed farmers have given up dairy herds since the 1950s in order to concentrate on crop production.[20]

19 Soper, *op. cit.* (1983); R. Treharne, 'The future of milk production in the United Kingdom', *The Milk Industry*, 58 (1966), pp. 35–7; A. E. Hirons and A. J. Quick, 'How many cows per cowman', *Agriculture*, 73 (1966), pp. 518–23.

20 Simpson, *op. cit.* (1957), pp. 141–62; 'Milk production in England and Wales: a study in the influence of collective marketing', *Geographical Review*, 49 (1959), pp. 95–111; W. B. Mercer, 'Two centuries of Cheshire cheese farming', *Journal of the Royal Agricultural Society of England*, 97 (1937), pp. 61–89; F. A. Barnes, 'Dairying in Anglesey', *Transactions of the Institute of British Geographers*, 21 (1953), pp. 137–155; Centre for Agricultural Strategy, *op. cit.* (1975).

Modern dairying is highly intensive – far more than any other type of farming except pig and poultry management, much of which is now more like industrial than agricultural production. Labour inputs are greater than in any other type of farming other than Horticulture and Pigs and Poultry, and farms are smaller than in all but these latter two types. Although net income *per acre* compares favourably with other livestock production, total net income does not, and the dairy quota cuts since 1984 are likely to hasten the continued decline in the number of dairy farmers. There are now only one-quarter of the number of registered milk producers that there were in the 1930s.

CHANGING LOCATION

Between the 1860s and the 1920s the rise of dairy production on arable farms in the east and south reduced the concentration of output in the grass-growing regions of the west. Since the 1920s there have been a number of changes in the location of milk output.

In the 1920s and 1930s the introduction of the lorry allowed remoter areas to market fresh milk; before they had either converted milk to butter or cheese or had not been involved in milk production. The introduction of standardized freight charges for the collection of milk by the MMB accelerated this trend, and the remoter areas of Wales, Cumberland, Devon and Northumberland, all of which had been engaged mainly in rearing, turned to dairying. But with the introduction of bulk collection of milk by the MMB from 1964 some of the remoter farms in these regions had to give up production, for tankers could not negotiate narrow winding lanes. Nor was this the only locational change. Between the 1920s and the 1980s milk output more than tripled, but the rate of increase was least in the east and the south – indeed in the post-war period milk production in the east has fallen – and greatest not in the traditional dairy regions of the north-west and Dorset, Somerset and Wiltshire (the mid-western region), but in the remoter regions of the north, Wales and the south-west – Devon and Cornwall (see table 17.6). Consequently arable England now produces a smaller proportion of milk sales than it did in the 1920s (see table 17.3). What may be called the pastoral core, the traditional dairy counties of the north-west and mid-west, has held its own. It is the remoter pastoral periphery that has gained; the west combined now has four-fifths of total output compared with only two-thirds half a century ago.

The westerly predominance in the dairy industry is apparent if either density or type of farming is considered. The density of dairy cows is greatest in the north-west and mid-west, as it was in 1875, and least in the east and south (see figure 17.5). Dairy farms occupy a greater proportion of the agricultural area in the north-west, mid-west and south-west, and are of little significance in the east (see figures 13.2, 13.3 and 13.4).

Table 17.6   Percentage increase in sale of liquid milk off farms, by regions

| Region | 1924–5 to 1954–5 | 1954–5 to 1984–5 | 1924–5 to 1984–5 |
|---|---|---|---|
| Far western | 296 | 168 | 966 |
| South Wales | 275 | 117 | 692 |
| Northern | 167 | 96 | 425 |
| North Wales | 231 | 50 | 400 |
| West Midlands | 142 | 81 | 339 |
| Mid-western | 87 | 89 | 253 |
| North-western | 70 | 64 | 178 |
| Southern | 74 | 27 | 121 |
| East Midlands | 48 | 36 | 101 |
| Eastern | 45 | −10 | 73 |
| South-eastern | 38 | 10 | 52 |
| England and Wales | 100 | 69 | 239 |

*Sources*: As for table 17.3.

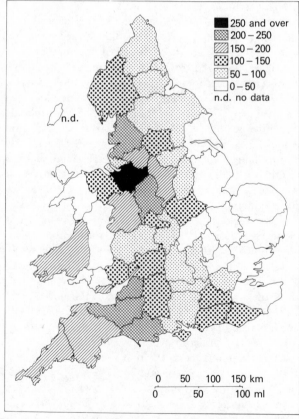

Figure 17.5   Dairy cows per 1,000 acres of total agricultural land, 1983.
*Sources*: Ministry of Agriculture, *Agricultural Statistics, United Kingdom 1983* (London, 1984); Welsh Office, *Welsh Agricultural Statistics, no. 6, 1984* (Cardiff, 1984).

SUMMARY

Dairy production was widespread before the mid-nineteenth century, but the edge of towns and the western lowlands were the principal locations. The spread of the railway and the import of cheap cheese and butter altered both the location and output, with liquid milk becoming the major product and the south and south-east increasing their dairy herds. Since the 1930s the marketing of milk has been transformed by the MMB, yield greatly increased by better health, better feeding and the replacement of Shorthorns by Friesians. However, demand has fallen behind the growth of output and in 1984 the EEC introduced quotas.

# 18
# Farming in the Uplands

Most of the uplands and hill regions of England and Wales (see figure 4.2) are given over to the breeding and rearing of sheep and cattle, and indeed always have been. The relatively few changes that have taken place in these regions, and the continuing poverty of farms – temporarily alleviated by the introduction of guaranteed prices for sheep-meat in 1980 – are due to the very harsh environment found at higher altitudes in Britain. As height above sea level increases, so it becomes difficult for farmers to grow horticultural products, cash grains or sugar-beet, oilseeds, or potatoes on a large scale. With further increases in height grassland productivity deteriorates and dairying and fattening becomes uneconomic; then all that is left to the farmer is the production of beef stores, and finally, in the highest altitudes, of lambs for sale to lowland graziers.

## THE UPLAND ENVIRONMENT

With increasing altitudes mean annual temperature declines in England and Wales at approximately 6.5°C per 1,000 metres, or 1°F for every 270 feet above sea level. As a result the grazing season contracts about one day for every increase of 50 feet in altitude. Consequently the type of crops that can be grown commercially diminishes, and above 800 feet the frequency of harvest failure increases exponentially. The shorter, cooler summers means grass growth begins later than at low altitudes and ends sooner, so that the output of dry matter per acre for upland pastures is only one-third to one-fifth that of lowland pastures. In the 1930s Sir George Stapledon estimated the meat output of average lowland pastures to be 5 to 15 times times that of the average upland pastures and the difference is much the same today.[1]

Temperature is not the only climatic hazard in the hills. As temperatures decline with altitude so mean annual rainfall increases. Thus in summer soil moisture content is high, and peat bog forms on flat, badly drained areas. Most of the uplands have an annual rainfall of 50 inches or more. Increased alttitude leads to more cloud, which reduces radiation receipts and the sunshine needed for ripening crops. In winter the upland areas have snow for quite long periods; few parts have less than three weeks of snow cover, while in parts of the northern Pennines it is over seven weeks. The snow buries the limited feed available to sheep and makes it difficult for shepherds to get to their flocks. In the terrible winter of 1947, 3 million sheep were lost.[2]

With increasing altitude and more rain, leaching gives very acid soils in much of the upland zone. High acidity limits the type of crop that can be grown; it also impairs the availability of nitrogen to plants. Soil type, acidity and type of vegetation changes with increasing altitude; both crop and grass productivity diminish. In the lower uplands a reasonable grass is possible, and clover can be grown; this gives way to a poor *agrostis* grass, then acid podzols with *nardus* or heather, then poorly drained peaty gleys with only *molinia* or *calluna* heath, and on the upland plateaux, peat bogs, which make up 7 per cent of the total area of Great Britain.[3]

1 S. J. Harrison, 'The elevation component of soil temperature variation', *Weather*, 30 (1975), pp. 397–409; J. A. Taylor, 'Upland climates', in T. J. Chandler and S. Gregory (eds), *The Climate of the British Isles* (London, 1976), pp. 264–87; M. L. Parry, 'Secular climatic change and marginal agriculture', *Transactions of the Institute of British Geographers*, 64 (1975), pp. 1–14; R. G. Stapledon, *The Hill Lands of Britain: development or decay* (London, 1937), p. 28; H. Evans, 'Marginal land – history and present policy', in D. A. Jenkins, E. R. B. Oxley and P. A. Gething (eds), *Marginal Land: integration or competition: 4th colloquium Potassium Institute Ltd* (Henley, 1974), pp. 1–9; J. Eadie, 'Increasing output in hill sheep-farming', *Journal of the Royal Agricultural Society of England*, 139 (1978), pp. 103–14.

2 G. Manley, *Climate and the British Scene* (London, 1955), p. 204; W. H. Pearsall, *Mountains and Moorlands* (London, 1965), pp. 42–3; P. E. Francis, 'The climate of upland Britain', in R. B. Tranter (ed.), *The Future of Upland Britain*, 2 (Reading, 1978), pp. 387–96; E. A. Attwood and H. G. Evans, *The Economics of Hill Farming* (Cardiff, 1961), p. 34.

3 D. F. Ball, 'The soils of upland Britain' in Tranter, *op. cit.* (1978), pp. 397–416; M. J. S. Floate, 'British hill soil problems', *Soil Science*, 123 (1977), pp. 325–31; J. A. Taylor, 'The British upland environment and its management', *Geography*, 63 (1978), pp. 338–53; E. Crompton, 'Hill soils and their production potential', *Journal of the British Grassland Society*, 13 (1958), pp. 229–37; Hill Farming Research Organisation, *Science and Hill Farming 1954–1979* (Edinburgh, 1979).

GRAZING AND SEASONS

In the lower hills good permanent pasture is possible, but with increasing altitude only rough grazing is available. This is the semi-natural vegetation of the uplands, which consists not only of the poorer grasses but also of heather and bracken. Until about 5,000 BC the hills were covered with deciduous forest up to 1,700 feet, possibly to 2,000 feet. This forest was cleared to provide grazing by Neolithic people in the period 3,300–2,500 BC, and later in the Iron Age. In the period of population growth AD 1,000–1,350, which was also a period of drier and warmer weather, there is evidence of cultivation and settlement at greater heights than at present. Since then the regeneration of woodland has been prevented by the grazing of sheep and cattle and the burning of heather. However, over the last 30 years the area of rough grazing has been reduced, for in the lower upland areas it has been reclaimed for farming, on much poorer upland there has been afforestation, and bracken has invaded many areas. As at the same time the number of sheep and cattle has increased, parts of the hills may now be overstocked.[4]

The relationship between livestock numbers and the carrying capacity of the land – whether improved or rough grazing – is at the heart of the problem of upland farming. In much of the higher regions only sheep are kept, which rely entirely upon rough grazing. In winter the only feed is heather, and the sheep rely upon this during the ewe's pregnancy and during the early days of lamb growth. Then there is a surge in the growth of grass – indeed 75 per cent of the year's growth takes place in three months – which fades in late summer and autumn. If the density of sheep is to be adjusted to the natural food-supply, then it should be to the low density of winter when there is little for the sheep to feed on; but this would leave much of the summer growth under-utilized. Numerous solutions and part solutions to this problem have been tried.[5]

The most common is for upland farmers to maintain only breeding herds of cows and flocks of ewes. Ewes, for example, are tupped in autumn and fend for themselves in winter; their lambs are born the following spring, fed on the abundant pastures of the summer and sold in the autumn to farmers at lower altitudes, who have either the fodder crops or better pasture to fatten the lambs for market   This is the simplest of strategies, followed by most hill sheep-farmers in the past. It can be modified, although the possibilities depend on the local environment and current costs and prices. Thus while it is normal

---

4 J. A. Taylor, 'Bracken: an increasing problem and a threat to health', *Outlook on Agriculture*, 10 (1980), pp. 298–304; D. F. Ball, J. Dale, J. Sheail, K. E. Dickson and W. M. Williams, *Ecology of Vegetation Change in Upland Landscapes*, pt. 1, *General Synthesis*, Institute of Terrestrial Ecology (Bangor, 1981), pp. 62–9; P. Anderson and D. W. Alden, 'Increased sheep numbers and the loss of heather moorland in the Peak District, England', *Biological Conservation*, 20 (1981), pp. 195–213.

5 Attwood and Evans, *op. cit.* (1961), pp. 90–5; Eadie, *op. cit.* (1978), pp. 103–14.

*Upland sheep farm in north Derbyshire. Buildings are surrounded by improved and enclosed grass, open rough grazing behind.* (Author)

practice to sell lambs or calves as stores after one summer, they can be sent to rented lowland pastures for one winter before being sold at the second autumn after birth. This 'wintering away' was practised in Wales, the Lake District, and on Bodmin and Dartmoor in the 1930s. Farmers with better land can sow improved grasses on their 'inbye' land or, in more favourable circumstances, grow fodder crops to see the animals through the winter. If prices for store animals or wool is very favourable, crops can be bought from lowland farmers to feed them during the winter.[6]

Not surprisingly – 10 to 15 per cent of the agricultural area of England and Wales is farmed in this way – there are considerable variations in farming practice in the hills. In the west, where the hills rise sharply from the coastal plain and face rain-bearing air streams, precipitation is greater than at equivalent heights in the east, and there is a rapid change from lowland farming to hill sheep (see figure 4.2). Further east, on the gentler slopes that fall from the Pennines to the North Sea, there is a

6 W. Dyfri Jones, *The Economics of Hill Sheep Farming: a study of hill flocks in Wales and the North of England* (Aberystwyth, 1973); T. W. Jenkins, *Hill and Upland Cattle and Sheep Farming in Wales*, Agricultural Enterprise Studies in England and Wales, Economic Report no. 88 (Aberystwyth, 1983); G. F. Copeman, 'Some agronomic problems and prospects for upland Britain', in Tranter, *op. cit.* (1978), pp. 14–22; T. H. Bainbridge, 'A note on transhumance in Cumbria', *Geography*, 25 (1940), pp. 35–7; E. H. Carrier, *The Pastoral Heritage of Britain: a geographical study* (London, 1936), pp. 17, 22, 62, 63; E. Davies, 'Sheep farming in upland Wales', *Geography*, 20 (1935), pp. 97–111.

broad transitional zone between the barren uplands and the agricultural lowlands. In both Wales and northern England the uplands are penetrated by valleys; home farms in the valleys can grow crops and grass as well as having rough grazing on the valley sides and interfluves. Hence many farms combine the characteristics of upland beef and sheep rearers with the hill-sheep type. In the past transhumance was practised; sheep and cattle were driven to upland pastures and kept there all summer, with the farmers living in temporary summer shelters. This form of utilization of seasonal pastures was of course far more common in Norway and the Alps, but was found in parts of Wales and the northern Pennines until the seventeenth century.[7]

BEFORE THE NINETEENTH CENTURY

The uplands of Britain have never been rich and have left few records before the nineteenth century. But in the seventeenth and eighteenth centuries they were utilized in ways not greatly different from the present. Most of the Lake District, the Pennines and the Welsh hills were used for the rearing of sheep and cattle. However, the cattle–sheep ratio was more inclined to cattle than at present. Although selling store sheep and cattle was the most import source of income, there were other products. Dairying for cheese was quite widespread. Because most of the upland areas were remote and communications with the lowlands were poor, a subsistence element persisted well into the eighteenth century. Cereals– oats and rye mainly – were grown on livestock farms to make poor bread. Many upland farmers also had other occupations. Most common was by employment in textiles – in Devon, in the Lake District and in the Lancashire and West Riding uplands – but there was also mining.[8]

The eighteenth century saw important changes in the upland economy. Before this century sheep were kept in both lowland and upland primarily for wool and only incidentally for meat. But in the eighteenth and early nineteenth centuries there was a growing demand for mutton, which was cheaper than beef and so more within the pocket of a population only slowly becoming wealthier. The lowland areas needed a supply of wethers

7 F. Emery, 'The farming regions of Wales', in J. Thirsk, *The Agrarian History of England and Wales*, vol. IV: *1540–1640* (Cambridge, 1967), p. 117; J. Thirsk, 'The farm regions of England', in Thirsk, *op. cit.* (1967), p. 22; Alun Roberts, 'Ecology of human occupation and land use in Snowdonia', *Journal of Ecology*, 47 (1959), pp. 317–23.

8 G. V. Harrison, 'The South-West: Dorset, Somerset, Devon and Cornwall', in J. Thirsk (ed.), *The Agrarian History of England and Wales*, vol. VI: *regional farming systems 1640–1750* (Cambridge, 1984), pp. 358–92; E. J. Evans and J. V. Beckett, 'Cumberland, Westmorland and Furness', in Thirsk, *op. cit.* (1984), pp. 3–30; P. Brassley, 'Northumberland and Durham', in Thirsk, *op. cit.* (1984), pp. 30–58; D. Hey, 'Yorkshire and Lancashire', in Thirsk, *op. cit.* (1984), pp. 59–86; F. Emery, 'Wales', in Thirsk, *op. cit.* (1984), pp. 393–428.

to fatten for market upon turnips and temporary grass, and the upland regions provided these sheep. Between 1695 and 1800 the number of sheep in England and Wales doubled, and the output of wool rose until the 1870s. In the uplands the ratio of sheep to cattle steadily increased; in Wales it rose from 2 to 1 in the sixteenth century to 4.2 to 1 in the 1860s. The breeds concerned, however, produced a coarse wool, suitable only for blankets and carpets. By the nineteenth century the uplands served primarily to produce sheep for fattening in the lowlands.[9]

Cattle had long been raised in the hills for fattening elsewhere, sometimes locally, sometimes for the fattening pastures around London, the major market. Thus, for example, by the middle of the eighteenth century there was a well-established link between cattle-rearing in the Devon and Cornwall uplands and the pastures of the Somerset Levels and the Blackmore Vale in Dorset. Welsh cattle had been driven to London since at least the thirteenth century, and after the prohibition of Irish cattle imports Scottish cattle were imported to be fattened in the southern lowlands. Until the reduction of duties on imported cattle and meat in 1845 and after, upland farmers had a hard but adequate market for their store cattle and sheep in lowland England.[10]

### THE UPLANDS IN VICTORIAN TIMES

During the period of High Farming the uplands became a reservoir of store wethers and young cattle for both the fattening pastures and the fodder crops of the lowlands. In Wales the enclosure of very large areas of common grazing in the uplands had led to the creation of independent farms; formerly this rough grazing had been part of lowland farms. In 1875 the highest sheep densities were to be found in Wales and the northern Pennines (see figure 18.1); but densities were nearly as high in the lowlands – in the limestone uplands from Lincolnshire to Dorset, where sheep were fed on turnips, and on the Sussex Downs and Romney Marsh.[11]

But from the 1870s sheep farming was undermined by the import of wool from Australia and elsewhere, and British wool output declined steadily. In the lowlands the very high cost of feeding led to a fall in sheep numbers, which reached a low point in 1947. Most of the national decline was in the lowlands, so that a steadily increasing proportion of

9 P. Deane and W. A. Cole, *British Economic Growth, 1688–1959; trends and structure* (Cambridge, 1962), pp. 68–71; A. H. Cowell, 'An approach to the history of upland country, ecology and habitat', *Agricultural History Review*, 32 (1984), pp. 63–74; R. Elfyn Hughes, J. Dale, I. Ellis-Williams and D. I. Rees, 'Studies in sheep population and environment in the mountains of north-west Wales, 1: The status of sheep in the mountains of Wales since medieval times', *Journal of Applied Ecology*, 10 (1973), pp. 113–32.

10 G. V. Harrison, *op. cit.* (1984), pp. 358–92.

11 Board of Agriculture, *Agricultural Statistics England and Wales, 1875* (London, 1876).

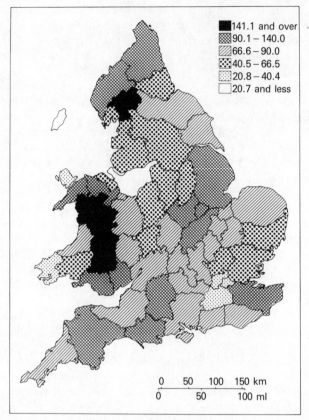

Figure 18.1   Sheep per 100 acres of crops and grass, 1875.
*Source*: Board of Agriculture, *Agricultural Statistics, England and Wales 1875* (London, 1876).

all sheep were to be found in the upland counties. Indeed the absolute numbers of sheep in the upland areas in 1949 was greater than it was in 1889, while that in the lowlands was less than a half (see table 18.1). The upland counties had less than one-third of all sheep in 1889, more than one-half in 1949. There had been an important change in the types of sheep. Whereas in the nineteenth century the uplands had flocks of breeding ewes and wethers, by the 1940s it was store lambs rather than store wethers that were sold to lowland farms. This pattern remains little changed. Although the highest density of ewes is in the uplands, that of lambs is in the lowlands and foothills.[12]

12 J. Fraser Hart, 'The changing distribution of sheep in Britain', *Economic Geography*, 32 (1956), pp. 260–74; J. T. Coppock, *An Agricultural Atlas of England and Wales* (London, 1976), p. 181.

Table 18.1 The sheep population of England and Wales, 1889–1973

| Region | 1889 | 1889–1919 | 1919 | 1919–49 | 1949 | 1949–73 | 1973 | 1889–1973 |
|---|---|---|---|---|---|---|---|---|
| Upland counties | 5,838,277 | | 6,327,498 | | 6,243,416 | | 9,438,395 | |
| % change | | 8.4 | | – 1.3 | | 51.1 | | 61.7 |
| Lowland counties | 12,842,294 | | 8,796,815 | | 5,501,023 | | 9,968,144 | |
| % change | | –31.5 | | –37.5 | | 81.2 | | –22.4 |
| All counties | 18,680,571 | | 15,124,313 | | 11,744,439 | | 19,406,539 | |
| % change | | –19.0 | | –22.3 | | 65.2 | | 3.9 |
| Upland counties as a % of all England and Wales | 31.2 | | 41.8 | | 53.2 | | 48.6 | |

Sources: E. J. T. Collins, The Economy of Upland Britain, 1750–1950: an illustrated review (Reading, 1978), pp. 92–4; Ministry of Agriculture, Agricultural Statistics, England and Wales, 1973.

It is more difficult to trace the changes in the cattle population of the uplands, for dairy and beef cattle were not distinguished until the 1950s. But the total number of cattle in the upland counties has increased steadily since the 1880s (see table 18.2); from 1889 to 1949 the number of cattle in the hills increased at precisely the same rate as in the lowlands, in the post-war period rather more rapidly, so that by 1973 the upland counties had rather more of the country's cattle, and much more of the beef cows than in 1949.

THE UPLANDS SINCE THE 1930s

In the 1930s the upland areas of Britain began to be recognized as a problem region, in much the same way as the depressed industrial areas of the north had become problem regions. Since the 1850s the uplands, never densely populated, had continuously lost population, establishing a spiral of decline as it became more expensive to provide services to a steadily declining number of people. In Victorian times some of the upland areas had income from non-ferrous mining, but this was undercut by imports in the late nineteenth century. By the 1930s the uplands were among the poorest regions in the British Isles. Since then, it is often said, technological change has passed the region by. This needs some qualification.[13]

The changes in the uplands since the 1930s have been partly technical, partly institutional. In the 1920s and 1930s research at Aberystwyth was aimed at improving grassland, and particularly grass in the hills. Since then the prime aim has been to reduce the proportion of each

Table 18.2　The cattle population of England and Wales, 1889–1973 (thousands)

| Region | 1889 | 1889–1912 | 1919 | 1919–49 | 1949 | 1949–73 | 1973 |
|---|---|---|---|---|---|---|---|
| Upland counties[a] | 1,375 | | 1,687 | | 2,095 | | 3,007 |
| % change | | 23.4 | | 24.1 | | 43.5 | |
| Lowland counties | 3,643 | | 4,506 | | 5,599 | | 7,336 |
| % change | | 23.7 | | 24.2 | | 31.0 | |
| All counties | 5,018 | | 6,194 | | 7,694 | | 10,343 |
| % change | | 23.4 | | 24.2 | | 34.4 | |
| Upland counties as a % of all counties | 27.4 | | 27.2 | | 27.2 | | 29.1 |

[a]Westmorland, Cumberland, Derbyshire, Durham, Northumberland, North Riding, West Riding, Breconshire, Caernarvonshire, Cardiganshire, Carmarthenshire, Merioneth, Montgomeryshire, Radnorshire, Flintshire, Denbighshire.
*Source*: E. J. T. Collins, *The Economy of Upland Britain, 1750–1950; an illustrated review* (Reading, 1978), pp. 92–4; Ministry of Agriculture, *Agricultural Statistics, England and Wales, 1973*.

13 E. J. T. Collins, *The Economy of Upland Britain 1750–1950: an illustrated review*, CAS Paper no. 4 (Reading, 1978), pp. 14–15, 18–20, 21.

farm under rough grazing and increase the area in improved grassland and fodder crops. Hence much rough grazing, particularly in Wales, has been ploughed up and reseeded with improved varieties of grass; other grassland has been limed, reducing acidity, while the spreading bracken area has been contained by the use of herbicides; in some areas peat bogs have been drained.[14]

All this has ameliorated the food supply of cattle and especially of sheep; but there have been other improvements. Farmers have tried to increase the ratio of land in forage crops to rough grazing and have begun to buy supplementary feeds for the winter; hay is put out on the moors for sheep and concentrates bought to feed cattle. More attention has been paid to the sheep themselves. In contrast to lowland farming there has been no change in the traditional upland breeds of sheep and artificial insemination is unknown. But ewes have been better fed at tupping and lambing times to try and increase the twinning proportion. Nonetheless, some 15 to 25 per cent of lambs still die at or near birth. On a few hill farms sheep have been kept indoors in winter, as they were in the lowlands in medieval times, but this is uncommon. Rather more of the grazing land is now fenced in to improve management and control grazing patterns. Such improvements have tempted many hill farmers to try and fatten their sheep and farmers lower down to finish their calves, rather than selling them to lowland farmers. Indeed, whereas in the 1950s only 15 per cent of hill lambs were sold fat, by the 1970s over half were sold ready for slaughter.[15]

FARM SUPPORT IN THE HILLS

The problems of the hills were recognized in the 1930s. Few farmers were prosperous at this time, none in the uplands. Hill farmers benefited from the decision to subsidize the use of lime in 1937, and in 1940 a subsidy was given on every hill ewe; in 1943 this was extended to each hill cow. After the war the 1946 Hill Farming Act added improvement grants to the headage payments. The hill farmer benefited rather less than most lowland farmers from the guaranteed prices established in the Act, but in 1967 the range of financial aids for improvements was extended. In 1975 the EEC introduced a policy of subsidies for Less

14 J. Eadie, 'Trends in agricultural land uses: the hills and uplands', in D. Jenkins, *Agriculture and the Environment* (Cambridge, 1984), pp. 13–20; Taylor, *op. cit.* (1980), pp. 298–304; A. J. A. Stewart and A. N. Lance, 'Moor-draining: a review of the impact on land use', *Journal of Environmental Management*, 17 (1983), pp. 81–99.

15 Agricultural Environment Research Group, *Agriculture in the North Pennines* (Newcastle, 1986), p. 27; Agricultural Adjustment Unit, *Hill Sheep Farming Today and Tomorrow: a workshop report* (Newcastle, 1970), pp. 56–61; Eadie, *op. cit.* (1984); pp. 13–20; Eadie, *op. cit.* (1978), pp. 103–14; W. Dyfri Jones, 'A review of some economic aspects of hill and upland farms', in Tranter, *op. cit.* (1978), pp. 50–74.

Favoured Areas, interpreted in Britain as being the hill regions. Under this the improvement subsidies continue and the headage payments are now called Hill Livestock Compensatory Amounts; in real terms they are greater than in the past. In 1980 the EEC, which had not hitherto supported sheep prices, introduced guide-line prices for sheep-meat; the variable premium paid on carcases below the target price goes generally to lowland fatteners, but this has worked back to improve the prices of store lambs, and has encouraged hill farmers to fatten their lambs for sale.[16]

## TYPES OF FARMING IN THE HILLS

Two types of farming are recognized in the uplands of England and Wales, and they show less change in the past than any other types.

First are the sheep farms of the higher and remoter hills. Nearly all the feed for livestock is grass and most of this is rough grazing (see table 18.3). Although some beef cows are kept, sheep are of overwhelming importance. Farms are large, mainly of rough grazing, but most hill farms are run by the farmer with little outside help (see table 18.4). Indeed in these remote areas labour, and particularly that of shepherds, is difficult to get. Sheep provide most of the farmer's income: wool is rarely more than 20 per cent, the rest comes from the sale of store lambs and of ewes too old to give more lambs. The type of sheep vary with the region – Swaledale, Scots Blackface, Derbyshire Gritstone, Welsh Mountain and, in the Lake District, Herdwick.[17]

Table 18.3   Land use in the hills and uplands by type of farming, England and Wales (million acres and percentage)

|  | Mostly sheep | | Sheep and cattle | | Both types | |
|---|---|---|---|---|---|---|
| Rough grazing | 1.01 | 75.9 | 1.28 | 45.2 | 2.30 | 55.2 |
| Grass | 0.30 | 22.6 | 1.31 | 46.3 | 1.60 | 38.4 |
| Tillage | 0.02 | 1.5 | 0.24 | 8.5 | 0.27 | 6.4 |
| Total | 1.33 | 100.0 | 2.83 | 100.0 | 4.17 | 100.0 |

*Source*: J. Eadie, 'Trends in agricultural land use: the hills and uplands', *Agriculture and the Environment*, Institute of Terrestrial Ecology (Cambridge, 1984), pp. 13–20.

16 Agricultural Environment Research Group, *op. cit.* (1986); Agricultural Adjustment Unit, *op. cit.* (1970), pp. 56–61; J. R. Crabtree, 'A trade and welfare analysis of UK sheepmeat exports within the European community', *Journal of Agricultural Economics*, 34 (1983), pp. 113–25; M. MacEwen and G. Sinclair, *New Life for the Hills* (Council for National Parks, 1983), pp. 8–16; P. Wathern, S. N. Young, I. W. Brown and D. A. Roberts, 'The EEC less favoured areas directive', *Land Use Policy*, 3 (1986), pp. 205–12.

17 J. T. Coppock, *An Agricultural Geography of Great Britain* (London, 1976), pp. 188–9, 210; Eadie, *op. cit.* (1984), pp. 13–20.

Table 18.4 Farm types in England and Wales, 1975 (acres)

| | Average size, crops and grass | Average size, total area | Grass | Tillage | Cereals | Beef cows | Breeding sheep | Farmers, etc. | Hired workers | Family workers |
|---|---|---|---|---|---|---|---|---|---|---|
| Livestock, mostly sheep | 134 | 421 | 118 | 15 | 10 | 9 | 570 | 1.1 | 0.2 | 0.2 |
| Livestock, cattle and sheep | 191 | 275 | 157 | 34 | 28 | 27 | 290 | 1.0 | 0.4 | 0.2 |

*Definitions: Livestock rearing and fattening: mostly sheep 75% or more of standard man-days in sheep.*
*Livestock rearing and fattening: cattle and sheep: other holdings with more than 50% of standard man-days in livestock rearing but less than 75% of standard man-days in cattle.*
*Source: Farm classification in England and Wales, 1975 (London, 1977).*

Second are the upland cattle- and sheep-farms, lying between the arable farms of the lowlands and the hill sheep-farms. The environment of these regions is more favourable than that on the hill sheep-farms and beef cows are kept as well as sheep. Farms are smaller than the hill farms, but they have more improved grass and cropland; indeed the area in improved grass is equal to the area in rough grazing (see table 18.3). These farms produce calves, suckled by the mother, as well as lambs; both are sold for stores, although in recent years upland farmers have been trying to fatten as well as rear. From the 1930s to the 1970s many of these farms added a dairy enterprise when the Milk Marketing Board's policy of uniform intra-regional rates was introduced and the spread of the lorry allowed collection of milk from the remotest areas. However, dairying has declined in the last decade.[18]

Until the introduction of the sheep-meat regime in 1980, hill and upland farms remained, as they always have been, the poorest of English farms. This was because of the harsh environment, the limited range of enterprises possible, and the lack of any major technological change comparable with those that have transformed the lowlands of England since the 1930s. But of prime significance has been the smallness of the businesses. This may be surprising, given the comparatively large acreage of these farms (see table 18.4). But the grassland is of very low productivity and the flocks and herds are small. In 1941 it was thought that 400 to 600 ewes was the minimum size to give an adequate living. But only 4 per cent of the flocks in England and Wales were then over 500 ewes. Although flock size has increased since then, many of the flocks in upland regions remain too small; by the 1960s a flock of 800 to 1,000 ewes was thought the minimum necessary in Wales, but 60 per cent of all flocks were of fewer than 200 ewes.[19]

SUMMARY

The importance of the hills in the agricultural economy is to provide sheep and cattle for fattening in the lowlands for meat. Of course, a considerable proportion of both sheep and cattle are currently bred and fattened in lowland regions, but the uplands still provide nearly two-thirds of the country's lamb and half the fat sheep, half the store cattle and nearly one-third of the fat cattle. If these animals were bred in the lowland regions it would require a considerable displacement of other enterprises. On the other hand, the upland areas require a large subsidy; indeed this has increased. In the 1950s 3 per cent of British government

18 Agricultural Environment Research Group, *op. cit.* (1986), p. 68.

19 E. G. Griffiths, 'Some aspects of the agriculture of Mid-Wales', *Journal of Agricultural Economics*, 20 (1969), pp. 69–75; Ministry of Agriculture, *Report of the Committee on Hill Sheep Farming in England and Wales*, London, HMSO, Cmd. 6498 (1944).

expenditure on agriculture went to the uplands, by 1981–2, 10 per cent; in the 1970s government grants and subsidies were 74 per cent of the net farm income of upland and hill farmers. Even with guaranteed prices, these areas provided a poor living for farmers before 1980. Indeed many upland farmers had a net income less than that of a farm-worker.[20]

20 J. S. Hall, 'Hill farming in the four northern counties of England', *Journal of the Royal Agricultural Society of England*, 127 (1966), pp. 17–28; Agricultural Environment Research Group, *op. cit.* (1986), p. 46; Attwood and Evans, *op. cit.* (1961), p. 139; W. Dyfri Jones, *op. cit.* (1978), pp. 50–74; N. H. Hall, 'The extent of store livestock trading in Great Britain', *Journal of Agricultural Economics*, 31 (1980), pp. 187–99.

# 19

# Conclusions

LOOKING BACK

The next two or three decades will be a continuing of the long process of modernization in English agriculture. This process began before the seventeenth century; by then serfdom had long been abolished, farming was largely undertaken for profit and feudal landlordism had given way to a more commercial approach. Since the early seventeenth century there have been three periods of change; from the 1620s to the 1860s, from the 1870s to the 1930s, and from the 1930s to the present.

Between the early seventeenth century and the 1870s there were two major changes in agriculture, the institutional and the technical. Slowly the open fields, the common pastures and the attendant restrictions on individual farmers were removed. Most of western and south-eastern England was already enclosed in the early seventeenth century; the later enclosure of open fields reduced the fragmentation of farms in the Midlands, and by the 1850s there was very little arable left in open fields, although upland commons remained. At the same time farms grew slowly larger, while small land-owners declined,and by the 1870s 70 per cent of English farmland was owned by only 13,000 landlords. Over most of this period, except for an interval in the early eighteenth century, the agricultural population steadily increased.

The major technical advance was the integration of crop and livestock production so that each benefited from the other; part of the cropland was used to feed livestock, but the year in turnips allowed weeding, and clover provided nitrogen for the soil as well as grazing for cattle and sheep, while the alternation of different crops in rotation reduced disease. The maintenance of soil fertility was almost entirely a function of the number of livestock kept and the area of legumes grown. The spread of this system of farming between the 1620s and the 1850s led to a steady if unspectacular rise in crop yields – a rise certainly greater than the increase in the farm population – so that the productivity of both land and labour rose.

Over most of these two centuries farmers were protected against imports by the Corn Laws, the perishability of much agricultural produce, and the high cost of transport. From 1845 this protection crumbled with the repeal of import duties, the spread of railnets abroad, the fall in oceanic freight rates and the use of refrigeration. In the 1850s and 1860s farm prices remained high in spite of the repeal of the Corn Laws, but from the 1870s to the 1930s the price of most of the staple farm products fell. This had important consequence for the farming systems that prevailed over much of lowland England.

First, wheat, wool and meat, the principal products, were undercut by imports. Farmers turned to less-threatened products such as milk, vegetables and fruit. Second, the fall in mutton, wool and wheat prices made the maintenance of soil fertility, both by folding sheep on turnips and feeding them in stalls to cattle, extremely expensive, and these practices declined; fodder crops were replaced by imported grains and oilseeds. Third, little attention was paid in this period to increasing the productivity of land. Drainage was neglected, the use of fertilizers fell behind that of Europe and crop yields showed only slight increases; in the case of some crops, yields actually declined. However, the rising real cost of agricultural labour did prompt advances in the use of machinery, and the self-binder and the threshing machine transformed the harvesting of cereal crops between the 1850s and the First World War. From the 1870s to the 1920s farm output stagnated, but during the period between 1900 and 1940 the knowledge accumulated which was used to allow the tremendous increases of output and productivity in the post-war period. The rediscovery of Mendel in 1900, the beginnings of nitrogen fertilizer manufacture in the 1920s, the development of pesticides and the first British experiments with herbicides in the 1920s and 1930s, the advances in animal feeding, the introduction of artificial insemination and the State sponsorship of agricultural research – all these and many other advances, such as the invention of tractors and combines, paved the way for the post-war explosion. Yet, of course, it was a change in economic policy, followed by the war, that prompted the *adoption* of known techniques. Britain's commitment to free trade in agricultural products, dating from 1845, withered with the sugar subsidy of 1925 and the Wheat Act of 1932. The war and the 1947 Agricultural Act ensured that the knowledge acquired in the first 50 years of the century would be adopted.

The third period, from the 1930s to the present, has seen not only remarkable increases in output and productivity, but the final undermining of Victorian farming. Chemical control of disease and the provision of plant nutrients by fertilizers has made mixed farming obsolete; specialization can now replace diversification. Fertilizers render livestock less necessary, as have herbicides the root crop and pesticides the rotation. Mechanization, less retarded by the bad times in the late nineteenth century and the inter-war period than yield-increasing innovations, has spread to crops other than the cereals, while tractor and combine have replaced horse and binder.

The poor times for arable farmers after 1870 arrested for half a century the growing importance of the large farm, but since the 1950s small farms have disappeared at an unprecedented rate. The farmer, overwhelmingly a tenant in 1870, has become more characteristically an occupier-owner; the break-up of the landed estate began before the First World War and was dramatic in the early 1920s, and the transfer of land to its occupiers has continued in the post-war period. In contrast, the trend in the agricultural population has been downwards since 1851, except briefly for the Edwardian revival and the Second World War; between 1951 and the early 1970s the decline was particularly rapid.

The declining labour-force has dealt with a far greater area of land per capita as the use of machinery has spread from cereals to the majority of cash crops. Yet it is worth recalling that the agricultural area is now substantially less than it was in the 1850s and 1860s, as is the area in crops. Indeed the current area in crops is less than it was in 1944, and the much criticized expansion of cropland since 1961 was dwarfed by the wartime plough-up.

LOOKING FORWARD

The future of agriculture in England depends upon any changes that may be made in the Common Agricultural Policy. This has become less favourable to farmers in the 1980s as quotas have been applied to dairy output and reduced prices are paid on excess cereal output, while, most important, annual target prices for a wide range of products have been increased at lower rates. Future trends in English agriculture depend primarily upon future decisions made in Brussels, and what these will be are not yet clear. It seems unlikely that there will be an end to the whole Common Agricultural Policy, with the abolition of price support and levies. This would allow the traditional food exporters, which still have a cost advantage in a number of products, back into the European market. There has not been such a situation in England since 1972, while a system without some guaranteed prices for farmers has not existed since 1931. It is impossible to predict what might occur in free-trade conditions upon the basis of the circumstances of over half a century ago. Over the next decade or so it seems unlikely that the EEC's protection against overseas producers will be relaxed. However, it does not seem probable that the Common Agricultural Policy will be as liberal to farmers as it has been in the past, and they will face a continuation of stagnant or slowly increasing producer prices and more rapidly increasing input prices. The economic outlook is not propitious; the decline in real net income for the industry as a whole is likely to continue.

The EEC is moving slowly on radical agricultural changes, but has suggested a number of ways of reducing surpluses. The cereal surplus is the major current problem and an attempt is to be made to reduce this by offering farmers payments per hectare not to grow crops on 20 per cent of their cereal area for five years. Surveys of farmers' intentions suggest that a significant proportion may take this up. Such 'set-aside' policies, a term borrowed from the United States, where they were first tried in the 1930s, can hardly be a long-term solution. Current suggestions are that set-aside may constitute the expansion of field margins, putting fields down to grass provided this is not used for production, or simply leaving land in fallow. In addition farmers are to be encouraged by subsidies to plant woodland on former cropland. However, experience from the United States suggests that set-aside will not lead to a radical reduction in output. Farmers may elect to put only their poorer land into set-aside and use more inputs on their remaining land. The only effective way to reduce surplus is to abolish levies and price supports, currently unlikely to occur, or to reduce target prices fairly rapidly.[1]

Both set-aside and woodland encouragement are devices to reduce the area in crops. In the past the first most powerful cause of a decline in arable land has been a drastic fall in prices, the second the expansion of the urban area. Since the end of the Second World War planning legislation has made it difficult to sell agricultural land for non-agricultural purposes, and some would argue that this is a major cause of accelerating house prices in the south-east of the country. Recent legislation aims at easing the sale of agricultural land for building development, which may reduce the arable area but not please conservationists.

The next decade, then, may see some decline in arable and cereal acreages in England. It is possible that proportionally more farmers growing small acreages of cereals on marginal land will take up the set-aside policies, thus emphasizing further the differences between the arable east and the grazing lands of the west, although not perhaps greatly reducing cereal output. An alternative method of reducing cereal surpluses, much discussed but not yet a matter for legislation, is to reduce the use of chemical fertilizers. Most of the fertilizer currently applied is nitrogen-based and a reduction in usage in eastern England would ameliorate the problem of nitrates in rivers and acquifers in this region and also reduce crop yields and hence surpluses. It would, however, also reduce farm profitability substantially at current prices. A less common suggestion, but one popular with conservationists, is to penalize the use of pesticides and herbicides. This would allow the spread of plant disease and weeds, unless these were controlled by traditional means, and hence reduce yields and contribute to the reduction of surpluses.

Cereal and other surpluses have arisen first because government policies have encouraged an increase in farm output, and second because

1 D. E. Ervin, 'Cropland diversion (set-aside) in the U.S. and U.K.', *Journal of Agricultural Economics*, 39 (1988), pp. 183–97; *Countryside Commission News*, 30 (Jan/Feb 1988); 29 (Nov/Dec 1987).

the use of pesticides and fertilizers have made yield increases possible. The adverse consequences of the use of chemical technologies has received much publicity, and consequently any policy that both reduces surpluses and conserves the countryside will be welcomed by many. The introduction of Environmentally Sensitive Areas, where farmers receive payments for pursuing traditional farm methods that do not damage the environment and encourage animal and floristic diversity, includes as yet only a few areas, and in 1987, together with sites of Special Scientific Interest, occupied 580,000 acres, a small proportion of England's farmland.[2]

These various financial incentives aimed at reducing English surpluses have not been available to farmers long enough to foresee future trends. Of particular interest is the possible regional variation in the uptake of set-aside; presumably it will be most vigorously adopted by farmers for whom cereal growing is least rewarding, and these farmers are mainly in the west, Wales and the Midlands where farms are small and the weather wet; thus the difference between the east, where most of the cereals are grown, hedgerows most frequently removed and problems of nitrates in water supplies is greatest, and the Midlands and west, still mainly grazing districts, will become greater. It has been estimated that if current practices are maintained some 23 per cent of the United Kingdom's agricultural land will be surplus to requirements by the end of the century. As yet little thought has been given to regional policy on this matter. Should extensification and set-aside be confined to the eastern arable areas, where most environmental damage has been done, or be applied throughout the country? The 1930s gives some indication as to what would happen if target prices were lowered; more land would go down to grass in the Midlands than the east (see above, pp. 39–45).

One of the causes of the cereal and other surpluses is the rapid technical advances of the last half century. Research in agriculture and promoting the adoption of new techniques among farmers have both been financed largely by government, particularly since 1945; the main institutes financed by the Agricultural Research Council have undertaken fundamental research, while the Agricultural Development and Advisory Service of the Ministry of Agriculture has promoted the adoption of new methods. Real expenditure on research increased very substantially after 1945, reached a peak in the late 1970s and is now in decline; indeed it currently (1988) faces the prospect of very substantial cuts in government expenditure. This is a result of the present government's aim to cut public spending rather than as part of any plan to halt future increase in productivity. Nor is it likely to halt innovation. The chemical and other support industries will undertake some research and techniques

2 Ervin, *op. cit.* (1988).
3 *Countryside Commission News*, 26 (April/May 1987).

will be available from overseas. Advances in animal biotechnology may make startling increases in output and productivity possible.[4]

If economic prospects for farming deteriorate, it is likely that the numbers employed in agriculture will continue to decline. The most rapid period of decline in this century was in the 1950s and 1960s, and the fall since then has been much less rapid. But as prospects dwindle so too will the number of small farmers, whose total will almost certainly fall; hence more and more of the agricultural area will become part of larger farms, a process that has been going on for at least a century and a half. It is likely that sitting tenants will buy their land less frequently, so much the same proportion of farmland will remain tenanted. The continued decline of the small farm may be arrested as farmers seek second incomes, not only outside the farm, but on the farm where campsites and farm shops and other activities currently receive government aid.[5]

Perhaps the most dramatic change in English agriculture since the Second World War has been the growth of mechanization in nearly every aspect of farm routine. A decline in profitability may slow, but is hardly likely to halt or reverse, this process. For the most part mechanization has been caused by the loss of potential farm-workers to better paid jobs in the towns, rather than by the sacking of farm labourers by farmers seeking to cut costs. It is unlikely that British agriculture could attract back enough labour to work the land even if mechanization became unprofitable. This is also relevant to the problems of pesticides. The use of pesticides is much criticized, but it is frequently forgotten that weeding required a very large labour-force and a quite different selection of crops. It is thus difficult to see English farming reverting to the traditional methods of the 1930s.

The next 20 years will be a period of further radical change in agriculture, and indeed in the English countryside. Farming occupies only a small minority of the work-force in rural areas and the future of farming is only one consideration in possible policies for these areas. Farmers have lost the battle for public opinion in much the same way as landlords lost it in the period before the repeal of the Corn Laws. By the twenty-first century England will be not only a post-industrial society, but a post-agricultural society as well.

4 D. R. Harvey, 'Research priorities in agriculture', *Journal of Agricultural Economics*, 39 (1988), pp. 81–98.
5 R. Gasson, 'Farm diversification and rural development', *Journal of Agricultural Economics*, 39 (1988), pp. 175–92.

# Index